# Military Intervention
# In
# European Conflicts

# Military Intervention
# In
# European Conflicts

Edited by
Lawrence Freedman

Blackwell Publishers

Copyright © The Political Quarterly Publishing Co. Ltd.

ISBN 0–631–19406–1

First published 1994

Blackwell Publishers
108 Cowley Road, Oxford, OX4 1JF, UK.

and
238 Main Street,
Cambridge, MA 02142, USA.

*British Library Cataloguing in Publication Data*
A catalogue record for this book is available from the British Library.

*Library of Congress Cataloging in Publication Data*
Cataloging in Publication data applied for.

Printed in Great Britain by Whitstable Litho, Kent.

# CONTENTS

Introduction                                                      1
LAWRENCE FREEDMAN

Nervous Bunnies—The International Community and
the Yugoslav War of Dissolution                                  14
JAMES GOW

Appeasement, Intervention and the Future of Europe               34
JANE M. O. SHARP

Military Intervention: Duty and Prudence                         56
KEN BOOTH

Disengagement by Stealth: The Emerging Gap between
America's Rhetoric and the Reality of
Future European Conflicts                                        76
THOMAS HALVERSON

The British Debate About Intervention in European Conficts       94
PHILIP TOWLE

The Debate in France over Military Intervention in Europe       106
JOLYON HOWORTH

Military Intervention for European Security:
The German Debate                                               125
HARALD MÜLLER

The Netherlands and Military Intervention                       142
JAN WILLEM HONIG

Russian Views on Military Intervention: Benevolent Peacekeeping,
Monroe Doctrine or Neo-Imperialism?                             154
ELAINE HOLOBOFF

Security Challenges in Post-Communist Europe                    175
PAUL HIRST

Index                                                           191

# INTRODUCTION

## LAWRENCE FREEDMAN*

### The Nature of Intervention

INTERVENTION tends to have one of two types of meanings. On the one hand there is action undertaken in the name of international peace and security. This now has a long history, involving a spectrum of activities from offering the services of mediators, providing monitors and peace-keepers to ensure that agreements are being honoured, supporting directly those offering humanitarian aid to the victims of warfare, inter-posing forces between the belligerents, and, at the extreme, entering a conflict on behalf of the most aggrieved party. On the other hand interven-tion can mean interference in another country's internal affairs. This too can take a variety of forms, from prodding its leaders in the directions of certain policies and deterring them from others, encouraging and sponsoring particular political tendencies and, at this extreme, attempting to take direct control of its affairs.

Whereas the first form of intervention, especially in its most active guise, is considered to be a rather special form of activity requiring elaborate rationales and covered by a defined body of international law and precedent, the second is treated more gingerly. At its most modest, interference in another's affairs is difficult to distinguish from much normal foreign policy activity, though it can potentially slide towards subversion. Furthermore, the United Nations has tended to take far more account of the rights of states rather than those of individuals or groups. This means that there is a well-established framework within which the responsibilities of the international community in the face of open conflict between two or more states can be understood, whereas the respons-ibilities when it comes to internal wars, persecution and repression are still evolving. At what point does a righteous intervention on behalf of a victimized minority become tantamount to aggression and who is to assess its true righteousness? Is it possible to put the national interests of the intervening parties to one side when they are asked to reshape another's internal politics and, if not, by what standards does one judge a successful intervention?

Many of these questions were first raised during this decade as a result of the crisis which erupted when Iraq occupied Kuwait at the start of August 1990 and which concluded with the liberation of Kuwait in February 1991. The Gulf War served to demonstrate that aggressive powers could still threaten international order. It also demonstrated that the major powers, acting under the aegis of the United Nations, could

* Professor of War Studies, King's College, University of London.

work together to ensure that aggression did not pay and that international norms were enforced. This led to President Bush's talk of a new world order, which did not seem so utopian at the time as it does now. The basic lesson of the Gulf was that if they were so minded, and so long as their objectives enjoyed broad support, the major western powers could take on and defeat all-comers in battle. Superiority in air power exhibited in spectacular fashion during the first weeks of Desert Storm, was likely to be decisive.

The confrontation with Iraq reinforced the traditional view that a functioning collective security system must demonstrate a capacity to rebuff aggression, but it also boosted the more novel view that elemental principles of political justice must also be supported. This thought was developed under the influence of the 'safe havens' policy, adopted in April 1991 to protect Iraq's Kurdish minority. The Kurds were then being hounded by the Iraqis and chased to the Turkish and Iranian borders after the failure of their uprising. The Kurds' plight was heart-rending in itself, but there was an additional basis for indignation in that they had been at least encouraged by the West to rise up against Saddam Hussein who was a common enemy.

Under the safe havens concept a degree of allied protection was accorded the Kurds when they returned home. This inevitably posed a direct challenge to the Iraqi state, though this was limited by the allies' reluctance to accept responsibility for the conduct of political affairs within the territory they were effectively controlling, which in turn meant that there was no long-term political settlement. Nonetheless, western leaders self-consciously used this episode to begin to amend traditional notions of sovereignty. The London summit of the Group of Seven in July 1991, after citing the 'exceptional action' taken to support the Kurds, urged 'the UN and its affiliated agencies to be ready to consider similar action in the future if circumstances require it'.

In practice, as Bosnia demonstrated, the key questions would revolve more around the permission of circumstances than their requirements. The safe havens concept itself was flawed in that by being described as a response to humanitarian concerns it provided no basis for addressing the underlying political conditions which stimulated the concern in the first place. This turned out to be a far more serious handicap in Bosnia than it had been in Iraq, because at least in Iraq it was practicable to establish safe havens and it was then difficult for either the Iraqi government or the Kurds to defeat the other. In the more dynamic and complex Bosnian situation, United Nations forces supporting humanitarian operations became virtually hostages and so prevented the governments which had supplied them taking action elsewhere (either in the form of lifting the UK embargo on arms supplies to Bosnia or mounting air strikes against Serb forces) to support the Bosnian government.

As this indicates, while these difficult questions have been gestating for some time, and not only in Europe, their European application has proved

2

to be peculiarly troublesome. This is a continent in which the bulk of the old great powers reside. They cannot be expected to take a disinterested view of conflict in their midst. Yet it is also one caught up in a struggle to reconstruct many states following the collapse of communism. These struggles have become intermingled with struggles to affirm distinctive national identities, often on a quite localised basis. The importance of the focus on Europe in this volume, therefore, is not simply that this is the region in which we live. This is also the part of the globe which served as the cradle of the contemporary international system. The system itself is now experiencing great change. Established rules, norms, conventions and procedures are coming to appear inadequate. If they are to be revised or replaced in a satisfactory manner then there is going to have to be much hard thinking about the overall management of European affairs, and the place of Europe in the rest of the world.

## Military intervention

This analysis must take into account a variety of economic, social and political factors. This volume focuses on the military dimension largely because it is here that the most extreme tests are going to have to be faced. The sort of intervention with which it is concerned can be described as the use of armed force to influence the character and course of a developing conflict which is neither taking place upon nor directly threatening national territory, and does not touch upon any specific obligations to allies.

The conflict may be within one particular state or involve a number. Its stage of development may be early or quite mature, with only sporadic fighting or large-scale battles. In this sense intervention is mainly distinguished from the many other contingencies for which armed forces prepare by the lack of a strategic imperative. Neither the intervening country nor its allies are directly at risk. There may be interests at stake but, at least in the first instance, they are not truly vital. Whether they might become vital if the flames fuelling the conflict are not dowsed is a critical, but extremely perplexing, issue.

Although the essays in this collection do not confine themselves to the Bosnian tragedy, each one of them is touched by it. At the time of writing (March 1994) the tragedy awaits solution, although recent events have been encouraging, following a toughening of NATO's stance on air strikes, a more active U.N. presence on the ground, and more energetic American and Russian diplomacy. As a result, Croatia and the Bosnian government are back in alliance, while the Serbs are making the task of supplying besieged cities much easier. Seventy per cent of the territory, and while anxious about the military situation if the Bosnian Muslims mobilise effectively against them, have shown little enthusiasm for many more concessions. One issue may be the ease with which they can incorporate

3

this territory into a greater Serbia. The Croatian government remains deeply unhappy about the Serbian enclave on its territory, Serbia is determined not to let the Albanian population of its Kosovo province enjoy the autonomy to which it was once entitled, while ethnic tensions simmer in Macedonia.

Those reading this will be aware of the later developments of this story. The fact that the fighting is not yet over and may even get worse does not preclude an interim account. Whatever else happens there is now no way that Bosnia, let alone the former Yugoslavia, can be reconstructed as a multi-national state. In terms of the objectives of the international community, as expressed in solemn resolutions from the United Nations Security Council and every other international body which has addressed the issue, Bosnia's wretched condition provides eloquent testimony to a failed attempt to shape the management of conflict in Europe.

## The European Context

In retrospect things might have been done using political and economic instruments earlier in the process, though most were tried. However, this volume is dominated by the question of whether the military instrument might have been used by the major powers to prevent the practices of 'ethnic cleansing' and the partition of a relatively liberal, secular state which at independence had been recognized by the international community. The question is relevant, not only for the Bosnian post-mortem, but because the Balkans have not been the only arena of conflict in post cold-war Europe. A number of civil wars have broken out within the area of the former Soviet Union and in some cases, as with Armenia and Azerbijan, these have led to hostilities between two states. There are other points of tension within central and eastern Europe. These have thus far been contained, though a combination of nationalist governments and deteriorating economic conditions could lead to serious confrontations. Overhanging this set of individual worries about particular problems is mounting anxiety over the prospects for Ukraine and Russia, for any large-scale violence involving these states would send reverberations throughout the continent.

Part of the difficulty with Bosnia-type situations lies in the choice that governments face in posing the real costs and dangers of intervention on the one hand with the more speculative consequences in terms of a more passive stance. The immediate images of suffering may appear compelling enough in terms of public opinion, but governments have to contemplate the long-term consequences of a short-term move to ease suffering, especially if the available actions are geared more to alleviating the pain than dealing with its causes. Another part of the problem facing governments is that once they have decided upon a course of action, their credibility is at stake if that course fails to produce results.

4

# INTRODUCTION

On the whole, the reluctance of western governments to intervene militarily must be seen in the context of a larger geo-strategic judgment which is central to their general policies towards central and eastern Europe. They undoubtedly wish these countries to succeed, with the consolidation of democratic practices and institutions and the restructuring of their economies. In a number of cases, most notably Poland, Hungary, the Czech Republic and, to a lesser extent, Slovakia, there is a widespread expectation that they will eventually be integrated into the western system through membership of the European Union and NATO. They also recognize that failure in many of these countries, and the aggravation of internal strife, could produce some terrible results and have a widespread impact through migration, environmental damage and the knock-on effects of economic and social dislocation. However, western governments do not consider that these dangers warrant them taking exceptional measures which will necessitate serious sacrifice by their people.

The unification of Germany has imposed significant demands on that country which, for the moment, is seen to be having a quite deleterious social, political and economic impact. Germany has an obligation to its eastern sister. An obligation of this seriousness is not felt elsewhere. Indeed the German example has encouraged the view that over-generous policies can both drag down the donor while providing insufficient incentive for the recipient to engage in fundamental reform. In short, interests in what goes on in the east are deemed significant but still limited. There is no greater sacrifice than going to war on behalf of another; limited interests do not justify such a sacrifice.

Yet western Europe cannot shut itself off from the consequences of events to the east. German unification was one of the spurs to the process which led to the Maastricht Treaty which saw the European Community turn into the European Union. It has since had an enormous impact on the internal cohesion of the Union. It was one of the main factors which made it impossible to sustain a system of fixed exchange rates as a prelude towards full economic and monetary union. The need to stimulate productive economic activity in post-communist countries has raised important questions about the barriers to trade erected by prosperous western states. Perhaps most damaging of all to the inner self-confidence of the Union has been its inability to design a new security system in which it would play a central role. From 1990 to 1992 there were heated arguments over whether a European defence entity could supplant NATO, and over whether the great issues of war and peace on the continent could now be handed over to some pan-European institution. Bosnia has silenced those debates, as it has become apparent that the system that can cope with these issues has yet to be designed.

# INTRODUCTION

## Bosnia as a Test Case

In June 1991 Slovenia declared independence from the Yugoslav federation. The attempts by the Yugoslav Army to prevent this were almost farcical and were certainly ineffectual. As the war reached Croatia, and Vukovar was destroyed and then Dubrovnik shelled, there was rising alarm, but a cease-fire, which has more or less held since, had been reached by the start of 1992. In an uneasy compromise Croatia, along with Slovenia, gained its independence but could not get back Serbian-controlled territory. The UN agreed to hold the ring.

Bosnia has been altogether more traumatic. The war has already lasted more than two years. The country has been shattered and brutalised, with an estimated 200,000 killed, hundreds of thousands injured or abused, and millions driven from their homes. There is, alas, no novelty in watching countries self-destruct from the relative comfort of western Europe, but the unravelling of Yugoslavia has been unusually painful because of the nagging sense that somehow it could have been prevented if only the international community had acted more effectively.

It is tempting to explain the anguish with which Bosnia has been viewed by reference to the vivid media coverage, which has certainly made it impossible to ignore the massacres, destruction and desolation in areas hitherto best known as favoured holiday resorts. However, the media role can easily be exaggerated. Despite official fears that an excitable public opinion was driving governments towards a bloody entanglement, governments proved themselves capable of resisting such pressures. Even if there had been no daily images of civilians being shelled, a conflict in Yugoslavia could not but have attracted high-level attention. This was not a faraway country, but one which had played a significant role in European politics throughout the Cold War period. Under Tito it had caused the first serious schism in the communist world, had carried the banner for non-alignment and had shown itself ready to experiment with a more libertarian socialism that might have been expected to give it a head start in the race among post-communist states to become Europe's first capitalist tigers.

The pain of the crisis was aggravated by its predictability. There was no need to be surprised. The main actors made little secret of their intentions and the political dynamics at play were transparent. At each stage serious commentators warned of what was to come. The history of the Balkans had given little encouragement to hopes that the region could settle down into a calm moderation, but the fact that traditional rivalries and hatreds reasserted themselves in such a stark form challenged the very idea of political progress in international affairs, despite the apparent boost provided by the end of the Cold War.

This was particularly poignant for West European politicians. For them it was the wrong crisis at the wrong time. Opinions differ over whether the European Community's intervention in Yugoslavia did more harm than

6

good, but there is little doubt that by the standards the Community had set itself the intervention was a complete failure, except for the fact that it did not fragment itself over the handling of the crisis. This was no mean achievement, given the consequences of the last time the main European powers fell out over a crisis involving Serbs and Sarajevo. However, the priority given to developing a *compromise* policy, accommodating widely divergent views and interests, may have come at the expense of an *effective* policy. This hardly conformed with the intended new image. After the debacle of the Gulf crisis, when all had been obliged to follow a stunningly decisive American lead, those who believed that the end of the Cold War created an opportunity for the European Community to assert itself as the premier security institution in Europe itself, seized on Yugoslavia as a chance to take such a role. The failure to find a European 'solution' cast a shadow over attempts to put a common foreign and security policy at the heart of the European project.

The European failure was not unique. All institutions with some claim on the security affairs of the new Europe have been damaged through their association with the Balkans crisis. The Conference on Security and Cooperation in Europe (CSCE) was just stirring as the crisis broke and was immediately sidelined. The Western European Union (WEU) showed that it could be used for the more symbolic forms of military action (such as the monitoring of the trade embargo on Serbia and Montenegro in the Adriatic), but that it could not handle serious military operations, for which only NATO had the capacity. NATO could also glimpse for itself an opportunity to assert a post-cold-war role for itself: it only belatedly identified military options which were severe enough to influence Serbian behaviour but not so severe as to risk embroiling the troops of member states in a protracted combat role. While the logistics and command demands of humanitarian operations were serious enough these still had to be under UN rather than NATO direction. More substantial operations depended upon large-scale American participation, which was not forthcoming.

Initially, the Bush Administration in the United States was happy to let the Europeans tackle Yugoslavia. It sensed that either this was a small enough problem to be managed using the Community's economic and political instruments, or else was such a can of worms that it should be grateful for an excuse to keep clear. However, the Americans could not escape. As the problem appeared unmanageable for Europe the up-holding of international norms depended upon Security Council resolutions, which could not but implicate the United States. As these resolutions were contemptuously ignored, questions of enforcement arose. This raised questions of military action which depended on American involvement. In early 1993, just as the Clinton Administration appeared prepared to lead its NATO partners down the route of tough action on behalf of the United Nations, it got cold feet, thereby creating a reputation for vacillation as soon as its policies faced resistance (a

7

reputation which was later reinforced in Somalia). The United Nations Security Council had its position confirmed at the top of the institutional hierarchy, but its responsibility for enforcing international norms in circumstances in which enforcement was extraordinarily difficult led to an image of impotence which drained its credibility.

This general failure has stimulated a worrying thought: if the events in Yugoslavia in general and Bosnia in particular are typical of those liable to be faced in Europe following the collapse of communist rule, does that mean that future conflicts may well rage unchecked, with local power deciding the outcome? In this sense, the specific features of the strife within the former Yugoslavia provide only part of the explanation as to why the question of intervention has become so vexatious. Involvement in any conflict where there is no direct threat to the intervening country or its allies is likely to invoke contradictory pressures which may again combine to produce equally unsatisfactory results.

## Principles of Intervention

Much of the debate that has taken place over both particular cases and general principles has been shaped more by consideration of moral and political imperatives than military doctrine and strategy. This has put military officers in something of a quandary. Many of them share the view that the best post-Cold War rationale for their continued existence is going to lie in this general area of what the British Army calls 'peace support' that is the distinctive role of: (a) helping to bring about a peace while fighting continues; (b) providing relief for those caught up in the fighting; or (c) helping to keep a peace once it has been agreed, along the lines of a traditional UN peace-keeping operation.

However, at the same time, they have grave misgivings. They accept the general view that armed forces should be a last resort, but are aware that by the time the 'last resort' arrives the situation may be so dire that the demands on armed forces if its is to produce results have become hopelessly high. They doubt that their governments will give them the resources, patience and rules of engagement necessary to achieve these tasks. One of the lessons of Desert Storm which may have some general applicability is that the best way to reduce the risks of limited engagements, especially when it comes to casualties and the possibility of a long-drawn out campaign, is not to put excessive limits on resources. The military wonder whether armed forces are really as suited to all these tasks as is commonly supposed. Humanitarian intervention may start with requests by civilian organizations charged with bringing relief needing protection, but many such organizations worry that any link with the military will undermine their reputation for impartiality and that they are still better off negotiating their way through trouble.

There is another respect in which the Gulf War precedent was mislead-

8

ing, in flattering the role of air power. The idea that the desired political effects could be achieved by exploiting air superiority without resort to land campaigns (or at least ensuring that land campaigns were conducted in the most favourable conditions) encouraged the Americans to accept a global role without the full liabilities that go with such a role. Unfortunately without a substantial commitment on the ground it is usually very difficult to get a grip on the course of conflicts which often revolve around the physical control of territory. Nonetheless, the preferred American measure was the no-fly zone, which was implemented (and enforced) in both the north and south of Iraq to protect Kurds and Shi'ites, and then also adopted in Bosnia, where it was not enforced.

The military like to work to a precise definition of aim against which they can plan and judge success, and then know when they are allowed to go home. The aspiration is understandable but misplaced. By definition civil wars are unlikely to be conflicts with clear-cut, let alone happy, endings. Most conflicts can be understood as power struggles, with one group seeking to improve its position *vis-à-vis* one or more other groups. The use of force swings the local balance of power in one direction. Any external interference, whether it be in setting rules for the conduct of the conflict, easing suffering, brokering a settlement, or intervening on one side, will influence the balance of power. When it ceases there will always be a tendency for the local factors to dominate once again. Thus intervention has to be recognized, not as being directed against a specific end, but as being part of a process.

## Interests in Intervention

The hardest question when considering intervention in Europe is whether the particular conflicts can be isolated and contained, or whether some might be much more substantial and widespread in their ramifications. The tolerance of the European system to major upheavals in Russia and/or the Ukraine should not be judged high. Even smaller-scale ructions can become dangerous if they start to threaten the equilibrium of a number of countries. If there is an underlying tendency towards instability, then the issue of intervention starts to be seen in a different light. The interest in the prevention of disorder takes on a higher value, because there can be less confidence that, left alone, most conflicts will peter out as the belligerents become exhausted. Whether or not this is the case with a particular conflict is a matter for careful analysis rather than simply the application of a gloomy disposition, but it becomes an important factor in assessing the risks of non-intervention as against those of involvement.

These are extremely difficult questions and it is unrealistic to expect clear and confident answers from governments. The contributors to this volume reflect different views of the underlying trends within the European security situation as on other issues, including interpretation of critical events in Bosnia. Inevitably also there is some overlap, although I hope that part of the interest of this book lies in how a series of events appear from different perspectives.

Because Bosnia looms so large in these essays, James Gow opens the volume with an analysis of why it was that so many institutions and states failed to get a grip on the situation. He describes its gradual deterioration and the responses of outside actors at each stage. He gives four reasons for their ineffectuality: poor timing, inconsistency, lack of coordination and an unwillingness to use force, making it difficult to enforce compliance. The failure to use force is explained by reference to the complexity of the situation as it appeared to outsiders, including the fact that this was never a straightforward case of inter-state aggression, and the inability to formulate objectives in such a form that they could be backed effectively by the use of force. The result was a futile hope that non-violent means could produce a desirable outcome.

The following two essays approach the fundamental issues raised by the Bosnia experience from contrasting perspectives. Jane Sharp examines the criteria for intervention and locates the recent debates in those that have long surrounded such concepts as Just War and Collective Security. She challenges persuasively the conventional wisdom that force should only be used as a last resort (for by this time the position may be so dire that the demands on the military would have been too severe) and notes the importance of confidence that armed force will succeed before this option will even be attempted. She also argues strongly that, however understandable the misgivings felt by Western leaders when contemplating intervention, non-intervention has carried with it high costs, including the long-term destabilization of the Balkans, the loss of credibility for both US leadership and the major institutions, support for the idea that changes to state structures and boundaries can be imposed by force and an undermining of the concept of multi-national societies as well as the terrific loss of life, casualties and wanton destruction within Bosnia itself.

Ken Booth by contrast explores the tension between our moral engagement in crises such as Bosnia and what he describes as technical prudence. He addresses the main arguments for intervention: to maintain international order, respond to a moral imperative, prevent deterioration of relations with the Islamic world, avoid setting a precedent for ethnic nationalism, and contain a threat to European peace: in each case he finds that either the dangers have been overstated or can be addressed by other means. His most substantial point, however, is that military intervention fails the test of technical prudence. He doubts whether there was an available political settlement in Bosnia which could have been imposed by the West, and certainly not by military means. Military power, he warns, is a blunt instrument and calamity often befalls those who exaggerate its potency or the vulnerability of their opponents. Instead he makes the cases for other duties such as isolating a conflict, supporting self-defence, promoting negotiations and fulfilling humanitarian obligations. He

10

concludes that little can be done with such conflicts until notions such as the 'international community' become genuinely 'infused by the world order values and universalist solidarities of global civil society'.

The studies of the debates within individual countries provide powerful evidence for the presumption that these countries are fully aware of the need for prudent, if not necessarily for alternative, forms of duty. Tom Halverson's analysis of American involvement in recent crises, including Somalia, leads him to conclude that the chances of substantial American military involvement in Europe is now remote. He quotes President Clinton's observation that the use of American force would be justified when 'our vital interests are at stake, when there is a clear, sharply-defined objective that is achievable at acceptable cost, and when you are sure you can build the support here at home'. These have become familiar features of the American debate. Presumably what is 'acceptable' will be related in some way to what is 'vital', but neither adjective is precise. The cumulative effect of the conditions is to make a case for intervention an extremely hard one to argue.

Philip Towle suggests British political culture is at least as receptive to the use of armed force as an instrument of foreign policy. The experience has been less unfavourable than that of the United States. Even Northern Ireland has encouraged some faith in the competence of the armed forces to handle politically delicate situations. But Northern Ireland has also warned of just how protracted and unforgiving these conflicts can be (and also of the danger of liberators coming to be viewed as oppressors). In this case, Towle notes, there was a failure to develop a national consensus on policy beyond support for humanitarian operations. In France too the government might have been expected to incline more towards intervention. Not only was French opinion genuinely outraged, but there was also an awareness that France had a greater political stake than others in demonstrating that mechanisms were available for handling such conflicts without calling in the United States. In this sense Bosnia was a rude awakening to the French establishment on the limited capacity of European countries acting alone. As Jolyon Howorth points out, one consequence of Bosnia has been to make it easier for France to accept the need for a transatlantic security structure. The problems of managing air operations confirmed for French leaders that any French action with allies would need to be coordinated by an integrated command.

In Germany and Holland the debates were different again, for Germany the rude awakening was of a different sort. German security policy has long been amenable to safe handling through NATO. This made it possible to avoid thought about independent action in Europe, where all the precedents were traumatic, and also any serious thought about war itself. As Harald Müller makes clear, the Germans had strong views on self-determination for Slovenes, Croats and Bosnians and were anxious to demonstrate the potential of pan-European institutions. Yet, as German politicians and editors saw clearly the need for the use of force, they could

11

only urge others to act. German public opinion was opposed to the very idea of German military operations of this nature. Even if it had felt that it had complete freedom of manoeuvre, Germany would have found Yugoslavia a very difficult place in which to intervene, given the memories of the Second World War. However, it did not even had a freedom of manoeuvre. Instead, the issue of principle was handled through the somewhat artificial mechanism of a constitutional debate over the interpretation of some limiting clauses in the Basic Law. As Müller observes, 'in the light of the German past' a reluctance to send troops abroad 'is not the worst possible case', but it nonetheless put a question mark against Germany's readiness to play a more assertive role in international politics and become a member of the Security Council.

In Holland there has been increasing awareness that military means might be necessary to stabilise Europe during its post-cold war convulsions, and this has been followed up with a high level of contributions to a variety of UN-sponsored operations. Jan Honig observes that the Dutch contribution to peacekeeping is proportionally higher than those of Britain and France, and larger in absolute terms that the smaller NATO allies, surpassing those of Canada and rivalling those of Italy. This allows it to cultivate a reputation for international responsibility. Honig raises questions as to the fragility of the public support upon which this effort is based.

Elaine Holoboff's analysis of Russian 'peace-keeping' reveals a very different situation from that in the western states. Here nervousness results from the partial and targeted nature of Russian involvement in countries which, until recently, were also run from Moscow. She describes the nationalist feeling as well as the desire to recreate something of the old Soviet Union, and then guides us through some of the 'peace-keeping' activities of Russian forces—in Georgia, Moldova and Tajikistan. Western countries have thus far shown themselves to be rather bemused by these events, recognizing the tendency to destabilize these countries in order to return as a stabilizer, uncertain as to what a more benign set of policies would look like and sure that they have no desire to be involved. The even more nationalist twist to Russian politics following Vladimir Zhirinovsky's success in the December 1993 elections means that the next challenges could be even more discomforting—in the Baltics or Ukraine. Holoboff concludes grimly that 'today's strategic advantage' may turn out to be 'tomorrow's neo-imperialism, or even neo-fascism'.

Lastly, Paul Hirst provides an overview of the security challenges facing the European Union. Now that the Cold War is over, the member states of the Union face no direct threat. The new challenges stem from the post-communist upheavals in the rest of the continent along with the comparable, though only loosely connected, turbulence in North Africa. There are a number of reasons to take a close interest in developments in these neighbouring areas, including concerns for democracy and violations of human rights. There is a desire to realise and benefit from the economic potential to fears that if eastern Europe and North Africa enter a down-ward economic spiral there could be serious political uncertainty and mass migration, in turn causing great social strains within the Union and encouraging local neo-fascism. If things go badly wrong, Hirst suggests that Western states will remain 'horrified spectators' rather than active interveners. Intervention would mean accepting a probability of costs and hazards far greater than the probability of being able to influence events to a satisfactory outcome. Hirst proposes a 'Euro-Keynesian' policy, involving trade credits and capital grants, targeted at Eastern Europe, as the best hope of calming the continent and promoting economic growth and prosperity, and so the best security policy. He does not claim to be optimistic that the European Union, in is current anxious and cautious state, will follow such a path.

In the end, the message of this book may be that the circumstances in which Western countries will feel it prudent and efficient to intervene with armed forces in European conflicts may be few and far between. This will be the case so long as they do not see any truly vital strategic interests being put at risk by events in their neighbourhood. One may suspect that by the time the interests at stake are recognized to be truly vital then the military option will appear even more hazardous.

# NERVOUS BUNNIES: THE INTERNATIONAL COMMUNITY AND THE YUGOSLAV WAR OF DISSOLUTION, THE POLITICS OF MILITARY INTERVENTION IN A TIME OF CHANGE

JAMES GOW*

IN Bosnia, bridges were burned, in Western capitals, they were not. Those capitals, either alone, or jointly, were not prepared to mount a full scale armed intervention, despite frequent calls for strong action to stop the shocking brutality and suffering in Bosnia, and to save either people or bridges. Whatever measures were taken, and with whatever conviction, they largely excluded the possibility of a major military intervention—although the matter was intensely considered at certain points. Whilst there was a major international effort to deal with the problems of the break-up of the former Yugoslav federation, involving strong commitments from a large number of countries around the world, the misery of Bosnia grew over eighteen months as various international actors failed to take a grip on the situation there.

Various reasons flow together to explain this general lack of success, as will be assessed below. However, chief among them is the reluctance to use force. Although there has been substantial international involvement in the former Yugoslavia, much of which has been on, or beyond, the borders of intervention (that is, action, whether political, economic, military or other, against the will of one or more parties), there has not been a significant international military intervention. The following is an attempt to site the place of armed intervention and the use of force in the context of international efforts to deal with the war in former Yugoslavia, especially, in Bosnia and Hercegovina, to analyse the fundamental weaknesses in those efforts—principally, the failure to ensure compliance with demands and agreements, through the use, or threat of the use, of force, and to explain why there was no military intervention.

* Dr James Gow lectures in War Studies at King's College, University of London.

## The Institutions of European Security and Their Roles in the Yugoslav War of Dissolution

The Yugoslav burden has fallen mainly on the shoulders of the EC and the UN. The Conference on Security and Co-operation in Europe (CSCE), which had initially carried the hopes of many in the post-Cold War age, was essentially confined to lending its backing to EC efforts to mediate between the various Yugoslav parties in 1992–92. The EC had immediately become involved in efforts to stop armed clashes following the declarations of independence by Slovenia and Croatia on 25 June 1991. The EC offered its own agency to the CSCE as a programme for action, including not only good offices and mediation, but also the organisation of a CSCE monitoring mission which operated in various parts of the former Yugoslav state and was still on the ground at the end of 1993.[1]

Both the WEU and NATO took limited back-up roles. The former, already involved in the autumn of 1991, drafted plans for a peace-keeping force (which were later passed on to the UN), whilst NATO was doing no more than maintaining a monitoring brief. Both became more deeply involved in the second half of 1992 as West European militaries became involved in three ways: humanitarian aid delivery; naval patrolling, monitoring and, eventually, enforcement of UN sanctions against the Federal Republic of Yugoslavia (Serbia and Montenegro) and a UN arms embargo on all parts of the former Yugoslav state; and finally the creation of a ground-breaking high-intensity peace-keeping, or military peace support, operation using well-armed ground forces to assist in the delivery of humanitarian aid to communities under siege in war zones. This last element was very much a NATO operation-by-another-name; although the initial troop commitments to the UN were made through the WEU, operations were organised by a core from NATO Northern Army Group Headquarters—Forward, a large part of which was transferred to a main HQ at Kiseljak in central Bosnia and Hercegovina, with a smaller element going to overall UNPROFOR Headquarters in Zagreb and a small advanced Headquarters unit established in Sarajevo, the Bosnian capital.[2]

However, these activities were supplements to the diplomacy of the EC and the UN. EC involvement took three forms. The most significant of these was that taken by the Council of Ministers. Acting in the context, first, of strengthening European Political Co-operation and, later, of the production model of Common Foreign and Security Policy,[3] the Council

---

[1] For more on these operations see James Gow and James D. D. Smith, *Peace-keeping, Peace-making: European Security and the Yugoslav Wars*, London Defence Studies No. 11, Brassey's for the Centre for Defence Studies, London, 1992.

[2] Général Philippe Morillon, *Croire et Oser: Chronique de Sarajevo*, Grasset, Paris, 1993, pp. 109–110.

[3] Although Common Foreign and Security Policy did not begin formally until the initiation of the European Union on 1 November 1993, the members of the EC had been practising it *de facto* since the signing of the Maastricht Treaty in December 1991.

first dispatched its presidential Troika to mediate in Slovenia. Having shifted from pure mediation to bullying (albeit not without vicious disputes among some of the Twelve) by the beginning of 1992, the Council was responsible for one of the boldest moves in the course of the crisis: the decision to grant recognition of independent international personality to Slovenia and Croatia; Bosnia and Hercegovina was later added to this list, whilst the Council because of a Greek veto on the issue, blocked granting of the same status to Macedonia.

In granting recognition to certain Yugoslav republics the Council undid one of its earlier initiatives: the EC Conference on Yugoslavia, initially in The Hague, later transferred to Brussels. That the Council undermined the Conference was clear in the assessment of the Conference's Chair, Lord Carrington, opined at the successor International Conference launched jointly by the EC and the UN in London in August 1992 and afterwards transferred to the UN in Geneva.[4] However, the prospects for the Conference were limited after its near-success but failure to gain an overall settlement in November.

The Conference had achieved the cardinal concession from the Serbian President Slobodan Milosevic at the start of October that the Yugoslav republics had the right to become independent and that borders were to be respected. It was this agreement in principle which cleared the way for the Council to move to recognition as a way of changing the political conditions of the dispute once the Conference had failed to achieve overall agreement and a majority of EC countries judged that there was little prospect of Serbia accepting an overall accord unless it had to. This was added to an analysis promoted most strongly within the EC by Germany that the way to halt the conflict in Croatia was to recognise Slovenia and Croatia. Events indicate that this analysis was correct— although Germany's advocacy of it alienated their Community *confrères*, as did the German announcement on December 23 that it would recognise the republics on 15 January which became a cause of friction and embarrassment when the Badinter Commission (a legal-advisory body set up as part of the Conference), asked by the Council to advise on recognition, deemed Croatia not to satisfy all of the five conditions laid down by the Council itself.[5]

The third way in which the EC played a role was operational. The EC was involved in a series of ceasefire negotiations in Slovenia and Croatia and responsible for organising a CSCE monitoring force to oversee the implementation of the agreements. In the main, the monitors were drawn from the CSCE Confidence and Security Building Measures talks in Vienna (and included representation from non-EC countries). They were

[4] Lord Carrington, 'Statement to the London Conference on Yugoslavia', 26 August 1992.

[5] For an excellent account of this from a legal perspective see Marc Weller, 'The International Response to the Dissolution of the Socialist Federal [*sic*] Republic of Yugoslavia', *The American Journal of International Law*, Vol. 86, No. 3, July 1992, esp. p. 586 ff.

16

no doubt instrumental in limiting the scope of the conflict in some parts of Croatia, as well as ensuring some local ceasefire agreements resulting in implementation, and successfully accomplished their mission in Slovenia. Nevertheless, the monitors were continually hampered by the general ineffectiveness of the international effort in stopping the fighting—something underlined by events in Bosnia and Hercegovina where the mission was extended in 1991 and almost completely withdrawn in the spring of 1992.

The problems faced by the monitors were in large part a function of the EC's inexperience and incompetence in negotiating ceasefires.[6] In addition, the EC increasingly found itself bullying the Serbian camp so as to make progress in the talks which undermined its ability to be a neutral mediator. After the UN became involved in ceasefire negotiations in November 1991, this situation began to improve, with the UN providing the Serbian camp with a more acceptable interlocutor on ceasefires, as well as one which was more competent—although it was not until recognition had created the conditions for a more viable ceasefire that there was an implemented agreement; this came into effect on 2 January 1992.

As a result, by the following spring, a UN peace-keeping force (UNPROFOR—UN Protection Force) had deployed 14,000 troops in four areas (UNPAs—UN Protected Areas[17]) in Croatia occupied by Serbian forces, as well as in the Bosnian capital Sarajevo (the latter partly in the hope that a symbolic presence would deter war there). The peace-keeping mission was successful in stabilising the cessation of open hostilities—although there were, on average, ten violations a day in the first year of operation. It was unable to secure implementation of two other crucial aspects of the ceasefire agreement negotiated by the UN's special envoy Cyrus Vance: demilitarisation of the UNPAs and the return of populations to them. This was the source of discontent in Croatia—which discontent continued to threaten a return to hostilities there intermittently, as its army incrementally regained control of Serb-held territories.

UNPROFOR was extended in the autumn and winter of 1992, with precedent-setting peace-keeping operations. The first of these was in Bosnia and Hercegovina and had little or nothing to do with traditional peace-keeping in which lightly armed soldiers patrolled an agreed ceasefire line between two opposing forces. Instead, a well-armed, armoured force was deployed to ensure the delivery of humanitarian relief to besieged communities in Bosnia and Hercegovina. In terms of peace-keeping, of UN activity and of the concept of humanitarian intervention, this was an extremely important innovation. A further innovation was the pledge by those countries supplying the troops involved to cover the costs of the deployments, rather than the finance having to be found from an

---

[6] Gow and Smith, *op. cit.*, pp. 13–25.

[7] United Nations Protected Areas was the name given to the four sectors into which UNPROFOR deployed in Croatia.

over-spent and under-paid UN kitty, although this arrangement was changed after a year of deployment, as the operation was being extended and enlarged.

The UK Security Council, in Resolution 770 of 13 August 1992, had empowered states to use any measures necessary for the delivery of humanitarian relief, including military measures. Discussion of the use of force made UN Secretary General Boutros Boutros-Ghali nervous. He expressed fears in a letter to the Security Council that the use-of-force resolution could endanger UN peace-keepers already operating in Bosnia and Hercegovina—and even those in Croatia—and hinted at their withdrawal by demanding 'adequate' advance warning of military intervention so that any threat to UN peace-keepers could be minimised. Those discussing the sending of armed escorts for the food and medicine convoys allayed some of his fears, however, by moving cautiously.

The second element of UNPROFOR was not charged with 'blasting its way through' to its point of destination. Instead, it was to escort the convoys in 'benign' ways, only using its armaments in self-defence, if fired upon first. This avoided the obvious difficulties that could be envisaged if convoys got into frequent fire-fights. However, it also meant that there were continuing problems ensuring the passage of aid where the way was blocked by combatants. Although the Serbian camp, as in most other matters, was easily the worst offender in this respect, the UN Civilian Affairs representative, Cedric Thornberry made it clear that all parties had frustrated the work of those attempting to deliver aid. This was especially the case after heavy fighting broke out between Bosnian Government forces and Croat forces in the spring of 1993, which fighting continued to the year's end and was a major impediment to the operation of UNPROFOR in the country.

Although there was growing impatience with the situation, there was not the will among those countries with troops on the ground to accept a shift towards enforcement, although the question was being debated again in the autumn of 1993, as France and the UK discussed French proposals for tougher delivery. UNPROFOR was undoubtedly alleviating some of Bosnia's misery and probably acting as, if not a deterrent, a presence which meant the level of violence was less than it might have been otherwise. However, neither it, nor the UNHCR and the International Red cross, with both of which it was working, could be expected to handle the scale of the problem presented by 2.7 million deportees, refugees and siege inhabitants in Bosnia without food, shelter and medicines—all dependent on the international aid effort. Whilst the Bosnia and Hercegovina operation was increased in the autumn of 1993, with additional troops being deployed, the prospects for the people of Bosnia really depended on an end to the fighting.

A third novel element of UNPROFOR appeared in Macedonia, where the UN set a further precedent by deploying its first-ever preventative peace-keeping force—all others had come into being after an armed conflict, usually only at its conclusion. However, the twin threat to Macedonia of war spilling over the border from the southern Serbian province of Kosovo and of an internal disintegration of the country in international limbo suggested that the precedent needed to be stronger and to include both a mandate to defend the country in the event of war rushing over its border and an internal policing mission to control the situation inside Macedonia. There was a hope that a symbolic presence would be enough. But, this had not been the case in Bosnia and Hercegovina, where UNPROFOR Headquarters for the operation in Croatia had been placed in Sarajevo in the hope that the international presence might deter war.

In this context, the further precedent of the US deploying its troops in a UN peace-keeping operation, adding 300 Marines to a 700-strong joint-Scandinavian battalion, added real weight to the symbolism. Nonetheless, the internal disintegration of Macedonia seemd to creep on. There could be little doubt, though, that as the Macedonian Command approached the end of its first year of operation, the prospect of war in the Yugoslav southern tier which had seemed near certain to come at the time UNPROFOR deployed in Macedonia, whilst not excluded as a possibility, had receded. Accompanying this was measured relief that the chance of a fireball of war blazing through south-eastern Europe had been limited at the same time.

The peace-keepers and the monitors, in all parts of the former Yugoslavia, played an important secondary role as a source of objective and independent information on events. This meant the frustrating task of witnessing the practice labelled 'ethnic cleansing' by the Serbian camp, first in the UNPAs where the ejection of non-Serbian populations was carried out under the noses of UN troops who had no mandate to prevent it, only to report it, and later in Bosnia and Hercegovina where from an early stage UN troops in Croatia were observing events across the border—this time without even a mandate to operate in the republic in question. Reporting from Bosnia enabled those involved in dealing with Bosnia in capitals to get types of information previously unavailable and a fuller picture of the war. In addition to the information provided directly by those on the ground, their presence also facilitated a large news media presence, which again increased the flow of information from the region.

That flow of information prompted both the humanitarian and coercive activity of the international community. However, these impulses constantly seemed to be in tension—whilst UNPROFOR in Bosnia was delivering aid, the UN Security council passed a number of more coercive resolutions, mostly against the Serbian camp. The biggest reason for this was the emergence of 'ethnic cleansing' on an enormous scale in Bosnia and Hercegovina in the spring and summer of 1992. This gave the prompt for US-led activity in the UN Security Council which included the imposition of comprehensive sanctions on the newly-declared Federal Republic of Yugoslavia (Serbia and Montenegro) in May (Resolution

19

757) to secure the withdrawal of the Yugoslav Army from Bosnia and Hercegovina, in compliance with an earlier Security Council resolution (752). Here one of the central difficulties encountered by the international community in its handling of events in Yugoslavia was faced: compliance. To secure compliance with one resolution, an enforcement measure—sanctions—had to be adopted. Yet, the Serbian camp found a way ostensibly to comply without altering the military situation: it split the Yugoslav army, half going to the new state, the other half remaining in Bosnia and Hercegovina to prosecute Belgrade's ambitions there.

Various other resolutions with an enforcement component were passed: the creation of an air exclusion zone over Bosnia and, later, its implementation; the imposition and implementation of a maritime blockade of Serbian and Montenegro; the declaration of 'safe areas' in parts of Bosnia; stronger mandatory sanctions against Serbia and Montenegro. Yet, none of these was completely successful; some, such as the 'safe areas' were bound to fail from their announcement, given the reluctance of those same Western governments which had declared them, to defend them with ground forces—largely because most of the 'safe areas' decreed were largely indefensible without other measures being taken as well. These areas might gain some respite, but that depended on Serbian compliance. Compliance tended to depend on how far the Serbians had to comply.

As the UN, led particularly by US initiative, continued to seek Serbian compliance, the situation in Bosnia and Hercegovina deteriorated, relations between the EC and the UN became fractious and a new, *ad hoc*, institution was created—the International Conference on Former Yugoslavia (ICFY). This was created following events in July 1992, when Lord Carrington seemed to have reached an agreement on a ceasefire and, in particular, on arrangements for the UN to take control of heavy weaponry. Tension between the EC and the UN reached breaking point. UN Secretary General Boutros Boutros-Ghali expressed his pique at the EC negotiating team's affront in making agreements on behalf of the UN—to look after heavy weapons—without even discussing the matter with UN representatives. Consequently, the tension was resolved by the establishment of a joint initiative. A new joint Conference was launched to replace the Carrington one. Carrington resigned and his place as EC Special Envoy was taken by Lord Owen, like Carrington, a former, UK foreign secretary. Owen was to become Co-Chair (alongside former US Secretary of State Cyrus Vance for the UN[8]) of an international conference on the former Yugoslav state which, unlike its EC predecessor, would go into full-time operation in Geneva, although it resulted from an initial conference in London.

Jointly, the EC and the UN pursued the cause of achieving peace in the lands which had been the old Yugoslavia. In addition to the EC and the

---

[8] Vance was later replaced by former Norwegian Foreign Minister Thorvald Stoltenberg.

UN Security Council, countries neighbouring the former-Yugoslavia were included in the mechanism of the ICFY, as was the Organisation of the Islamic Conference.[9] Although the ICFY was established to deal with dissolution of Yugoslavia as a whole and comprised a plenary forum and six working groups, it was the continuing war in Bosnia and Hercegovina which engaged Conference Co-Chairmen the most.

Vance and Owen's mission was to negotiate a settlement acceptable to all parties, but one which, by the principles on which the ICFY was established, would defeat cardinal Serbian war aims. This mission-impossible seemed to be on the verge of completion with the elaboration of the so-called Vance-Owen Plan, which would have divided Bosnia into ten provinces (see below). Whilst in practice the delineation of these provinces would have made some concession to ostensible Serbian war aims, their implementation would also have denied the cardinal Serbian war goals of contiguous territory and ethnic purity. Remarkably, through a mix of persuasion and bullying in January and, again, in May 1993, the Co-Chairmen appeared to be millimetres away from agreement. However, this did not happen and the Vance-Owen Plan was effectively killed off by the US Administration in May.[10] A subsequent initiative, derived from joint Serbian-Croatian proposals and with little pretence to a just settlement, also appeared to be close to success in July 1993. However, the Union of Republics plan, like its predecessor failed. Yet again, the international effort to halt war in the region had run into the ground.

## The Fundamentals of Failure:
## Assessing International Peace-making Efforts

There were important ways in which the activity of the institutions concerned with European security made a positive difference in the course of the Yugoslav crisis. Moreover, ill-equipped and inappropriate institutions predicated on the Cold War division between East and West were clearly pitched against a multiple problem of historic proportions. In difficult circumstances, with limited means, some of the bodies involved

---

[9] The role of the Organisation of the Islamic Conference (OIC) is worth note. The various Islamic countries had diplomatically backed the position of the Bosnian Presidency and Government, led or dominated by Slav Muslims from Bosnia, although in each case including Serbs and Croats. On occasion this played into the hands of the Serbian camp as it attempted to paint Bosnian President Alija Izetbegović and Foreign Minister Haris Silajdžić as agents of Islamic fundamentalism. The value of OIC backing, aside from financial support by Saudi Arabia, diplomatic support from Turkey and both strong financial and political backing from Malaysia (seeking to develop and sustain a European outpost for ideological Islam) was, in any case, limited. This was most clearly shown by the fact that, for this first time in history, the OIC had a unanimous collective view on an issue, yet it was unable to bear on the international handling of Bosnia in a major way, although its inclusion in the ICFY mechanism indicated that it was not completely sidelined.

[10] Lord Owen, 'Yugoslavia', Churchill Lecture, The Guildhall, London, 25 November 1993.

achieved more than was generally credited to them by critics (this is particularly true of the EC). However, the undeniable bottom line is that the institutions were not adequate to the challenge.

Overall, international action was not effective, or only of limited effect, for four reasons: timing was wrong, there was inconsistency, there was a lack of co-ordination and agreement, and, finally, there was an ever-present weakness with regard to the linked issues of ensuring compliance and the use of force.[11] International efforts suffered from the start because by the time the EC arrived to mediate between Belgrade and Ljubljana after the declarations of independence—and later tried to broker an agreement based on the confederal positions previously advocated by the republics which had declared independence, but rejected by Belgrade—it was already too late: once force was used against Slovenia and Croatia, there was no real prospect of their being able to accept re-integration into a Yugoslav state. This involvement came late in the day considering that for several months, if not three years, there had been clear signals that there was a situation developing which required attention.

At virtually every stage, the international community reacted to rather than anticipated events. The consequence was that at every stage action which could have made all the difference three or six months earlier came late and, usually, with too little commitment. The clearest example here is the fate of Bosnia and Hercegovina. Although there had been unmistakable signs that the republic was teetering on the verge of war for over a year—in August and September 1991, the Yugoslav Army had completed the deployment of tanks at major communications points throughout the country and had all-but abandoned barracks in the major towns in non-Serbian populated areas and had dug in heavy artillery on high ground around towns.[12] At the time this arsenal began the last and worst phase of the attempt to destroy Bosnia and Hercegovina in March 1992, the inter-

[11] The following benefits greatly from discussions with Cathèrine Guicherd of the North Atlantic Assembly, who has also written two excellent studies of EC involvement, the shorter in English, the longer in French: 'The Hour of Europe: Lessons from the Yugoslav Conflict', *The Fletcher Forum of World Affairs*, Vol. 17, No. 2, Summer 1993; *L'Heure de L'Europe: Premieres Leçons du Conflit Yougoslave*, Les Cahiers du CREST No. 10, CREST-ÉCOLE Polytechnique, Paris, 1993. Whilst we would agree absolutely on timing and coherence, my 'compliance', although underpinned in large part by the idea of military action, is broader; in addition, I think the appropriateness of measures has to be taken into account.

[12] It is important here to correct a widespread false apprehension: international recognition did not cause war in Bosnia and Hercegovina, although the Serbian camp used this as a pretext and it fuelled their campaign. The fact was that most preparations for the destruction of Bosnia and Hercegovina were in place nine months before the international community granted diplomatic recognition to Sarajevo on 7 April 1992. By September 1991, US Secretary of State James Baker was in a position already to warn the UN Security Council of the aggression 'beginning to take shape in Bosnia', at a time when the Bosnian Presidency was still working urgently to obtain a new Yugoslav framework through the EC Conference in The Hague. UN Doc. S/PV 3009, 25 September 1991. See James Gow, 'One Year of War in Bosnia and Hercegovina', *RFE/RL Research Report*, Vol. no., 4 June 1993.

national response was meagre: there was an internationally co-ordinated move to grant recognition of independence to the country.

That there was a threat of widespread violence could not be denied—Radovan Karadžić, the local Serbian leader, had made the threats obvious. That the EC, as well as those in other parts of the international community, were aware of the threat was clear in the fact that from February 1992 onwards, the EC Conference and other international efforts were geared towards avoiding war in Bosnia and Hercegovina. The EC effort was essentially based on the adoption of an idea—ethnic territories, or 'cantons'—which had been propounded by the Serbian camp.[13] Understood by the EC negotiators as a means to propitiate the Serbs and avoid war, it was really a charter for 'ethnic cleansing': ethnically designated cantons created the basis for ethnically pure territories.

Some months later, in the wake of the terror which swept the country in the spring and summer, the EC-UN backed ICFY in Geneva came up with a plan which might have been appropriate to the acommodation of any genuine fears in the Serb communities in Bosnia and Hercegovina. The constitutional plan, devised by a working group under a Finnish diplomat, Marrti Ahtisaari, was much better in that it did not take ethnicity as a starting point, although it was a factor taken into account. The end product was a set of regions which had ethnic majorities, but were constitutionally designed to be multi-cultural.[14] However, by the time the Ahtisaari plan was called the Vance-Owen plan and placed on the negotiating table, 'ethnic cleansing' had been realised.

The way in which the international response lagged behind events can be explained in large part in terms of the nature and composition of the various bodies involved. All are intergovernmental organisations. They all require discussion and agreement between the member states; most require consensus before decisions can be taken. Therefore, with regard to a controversial question such as the collapse of Yugoslavia, there was much disagreement between the individual governments which comprised the international agencies. This made it impossible for there to be quick responses to situations which required them.

Such differences of opinion were most notable with regard to the questions of recognition, the deployment of military personnel and the use of armed force. Even where there was some kind of agreement on what was to be done, there were different perspectives on implementation. Once it had been decided that the European countries would offer troops

[13] See Milan Andrejevich, 'The Future of Bosnia and Hercegovina: A Sovereign Republic or Cantonisation?', *RFE/RL Report on Eastern Europe*, 5 July 1991.

[14] See 'Report of the Secretary General on the International Conference of the Former Yugoslavia' UN Doc. S/24795, 11 November 1992. Most people closely involved accepted, at least unofficially, that there would be some areas in the country to which ejected populations would never return and in which the multi-cultural provisions would have little meaning in reality, at least in the near future.

to support the UN's humanitarian effort in Bosnia and Hercegovina, there were differences of emphasis between the French who wished to use the WEU to plan the operations and the UK which favoured NATO for the role. Later, on the question of enforcement of a UN air exclusion zone over Bosnia and Hercegovina, the US wished to have the right to strike targets on the ground and in Serbia itself, whereas the French preferred to limit operations to Bosnia and Hercegovina and, if possible, aerial targets. This was a reflection of the general tension between the aerial bullishness of the US and the greater caution of those carrying out the humanitarian mission with troops on the ground.

The crucial problem concerned compliance and the use of force. The pattern of international activity indicated that, although there were numerous efforts to mediate, progress towards either ceasefire or political agreement only emerged after some form of coercion had been applied, usually against the Serbian camp.[15] However, the logic of this pattern was not readily extended into the sphere of the use of armed force.

Even after almost one year of war, the Vance-Owen Plan, in spite of considerable complexity, had a role to play in moving towards an end to hostilities in Bosnia. The plan involved the creation of ten provinces in a single Bosnia and Hercegovina, within each of which there would be a multi-ethnic government and, in nine of these, a governor nominated by one of the three constituent ethnic groups (the capital, Sarajevo, would have had a separate status). Yet, both in January and in May, agreement on all elements of the Vance-Owen Plan appeared close. On both occasions, an apparently growing threat of US-led air strikes helped to induce Serbian co-operation. However, at both stages, that co-operation proved to be short-lived once it became clear that the organisation of a force to implement the plan was still subject to debate and that some crucial countries, notably the US, were reluctant, if not opposed, to involvement both if it required their own ground troops and if it appeared to be morally unacceptable in their terms.

The reluctance of relevant governments to commit armed forces in the Balkans, for good and bad reasons, had the effect of giving a green light to those who would do whatever they could get away with without being brought to account. As one senior UN official engaged in the handling of the Yugoslavia break-up observed: 'Force is the ultimate arbiter and any diplomatic policy that does not rely on carrots and sticks will not really get you very far. Without a club in the closet, without a credible threat of force, policy becomes bluff, bluster.'[16] From the outset, categoric declarations that there would be no use of force stripped diplomatic efforts of one of

---

[15] See James Gow, 'The use of coercion in the Yugoslav crisis', *The World Today*, Vol. 48, No. 11, November 1992, pp. 198–202.

[16] Herbert Okun, UN Special Adviser and Deputy-Head of Civilian Affairs UNPROFOR, Interview, 'Diplomacy and Deceit' Channel 4 TV, 2 August 1993, Media Transcription Service, *Bloody Bosnia*, MTS/M2578, WPS, p. 4.

their key instruments: the threat of the use of force in circumstances where other means proved inadequate or unpersuasive.

### Intervention: Practicalities, Principles and Politics

The question of the use of force was much debated, even from the earliest stages of the Yugoslav break-up. Whilst Slovenia experienced ten days of armed conflict in the summer of 1991, the issue was raised, but never gained momentum, given the short duration of hostilities. During the war in Croatia, especially, during the siege and bombardment of Dubrovnik, the chorus of calls for intervention swelled; the chorus included political figures as senior as the former UK Prime Minister, Margaret Thatcher. Finally, the cries were repeated during the war in Bosnia and Hercegovina, with the practice dubbed 'ethnic cleansing' ravaging that country, as the Serbian forces carried out a campaign of terror in order to create the boundaries of a new state, free of potentially hostile, non-Serbian populations.[17]

Even, as late as September 1993, the debate on international armed intervention continued, with Thatcher, again, this time accompanied by a host of luminous international political figures, calling for NATO air power to be used against the Serbian forces in Bosnia, via *The Wall Street Journal Europe*.[18] Even, the prospect of an ostensibly limited use of force, such as this was intended to be, did not result in action. Among the major reasons for this were the state of diplomatic efforts in Geneva and elsewhere to bring the fighting to an end, as well as the prospect that any intervention begun in this way would not only risk compromising troops already deployed with UNPROFOR, but could well lead to a subsequent full-blown intervention involving ground forces.

Large scale external armed intervention including ground forces never emerged. Discussion of the various aspects which featured in the debates on this can be made in three categories (although the various aspects may be readily interwoven in a web of reluctance). These debates concerned the practicalities of intervention, the bases of intervention and the political direction of intervention.

A variety of practical impediments to intervention appeared at one time or another in the debate on armed intervention in Bosnia. These were summarised by the UK Foreign Office in a briefing which made out the 'Case Against Military Intervention'.[19] Those reasons included the experience of World War II in Yugoslavia, particularly, in Bosnia, where communist-guerrilla forces won victory over the Axis occupiers, Italy and Germany. This was supplemented by fears that the mountainous terrain in Bosnia favoured extended guerrilla resistance to external forces.

[17] Once it became apparent that the Serbs would not face an international intervention to stop this process, Croat forces in Hercegovina began extensively to follow the Serbian lead.
[18] 2 September 1993.
[19] November 1992.

A further addition was the complexity of the situation, with three sides involved, either fighting all against each other, or forming shifting and temporary tactical alliances. Moreover, as the UK Foreign Secretary, Douglas Hurd, often reminded everybody, this was a war where there was no front line, where fighting was village against village, street against street, even neighbour against neighbour. Not only did this mean that it would be hard to distinguish one group from another, but it meant, the argument continued, that intervention would risk heavy 'collateral damage'—that is, civilian casualties which would not be tolerated by electorates in Western countries. In short, according to this view, the task was simply beyond the capacity of an international intervention force.

This was a partial picture. The war, whilst containing those elements, was not the natural disaster, or act of spontaneous combustion, that Mr. Hurd seemed to characterise. For those paying some attention, it was clear that the Serbian side had initiated a large scale use of armed force, in a planned and organised way, with a view to realising new state borders and that, where the Serbs met resistance, there were frontlines.[20] Nor did any side in Croatia, or Bosnia, even adopt guerrilla techniques, let alone show proficiency in them, until February 1993, when Muslim groups in eastern Bosnia began to organise and carry out hit and run raids. Indeed, the social structure underpining successful guerrilla operations had been eroding since the end of World War II.[21]

However, what was more important than the reality of the situation was the perception of it. This conditioned the thinking of many on the question of intervention. Whilst few probably though that a successful intervention was impossible for these reasons, it was thought that, to be successful, the scale of intervention would have to be prohibitively large—the troop numbers discussed never fell below 120,000 and were more usually in the region of 400–500,000.

The potential cost of this size of operation, both in human and financial terms, was felt to be a constraint. In the UK, great importance was quietly attached to avoiding involvement which would call into question the scheme known as Options for Change by which cuts were to be made in the armed forces and defence expenditure reduced. At the same time, it is also not unreasonable to suppose that, had intervention, or the deployment of larger forces than those already in UNPROFOR to implement the Vance-Owen plan, become a realistic option, the necessary resources would have been found, as they were for the Falklands and Gulf Wars.

In addition to this, the putting together of such a force would not necessarily be straightforward. A force of that size would have had to be multinational. In the Gulf War, where there had been a sense of conviction about what the problem was, as well as about what had to be done, there

---

[20] I have described and analysed the war in Bosnia, including the preparations made several months before independence, in 'One Year of War in Bosnia and Hercegovina'.

[21] See James Gow, *Legitimacy and the Military: the Yugoslav Crisis*, Pinter, London, 1992, pp. 112–14.

were many problems in assembling, harmonising and using such a force. Where the commitment was lacking and the public perception of the problem unclear, the sheer difficulty of putting together a suitable force in itself became an obstacle to intervention.

A further practical obstacle to armed intervention was the deployment of UNPROFOR. This was true with regard both to the original Croatian Command and to the later Bosnia and Hercegovina Command. Before the deployment in Bosnia, any armed action there had to be pitched against the fragile cessation of hostilities in Croatia which held the threat of break-ing into war again and the security of the UN troops deployed to supervise the ceasefire. Once further international military units were deployed in Bosnia to assist in the delivery of humanitarian aid to cut-off and besieged communities, the question of the UN troops' security became even more acute. Any decision to use force would have either put those forces at risk, or required their withdrawal. Neither was a palatable option, especially, where the countries deploying troops were, anyway, generally reluctant to use force.

The reluctance to mount an armed intervention expressed through analyses of the cost and complexity, was also evident in a lack of clarity on the bases for an intervention. Calls for intervention were made on two grounds—the principles of human rights and of international security and the inviolability of state borders. In both cases, however, there was uncertainty about the legality and morality of intervention (although it is difficult to suppose that, had there been a will to intervene with armed force, legal and moral uncertainty would have been overcome).

To many, the Serbian strategy of genocide in Bosnia in itself constituted a reason for intervention. Although the idea of humanitarian intervention was far from new, it gained new life as a result of Operation Provide Comfort in the wake of the Gulf War—an operation to prevent Saddam Hussein's troops carrying out genocide against the Kurds in northern Iraq.[22] The gradual withering of that operation, as the UN decided to halt it for lack of funding, generally went unnoticed as the Bosnian case was discussed repeatedly.

The legal and moral basis to prevent an act of genocide was not clearly established. Articles I and 55 of the UN Charter greatly emphasise the need to ensure that human rights are respected; the advancement of norms and legal documents based on this principle in other fora has added significance to questions of human rights; finally, international humanitar-ian law in armed conflicts, whether international or internal, 'could provide a separate justification for intervention in certain cases',[23] a point

[22] On the humanitarian intervention generally, see Nigel Rodley ed., *To Loose the Bands of Wickedness: International Intervention in Defence of Human Rights*, Brassey's, London, 1992; on the specific case of the Kurds in northern Iraq, see the contribution to that volume by Lawrence Freedman and David Boren.

[23] Christopher Greenwood, 'Human Rights and External Intervention', Ditchley Con-ference Report No. D93/8.

made with reference to the Geneva Conventions and the duty of all parties to those Conventions to 'respect and *ensure respect* [original emphasis] for the Conventions', including that on genocide.

These provisions, however, were in tension, at least in terms of the prevalent interpretation of the international order, with the cardinal principle of state sovereignty. Embodied in Articles 2(4) and 2(7) of the UN Charter, this principle rejects the possibility of the UN, or other external agents, interfering in the internal affairs of a state, unless the UN Security Council has determined a threat to international peace and security and taken enforcement measures under Chapter VII of the Charter which override the state's sovereignty. Whilst the events in former Yugoslavia, along with those in other places such as Somalia, were helping to shape thinking on and re-interpretation of these principles and, at least the point at which abuses of human rights, or breaches of international humanitarian law, in themselves, become threats to international peace and security, it is evident that no clear understanding of this problem existed.

Indeed, at the time of writing, the process of re-evaluation of the norms and principles relating to humanitarian intervention seems far from complete. Whilst it may be noted that the Geneva Conventions entail some duty to ensure respect of them, including that on genocide in war, it is by no means clearly established what the obligation entails in reality. It does not appear to necessitate military intervention—which would, in any case, be at odds with the cornerstone provisions of the UN Charter, unless there had been a Security Council resolution to support it. The provisions of the UN Charter, the Geneva Conventions and other documents in international law concerning human rights could be invoked to *permit* an international armed intervention. However, they do not, as many making the argument with regard to Bosnia believed they should, require such intervention.

Similarly, in the moral domain, exactly the same arguments were pitched against each other. The requirement to prevent genocide was set against the principle of non-intervention. The question of intervention was also subject to moral and philosophical questions of the just war—not only would there have to be sound ground for intervention, but there would have to be consideration also of other matters which would determine the justice of an intervention, such as the prospect of success and the likely price that would be paid for it.[24] This point, made normally, was related to some of the practical considerations detailed above.

If the basis for a military intervention appeared uncertain and, therefore, not compelling, in terms of human rights and humanitarian law, it was no more sure in terms of international security. Whilst the events in former Yugoslavia quite palpably presented a threat to international peace and security, they did not completely do so in terms of prior conventional

[24] See *ibid.*

28

interpretations of what constituted such a threat—principally, military aggression across a border by one member of the UN against another. In the first six months of war, hostilities were conducted, from the legal point of view, within the boundaries of one state, although, *de facto*, Yugoslavia had evolved into a set of mini-states. This meant that an intervention at the time of the fighting in Slovenia, or in Croatia, would have been made at variance with the provisions and interpretations of international law and the UN Charter at that stage. Many people, in retrospect, have argued that there should have been an external intervention at the time of the bombardment of Dubrovnik in Croatia, during the Autumn of 1991. Those making these arguments tend to forget that, at that stage, Croatia formally remained part of Yugoslavia for the international community and that the circumstances for an intervention were not so clear cut as they can seem looking back.

In Bosnia, however, the situation was a little different. This was the case because the US, the EC and its Member States, as well as numerous other countries had accepted Bosnia into the family of nations and were helping its entry into the UN. As an internationally recognised state and a member of the UN, to many observers, as well as the Bosnian authorities, it seemed that the international community would have to take action, not only to prevent attempted genocide, but to protect the Bosnian state from dismemberment resulting from armed aggression managed by the Serbian political leadership in Belgrade.

From the point of view of those in Western capitals facing the question of an armed intervention, however, the matter was, again, not clear-cut. Whilst it was evident that Belgrade carried responsibility for the initiation of large scale, organised campaigns of violence in Bosnia (something recognised in the UN Security Council Chapter VII resolutions, especially relating to sanctions, against Serbia), the aggression was not a classical cross-border adventure involving a well-established member of the UN— as had been the case with Iraq and Kuwait. It was, rather, a hybrid war. The continuing presence of the Yugoslav People's Army (YPA), loyal to Belgrade, in Bosnia after independence, meant that, although there were significant incursions across the River Drina between Serbia and Bosnia, there were also 80,000 troops already based in Bosnia. These troops were a consequence of Bosnia's predicament as a state emerging from the Yugoslav federation to become independent.

The transitional nature of the situation in Bosnia fuzzed some of the questions relating to the basis of intervention. So, too, did the fact that it was only in part a war of external aggression. The fact that the bulk of, first, the YPA and, later, its successor, the Army of the Serbian Republic (in Bosnia), comprised Serbs from Bosnia gave the war a strong element of internal conflict. Civil wars have been conventionally (to some extent prudentially) judged to be matters internal to the state and, therefore, subject to the general proscription of interference in domestic affairs— although, in reality, there is often external backing for different sides in

29

civil wars. Even though there was a critical question concerning the inviolability of the state's borders, the internal dimension was a counter-weight to the need to take similar action, particularly where there was little appetite for doing so.

However, for all the factors relating to practicability and principle which complicated the question of military intervention in Bosnia, the crucial matter was the politics of intervention. Whilst experts and officials generally recognised the complexities of the situation in Bosnia and the region, there was also a general awareness that only the use of force, or the threat of its use, perhaps, would decisively affect events on the ground. Whilst much was made of comments by military figures about their fears concerning the sending of troops to Bosnia, those fears, in general, were not so much to do with the strictly military factors involved, but rather were concerns about the relationship of the use of force to political objectives.

For example, Sir Richard Vincent, Chair of the Military Staff Com-mittee at NATO was widely reported when he took the rather unusual step of publicly voicing worries that, without a proper political dynamic, military intervention in Bosnia could parallel the Charge of the Light Brigade. Less noticed was that his point concerned not the use of force, but its linkage to a political objective. Even less noticed was his reported private assessment that intervention was possible and necessary at different levels.[25]

That opinion could be heard from many, if not all, corners of official-dom, both civilian and military, in private discussion. The assessment was that politicians were the major constraint on policy. In a different way, this is a point that was conceded by Douglas Hurd: 'The only thing which could have guaranteed peace with justice would have been an expeditionary force, creating if you like a new Northern Ireland, being there for how many years? And no government, no government has at any time proposed that.'[26] More strikingly, was the understanding expressed by NATO Secretary General Manfred Wörner who pointed that the reason there had been no military intervention was the politicians making up those governments and their lack of 'political will'.[27] Various plans had been made and policies recommended of a more interventionist nature, but various ministers had not had the stomach for them. If there was an overall policy failure, its central feature was the absence of armed force as a bottom-line. The reason for that absence was a lack of the 'political will' to act forcefully in a transitional situation that appeared to be both laced with risk and not absolutely indispensable.

[25] See, for example, Andrew Marr, 'Politicians let NATO down over Bosnia', *The Independent*, 11 September 1993.
[26] Douglas Hurd, Interview, 'Diplomacy and Deceit', Channel 4 TV, 2 August 1993, Media Transcription Service, *Bloody Bosnia*, MTS/M2578.WPS, p. 4.
[27] Manfred Wörner, Secretary General, NATO, 'NATO's Role in a Changing Europe', 11SS Adelphi Paper 284, 1994, p. 98.

The fact that, from an early stage of the Yugoslav break-up, politicians in virtually every significant country had decided that the situation was practically and politically uncertain, unclear, complex, too danger-ridden and potentially costly, meant that armed intervention was always highly unlikely. Where the only clear, common perspective was that the problem was too difficult to be dealt with using the kind of armed force which might be made available, it was more or less ruled out. It was that mixture of no intelligible political aim and political queasiness which most prompted the fears of senior military personnel.

The political worries of Western politicians concerned popular opinion and the need to win votes at the next election. The prospect that the mission might go wrong, given the complexity of the problem and its apparently intractable nature, made these political leaders reluctant to contemplate intervention seriously enough. The fear that it could be another Northern Ireland, Dien Bien Phu or broader Vietnam weighed heavily on the minds of politicians wanting to avoid similar problems.

In particular, in this respect, the shadow of Vietnam hanging over US political and military leaders was critical. For, because of the US's crucial role in NATO, as well as the size of its armed forces, no sizeable military intervention with ground forces was conceivable without US involvement.[28] Had the US been prepared to commit its ground troops, then there would have been little prospect that the UK, for all the worries shared by the Secretaries of State for Foreign Affairs and Defence, would not have been involved alongside. Likewise, whatever French rhetoric may suggest, in practice France has shown itself committed to international operations in a way which makes it hard to imagine Paris not, with special considerations, associating themselves with an intervention such as could have been in Bosnia.

The US, therefore, was (and remains) the linchpin of any concerted international military operation. The two US Administrations were both hamstrung by domestic considerations. These fell between the need to deal with the country's own economic difficulties, the lack of strong enough opinion that there should be intervention—in February 1993, 60 per cent of US citizens were reported to be opposed to intervention[29]— the absence of a perceived interest significant enough to warrant overcoming Vietnam sensitivity and making a commitment to forces anyway, and, lastly, a political campaign to explain that force commitment to public opinion.

American concern about Vietnam was well understood by the Serbian camp. They took every opportunity to remind the US and its potential

---

[28] Of course, much of this discussion was based on the notion of large-scale intervention. One alternative for the future for armed forces such as those of the UK and France would be a modernised return to the practices of their imperialist pasts—small, high quality forces designed for raids directed at the centre of gravity of opposing forces, something which could have been relevant had there been a decision to use force in Bosnia.

[29] *Washington Post*, and ABC Poll, reported in *Mladina*, 23 February 1993.

allies of the Vietnam spectre—however important—in any armed international action which would block them.[30] The Serbians managed to add to Western apprehensions about an armed intervention in the republic: intervention would be variously another Northern Ireland, another Beirut, or another Vietnam. Of course, Serbian reminders were just that: they were playing on those already present concerns and fears of politicians and military planners in the West. The message that an armed intervention would result in too many problems was well received and the continuing importance of the 'Vietnam syndrome' in the US confirmed.

In the final analysis, the critical factor in the failure of Western countries to intervene was the refusal of the US to put ground troops into the ring. That refusal stemmed in part from the absence of a compelling interest to commit ground troops and partly out of the anxieties about committing them to something which was perceived to contain the material of another Vietnam. However, the US was not alone in this. Whilst the UK and France would almost certainly have lent their support to a mission based around US troops, both they and other European governments (east and west) shared the same lack of confidence about military intervention and a similar, but different, weak sense of interest.[31]

If there was no compelling reason for the US to put its troops on Bosnian soil, there was no necessary reason for the Western Europeans to mount, or demand, a major military intervention there. It was Bosnia's fate, indeed, Yugoslavia's, that it presented a problem for the whole of Europe, in particular, for those integrating in the West in the European Community which was close enough that it could not be ignored—it had to be given attention, something had to be done. Bosnia was, however, not so close, nor so immediate, that there was an overriding need to decide to take the kind of action necessary—the use, or the threat of the use, of armed force—to resolve the situation.

In this sense, both the US and the various Europeans, for all they sometimes had radically different ideas about the situation in former Yugoslavia, knew and understood most of the detail in it. However, they still failed, individually and collectively, to gain a sharp political focus on events in Bosnia and to establish a perspective on the political future of the country. Without such a perspective, none of them could clearly begin to sort the wood from the trees and seriously address the question of military intervention. It seems likely that there was no desire to do so.

Much of the international involvement in the former Yugoslavia constituted something close to intervention, not necessarily purely military,

---

[30] See Patrick J. Garrity, *Why the Gulf War Still Matters: Foreign Perspectives on the War and the Future of International Security*, Report No. 16, CNSS, Los Alamos National Laboratory, LA-12592, July 1993, p. 36.

[31] A further consideration here was that the Russian Federation, whilst officially backing most UN Security Council initiatives was always sensitive to certain relatively small, but vocal pressures which would have made it reluctant to back the use of force against the Serbs in most circumstances, although it might well have done so in particular circumstances.

but it was never outright. By this, I mean that the deployment of UNPROFOR in Bosnia and Hercegovina was something accepted under pressure by the parties, against their will (the Serbs, in particular), rather than welcomed by them. It was only welcome to the Serbian camp in so far as it was a deployment of armed forces which did not threaten to stop their campaign through combat. Nonetheless, the presence of armed international troops was an impediment which they would rather have avoided.

However, the kind of large-scale military intervention often debated never materialised. There are numerous components of an explanation for this. They include the various complexities of the situation in Bosnia itself and the transitional period in which the war has taken place and the reality that, because of this, the war has not been an open case of inter-state aggression. The relative complexity both of the former Yugoslav state and of the process of dissolution through war meant that little if anything was straightforward—and anything which was so could easily be blurred because of other intricacies. Beyond this is the lack both of clarity and of vision in Western political perceptions of the war—the kind of vision which could represent a meaningful political objective for military intervention, or even the use of force by an implementation force.

Bosnia is, in the end, not only the borders of the former state and those of the ironically named Union of Republics which is set to succeed it, shaped by the efforts of international mediation, nor is it only the borders of the entities likely to succeed the Union republics after a relatively short period. Bosnia also represents the historic boundary between east and west, that between Islam and Christianity. And it represents the limits of European integration, of humanitarian concern and of political interest.

Nor was it important enough that the various governments and agencies dealing with the break-up of Yugoslavia were obliged to be decisive, cohesive and coherent in their actions. The bottom line, though, is that much good work and good-will, have looked like a shambles, because among al the different governments of the Western world affected in various ways by all the other factors which have been discussed, especially the US, there was not one which was clear and confident enough to bite the bullet. Rather, all were like losing gamblers, constantly hoping that diplomacy and non-violent pressures would be enough, or like rabbits frozen in the glare of Bosnian headlamps, afraid to jump. Political nervousness dictated the international response. In short, through a jungle of deliberation and a forest of procrastination, the leaders of the international community saw several Yugoslav doors, but could not decide if they should be opened or closed.

# APPEASEMENT, INTERVENTION AND THE FUTURE OF EUROPE

### JANE M. O. SHARP*

THREE dichotomies need to be addressed in order to understand the theory and practice of military intervention. The first is between intervention viewed as intrusive and improper interference, and intervention as a positive and affirmative mode of conflict resolution. The second is between the values being protected by an intervention, whether they should be state values like territorial integrity, or human values like individual and minority group rights. The third is between unilateral and multilateral intervention.[1]

The essence of an effective collective security system must be preventive diplomacy to settle disputes wherever possible without resort to force. Ideally, the system should also restrain great powers which are tempted to intervene unilaterally to defend their own national interests at the expense of international peace and stability. But when force is needed to discipline rogue nations the system must provide for the major powers to intervene for the common good, even when their own short term national interests are not at risk.

Recognised spheres of influence circumscribed interventions by the major powers during the Cold War years. But the emerging international system could adopt a new norm of intervention and generate multilateral forces capable of intervening, at short notice, to prevent abuse of minority group rights in parts of the globe previously off limits.

This paper takes the doctrine of Just War as the starting point for an exploration of the criteria for Just Intervention, for we should have no illusions that traditional peace-keeping operations can work in a war situation. Intervening to end a war means going to war on behalf of others. Just War doctrine suggests that five preconditions must hold to justify intervention in an ongoing conflict:[2]

1. the operation must be conducted under a competent authority,

* Jane M. O. Sharp is a senior research fellow, Department of War Studies, King's College London, and directs the Defence and Security Programme at the Institute for Public Policy Research (IPPR). She is the author of *Bankrupt in the Balkans: British Policy in Bosnia* (IPPR, 1993).

[1] Lori Fisler Damrosch, 'Changing conceptions of intervention in international law', Laura Reed and Carl Kaysen, eds, *Emerging norms of justified intervention*, American Academy of Arts and Sciences, Cambridge, Mass: 1993, pp. 93–110.

[2] Hugh Beach, *Just Intervention?*, London: Council for Arms Control, 1993; Jean Bethke Elshtain, ed., *Just War Theory*, Blackwell, Oxford, 1992.

2. for a just cause,
3. after peaceful means have been tried and failed,
4. if there is a reasonable chance of success,
5. and with a sense of proportion and discrimination, i.e. not merely for revenge which will, inter alia, harm innocent civilians, but to produce a better result.

## Searching for a competent authority: collective security or collective defence systems?

After wars and other upheavals the major powers usually try to re-establish order with new security arrangements designed to protect human rights for all citizens within secure borders. The emphasis has oscillated between universal systems of collective security which have no predetermined enemies, and military alliances organised for collective self defence against well understood (if not always explicit) threats.[3]

The efforts to establish collective security systems have not fared well. In the aftermath of the Napoleonic Wars Russia, Prussia, Austria, Britain and (later) France formed a Concert of Europe which without any formal machinery met for periodic conferences and congresses to manage the affairs of Europe from 1815 to 1878.[4] These five powers assumed the right to intervene multilaterally to maintain order where necessary, but also to curb the tendency of some of the five to intervene unilaterally where their own interests were heavily involved.

As British Foreign Secretary, for example, Lord Castlereagh opposed Russian proposals to intervene to restore the Spanish government in the 1920s. Then, as now, the major European powers were bitterly divided on the status of Serbia.

After the First World War the League of Nations emphasised the need for all sovereign states to protect the rights of minorities to equal treatment in law, religious freedom and use of their own language. Few states took these obligations seriously, however, and the League proved powerless to enforce them, taking no action to prevent either the Japanese invasion of Manchuria or the Italian invasion of Ethiopia. The League was plagued

---

[3] I am indebted to David Carlton for useful discussions on the differences between collective security and collective defence. See also Stephen Walt, *The Origins of Alliances*, Cornell University Press, Ithaca, New York, 1987; Samuel P. Huntington, 'Democratisation and Security in Eastern Europe', Peter Volten, ed., *Uncertain Futures, Eastern Europe and Democracy*, Institute for East-West Security Studies, New York, 1990, pp. 35–49. Charles and Clifford Kupchan, 'Concerts, Collective Security and the Future of Europe', *International Security*, Vol. 16, no. 1, pp. 114–61.

[4] The early years of the Concert were better managed than the later ones; see Henry A. Kissinger, *A world restored: Metternich, Castlereagh and the Problems of Peace*, Houghton Mifflin, Boston, 1973; Marc Trachtenberg, 'Intervention in historical perspective', Laura W. Reed and Carl Kaysen, *Emerging Norms of Justified Intervention*, op. cit., 1992, pp. 15–36; Charles and Clifford Kupchan, *op. cit.*

with a double standard: in the minority treaty system, for example, the lesser European powers (in the Baltics, the Balkans and central Europe) were subject to restrictions, but the 'civilised' countries in western Europe could treat their minorities as they wished; although flagrant violations were ignored even in the states that were subject to the treaties. The result was that the smaller European states began to seek protection in bilateral arrangements with powerful neighbours, producing a set of alliances culminating in the Second World War.

In 1945, after the genocidal aggression of Nazi Germany, the United Nations again focused on human and minority rights. UN Conventions were concluded on The Prevention and Punishment of the Crime of Genocide (1948), to Protect Economic, Social, and Cultural Rights (1966), and to Protect Civil and Political Rights (1966). In order to protect the sovereignty and independence of former colonial peoples, the UN Charter also embraced the principles of self-determination and non-intervention (Articles 1(2) and 7), and made provisions for the peaceful settlement of disputes under Chapter VI (articles 33–38).

These articles are often invoked by those who argue against intervention, notably by scholars from Third World countries with histories of intervention by former imperial powers.[5] Not surprisingly, former colonies see intervention as incompatible with their new-found sovereignty. Nevertheless, under Chapter VII (Articles 39–51) the UN provides for intervention by member states in the event of breaches of the peace and acts of aggression. Article 41 allows for economic sanctions and Article 42 for military action. Article 43 called for negotiations among the member countries to provide the force necessary for a UN intervention. Article 45 calls for such force to be 'immediately available' the numbers to be determined by agreement. Article 47 stipulates that a Military Staff Committee be established, consisting of the Chiefs of Staff of the five permanent members of the Security Council (China, USSR, USA, UK and France) which would direct armed forces placed at the disposal of the Security Council, and may establish regional sub-committees.

Article 51 provides for the right of self-defence if a state is attacked and until the UN Security Council has taken the necessary measures to restore peace. In a speech to the Russian General Staff in September 1993 the British Defence Minister, Malcolm Rifkind, reminded his audience that Article 51 was the authority under which Britain retook the Falklands Islands, after invasion by Argentina in 1982.[6] Article 51 was also seen as providing the right for collective defence in both the North Atlantic Treaty

---

[5] Virginia Gamba, 'Justified intervention? A view from the South' in Reed and Kaysen, *op. cit.*, pp. 115–25; Olaro Ottunno, 'Maintaining broad legitimacy', John Roper, Masashi, Enid Schoettle and Olara Otunno, *Keeping the peace in the post-cold war era: strengthening multilateral peace-keeping*, Trilateral Commission Report, Washington D.C., March 1993, pp. 69–82.

[6] UK FCO, *Arms Control and Disarmament Quarterly Review*, 31 October 1993, pp. 32–7.

and the former Warsaw pact, to justify the right of one party to the alliance to come to the aid of another if the latter comes under attack. The definition of self-defence has on occasion been stretched to justify pre-emptive attacks on states deemed a serious threat, as for example the Israeli attack on Egypt in 1967.

In the mid-1940s the US responded to its obligations under Article 43 by offering to supply 20 divisions of ground troops (over 300,000 men), a large naval force, 1,250 heavy bombers and 2,250 fighter aircraft. The arrangements envisaged under Articles 43 and 45 were never carried out, however, because of tensions between the former Soviet Union and the West. The Soviet leaders took the view that without agreements concluded under Articles 43 and 45 the UN had no business intervening anywhere with military action. The rest of the UN community took the view that without agreements concluded under Articles 43 and 45 Member countries were not obliged to participate in military enforcement action, but could volunteer to do so.[7]

Chapter VIII of the UN Charter provides for regional security arrangements to act under UN authority to maintain peace and security. During the Cold War, UN actions were primarily in Third World trouble spots because regional organisations like NATO and WTO rarely challenged overtly what each did within its own half of Europe.[8] NATO governments did not try to intervene, for example, when Soviet troops crushed the Hungarian and Czechoslovak uprisings in 1956 and 1968, because they judged that to do so might trigger a nuclear war. Nor did the Soviet Union interfere overtly with American interventions in Latin America.

During the Cold War the prevailing norm was against intervention, which was generally seen as an intrusive remnant of imperialism. In the 1990s, if conflicts continue to erupt throughout the former communist world, a new norm could begin to see intervention as a positive means to resolve conflict and protect the human rights of vulnerable civilians. But we are not there yet. In the 1990s, the NATO, WEU and CSCE powers were only prepared to conduct peace-keeping operations under UN authority on a case by case basis. In their CSCE capacity, states ruled out any peace enforcement missions. NATO Secretary General Manfred Worner repeatedly emphasised during 1992 and 1993 that NATO had done everything the UN asked it to do. This is technically true: NATO deployed naval forces (with those of the WEU) to the Adriatic in Operation Sharp Guard to prevent unauthorised shipping entering the waters of rump Yugoslavia (Montenegro and Serbia), as well as aircraft to Italy to be available for the Deny Flight, and Close Air Support operations. The problem was that military commanders on the ground were unwilling to

[7] Brian Urquhart, 'For a UN Volunteer Military Force', *The New York Review of Books*, 10 June 1993, pp. 3–4.

[8] Covertly, both sides sought to undermine the influence of the other in a number of ways. See 'The Secret War', in Gabriel Partos, *The World that came in from the Cold*, RIIA, London, 1993, pp. 183–92.

call for air strikes against the Serbs and Croats for fear of endangering their own men serving with UNPROFOR. Until February 1994 the No Fly Zone was violated hundreds of times by Serb and Croat aircraft without NATO forces making any attempt to shoot them down.

### Intervention under United Nations auspices since 1945

The UN is clearly not yet able to conduct effective military operations, even though it remains the only widely acceptable legitimating authority. Since the end of the Second World War, the UN Security Council has authorised four categories of intervention: peace enforcement, first generation peace-keeping, humanitarian intervention (sometimes referred to as second generation peace-keeping), and peace enforcement.[9]

The rarest has been peace enforcement, i.e. intervention to stop a war in progress and establish order, as provided for in Chapter VII of the UN charter. Chapter VII stipulated that military forces be contributed at short notice by member governments.In fact, however, during the Cold War the ideological conflicts between the US and the Soviet Union precluded the establishment of the Military Staff Committee and the only peace enforcement operation (against North Korea in the 1950s) was authorised in the absence of the Soviet delegate to the UN Security Council. With the end of the Cold War and the development of a more cooperative relationship between the former Communist countries and the west, new possibilities emerged for the UN to authorise *ad hoc* multilateral enforcement actions. This was the message George Bush tried to convey in his annual address to the United Nations General Assembly in September 1990.[10] One of the first actions of the new consensual Security Council was to legitimise the war to liberate Kuwait from occupation by Iraq in 1991. This carried a mixed message to the Third World and the Russians, however, as it reinforced their earlier impression that the UN had always been a tool of the United States.[11]

### First generation peace-keeping

When conflicts erupted in the Third World during the Cold War years the UN deployed 'peace-keeping' forces, the Blue Helmets, to freeze the conflict and separate as far as possible the warring factions. Peace-keeping was not specifically provided for in the UN Charter, but was designed by

[9] Of course these categories are not clear cut, some operations are a mixture of peace-keeping and humanitarian intervention and some peace-keeping operations are given Chapter VII responsibilities.
[10] Address by President Bush, 'The UN: world parliament of peace', *Current Policy No. 1303*, UN General Assembly, New York, 1 October 1990.
[11] Jonathan Eyal, 'The Gulf War is a disaster for the Soviet Union', *Guardian*, 28 February 1991; Colonel O. Falichev, 'The Shilka versus the B-52: Experience from the Gulf War', *Krasnaya Zvezda*, 5 April 1991; see also 'Military Lessons of the Gulf analysed', *Krasnaya Zvezda*, 17 May 1991.

38

former UN Secretary General Dag Hammarskjold for use in situations where Chapter VI settlement of disputes was inadequate and intervention under Chapter VII impossible. The main elements of peace-keeping (which Hammarskjold used to refer to as Chapter VI and a half) are intervention by military forces under passive rules of engagement to keep a peace already agreed by the previously warring parties.[12]

The UN lists the principal characteristics of traditional peace-keeping as follows:

1. the parties must consent to the presence of UN troops;
2. the UN must maintain impartiality between the parties to the conflict;
3. the parties must cooperate with the UN troops;
4. there must be a clear mandate from the UN Security Council;
5. any changes in the mandate must be accepted by the parties;
6. the mandate must be practicable;
7. the operation must maintain the support of the parties;
8. military personnel provided by Member governments must pass under the exclusive command of the UN Secretary General; and
9. the operation must have sound financial backing.[13]

Even for this relatively soft option, UN Security Council authority was difficult to organise in the Cold War because of the 279 vetos cast in the Un Security Council between 1945 and 1990. Between 1948 and 1988 there were only 13 UN peace-keeping operations. Since 1988 there has been a quantum leap in requests for peace-keepers, straining the UN bureaucracy to breaking point.[14] At the beginning of 1994 these numbered fifteen, more than at any other time in UN history.[15] In addition to UN Protection Forces in former Yugoslavia (UNPROFOR), other UN peace-keeping missions include: a truce supervision organisation (UNTSO) in the Middle East; a military observer group in India and Pakistan (UNMOGIP); forces to separate Greeks and Turks in Cyprus (UNFICYP); a disengagement observer force between Israel and Syria (UNDOF); an interim force in Lebanon (UNIFIL); an observer group in Central America (ONUCA); an observer mission in El Salvador (ONUSAL); an observer mission in Kuwait (UNIKOM); a mission for the referendum in Western Sahara (MINURSO); a verification mission in

[12] On traditional UN peace-keeping missions, see Marrack Goulding, 'The Evolution of United Nations Peacekeeping', *International Affairs*, Vol. 69, 3 July 1993, pp. 451–64; Trygve Lie, *In the cause of peace*, Macmillan, London, 1954; William J. Durch, ed., *The Evolution of UN Peacekeeping: Case Studies and Comparative Analyses*, St Martin's Press, New York, 1993. The best account of recent UN operations is in Mats Berdal, *Whither UN Peacekeeping?*, IISS, London, Adelphi Paper No. 281.

[13] UN Department of Public Information, *Blue Helmets: A Review of United Nations Peacekeeping*, New York, 1990.

[14] Cedric Thornberry, *The lessons of Yugoslavia*, paper presented at the Centre for Defence Studies, Kings College, London, 7 December 1993; see also Mats Berdal, *op. cit.*

[15] Koli A. Annan, 'UN Peace-keeping Operations and Cooperation with NATO', *NATO Review*, October 1993, pp. 3–7.

Angola (UNAVEM); a transitional authority in Cambodia (UNTAC); an operation in Somalia (UNOSOM).

## Humanitarian intervention

Humanitarian intervention is a recent innovation of peace-keeping in which operations are mounted without the agreement of the warring parties, but are still passive in the sense of keeping peace rather than making war. Operations in Bosnia, Somalia and Cambodia in the 1990s sought initially to protect convoys carrying humanitarian aid to civilians in war zones, with the focus on moral authority and only minimum military force, certainly not sufficient to curb the fighting. Christopher Greenwood defines humanitarian intervention as 'armed intervention in a state, even against the wishes of the government of that state to prevent widespread death or suffering among the population'.[16] Without the consent of, indeed sometimes in direct opposition to, the local warring parties these humanitarian operations are easily overwhelmed. Extra tasks the UN missions were unable to perform adequately included the resettlement of refugees, supervision of elections, clearing of mines, monitoring of cease fires and defence of convoys against hostile forces.[17]

## Preventive deployments

In the late 1990s, UN officials were claiming success for their first venture in preventive deployment of force (the mission to the Former Yugoslav republic of Macedonia, FYROM). Cedric Thornberry attributed this to the support of the Macedonian government, the high level of competence of the troops, and especially to the presence since July 1993 of 315 American ground troops, a commitment that President Clinton was unwilling to make to Bosnia. Observers on the ground reported, however, that both Greece and Serbia were supplying the different ethnic factions in Macedonia with arms and warned that the situation could explode.[18] Many feared the Clinton Administration would then withdraw US forces as it did so ignominiously from Somalia.

## What constitutes just cause for intervention?

UN conventions need credible enforcement procedures and without the quiver of a credible intervention capability in its bow, the UN Charter is worthless. Nevertheless intervention cannot be undertaken lightly and

---

[16] Christopher Greenwood, 'Is there a right of humanitarian intervention?', *The World Today*, February 1993, p. 34.

[17] Berdal, *op. cit.*

[18] Kim Mehmeti, 'The Balkan Arms Bazaar', *Balkan War Report*, December 1993, no. 23, pp. 1–9; see also Tasos Kokkinides, 'Arming Greece and Turkey: NATO's contribution to the Balkans', *ibid.*, p. 11.

must be justified to parliaments and treasuries on legal, moral and strategic grounds.

There are two main reasons why the western security community should have intervened with a serious military operation to halt Serbian and Croatian aggression against Bosnia. The first was to uphold the principle that borders must not be changed by force, but only by negotiation and consent of all the interested and affected parties. The second was to demonstrate unambiguously that genocide must not be tolerated.

One of the dominant themes in the debate about whether and how the international community should intervene in Bosnia was the question of whether the conflict there was a civil or an interstate war. And if the former, whether there was any legal right of intervention, given the UN principle of non-interference in the domestic affairs of states.

The war in Bosnia is a hybrid conflict with aspects of both civil and interstate conflict. The principal aggressors are Croatia and Serbia directing their proxies, as well as their own national armies, against the territorial integrity and the civilian populations of Bosnia-Hercegovina, a state which the US and the EC and most of the international community recognised in late 1991 and early 1992. In that sense, a western-led coalition of states had as much right to intervene against Serbian aggression in Bosnia as they did against Iraqi aggression of Kuwait. A British legal scholar said in early 1993 that political and military considerations, rather than lack of a legal basis, precluded military measures against the Serbs.[19]

But even if Bosnia, Serbia and Croatia were still autonomous republics in a federal Yugoslavia, the other European powers (as members of both the UN and the CSCE) could hardly justify washing their hands of the atrocities Serbs and Croats committed against the multi-ethnic Bosnian community on the grounds of non-intervention in the domestic affairs of a sovereign state. Genocide is wrong whether or not it crosses international borders. Until the Second World War genocide was considered largely a matter of domestic concern, not subject to interference by other states. The Genocide Convention was a response to the wholesale murder of Jews by Nazi Germany. Since then, genocide has been a crime under international law.[20] There is thus no longer any justification for passivity and indifference in the face of systematic killing, torture and rape of people because they belong to a religion, a race or a nation that has been arbitrarily defined as 'unclean'.[21]

---

[19] Christopher Greenwood, *op. cit.*

[20] Genocide is defined as 'acts committed with intent to destroy a national, ethnic, racial or religious group, by killing members of the group, causing serious bodily or mental harm to members of the group, deliberately inflicting on the group conditions of life calculated to bring about its physical destruction, imposing measures intended to prevent births within the group or forcibly transferring children from one group to another group'.

[21] Henry Siegman, 'Bosnia's holocaust puts churches to shame', *IHT*, 5 January 1994.

In addition to the moral and legal grounds for intervention are a set of strategic factors. One important objective, in the interests of global security (bearing in mind the long history of conflict in the Middle East as well as the current instabilities between Russia and the central Asian states), should be to avoid further exacerbating the existing tension between western Judeo-Christian states and the Muslim world. Since the majority of those suffering in Bosnia are Muslims, western reluctance to intervene reinforced a widely-held view in the Islamic countries that the West in general, and the US and Britain in particular, are anti-Muslim. This view was reinforced by the 1991 Gulf War and especially by the US, French and British bombing raids over Iraq in January 1993. The coordinated allied response to violation of the No-Fly Zone imposed over southern Iraq was in sharp contrast to the indecision and inaction among the allies about how, even whether, to respond to three months of daily violations of the No-Fly Zone imposed by the United Nations over Bosnia. Western indifference risks uniting the currently-divided Muslim governments into an anti-western coalition and further radicalising the Muslim Diaspora to produce another generation of rootless terrorists.

Another major reason to punish Serbian and Croatian aggression is to deter other potential ethnic cleansers and land grabbers especially in the former USSR. Western inaction in Bosnia suggests that we are indifferent to the bullying of the weak by the strong anywhere. This view was strengthened during 1993 by the extraordinarily simplistic view of foreign policy adopted by the Clinton Administration, which appeared to consist of mindless approbation of whatever policy Boris Yeltsin stumbled into, be it undemocratic practices at home or invasion of new states on the Russian periphery.[22]

In Ukraine the combination of US policy towards Russia and western inaction on Bosnia was cited by those making the case to retain independent nuclear weapons, on the grounds that Ukraine obviously could not count on western help should Russia treat Ukraine as Serbia treats Bosnia. Pandering to Russian opposition to the expansion of NATO also sent a message to the weaker nations in Eastern Europe, that they had better look to one of the regional great powers for bilateral protection as it apparently is not forthcoming from the western alliance; an ominous repetition of history.

It was also in western interests to prevent a widening of the war in the Balkans. A pan-Balkan War is not inevitable, but each passing day without resolution of Serbian war aims makes a wider war more likely. If the fighting in Bosnia spreads to the Muslim areas of Sandzak on the Serbian Montenegran border, for example, and from there to Kosovo, Serbian forces could be even more brutal to the ethnic Albanian population

---

[22] Jane M. O. Sharp, 'The Bill and Boris show', *The Bulletin of Atomic Scientists*, January–February 1994, pp. 12–13.

42

there.[23] Albania might then be tempted to intervene. Macedonia with 30 per cent Albanian population could also join in, at which point Greece would enter on the Serbian side, after which Turkey and Bulgaria would come in to counter and balance Greece.

## Shaping post Cold War Europe

Perhaps the most important reason to intervene in Bosnia, given the fragile transitional state of the international system, was to uphold the vision of a federal pluralistic multi-ethnic Europe. The worsening violence in Bosnia showed that the veneer of civilisation in parts of the Balkans is wafer thin. If European security is to be indivisible, western societies must shore up and share with their neighbouring post-Communist societies a model of strong pluralistic central government, tolerance of diversity and respect for human rights. Without these core values, inter-ethnic conflict will continue in the Balkans and could soon spread north and west.[24] As the German Defence Minister rightly asserted in early 1994: if western Europe does not export stability it will import instability.[25]

When the Cold War ended in the late 1980s, various scenarios were offered for the future structure of the European security system. Structural realists believed that what kept the peace during the Cold War was the balance of power between NATO and the WTO with each side respecting the others sphere of influence. They hoped for a continuation of a bipolar system in which the US would lead the North Atlantic Treaty Organisation (NATO) in which the west Europeans would assume a more equal weight, and a more democratic Soviet Union would lead a more equitable Warsaw Treaty Organisation (WTO).

A second scenario assumed a much weaker Soviet Union with a strong US leading a pan-European Security system that would develop either from the Conference on Security and Cooperation in Europe (CSCE) or from a gradual extension eastwards of the western zone of peace comprising the western democracies in NATO, the European Communities (EC) and the European Free Trade Association (EFTA). A third scenario assumed both Cold War superpowers much weakened in a fragmented Europe as states renationalised their foreign, economic and security policies. In the second scenario (a pan-European security system) united Germany was seen as a stabilising factor, but in the third (fragmented Europe) united Germany was likely to be destabilising.[26]

[23] Ethnic cleansing continued unabated in Kosovo during 1993; see Julie Mertus, 'Like rabbits in the Serbs' gun sights', *IHT*, 20 January 1994.

[24] Pierre Hassner, 'Beyond nationalism and internationalism', *Survival*, Vol. 35, no. 2, Summer 1993, pp. 49–65.

[25] Cited by Neal Ascherson, 'NATO is bungling its last chance to create security amid disorder', *The Independent on Sunday*, 9 January 1994.

[26] On post Cold War models, see Jane M. O. Sharp and Gerhard Wachter, *Looking Beyond the Blocs: European Security in 2020*, Institute for Peace and International Security,

Prospects for a continuation of stable bipolarity diminished in 1991 with the collapse of first the WTO then the Soviet Union. They were revived somewhat after the Russian elections in December 1993, amidst growing apprehension about the rise of aggressive fascism. East European governments hoped that a silver lining in this otherwise very dark cloud could be an end to the reluctance in some western capitals about whether to expand NATO eastwards.[27] These hopes were dashed at the NATO summit in January 1990, however, when the US offered only more consultations in the form of the Partnership for Peace, adding little to what had already been offered in the North Atlantic Cooperation Council (NACC) a year before.[28] During 1993 there was precious little cooperation between east and west in Europe as the 12 European Union states continued to close their markets to the former CMEA countries and the 16 NATO states dithered about whether or not to embrace the former WTO powers in Eastern Europe. This western indifference made the Central European aspirants to NATO feel that Boris Yeltsin was exerting a veto on their alliance prospects, just as former Soviet Foreign Minister Kvitsinsky tried (but failed) to do in 1991.[29]

Despite regular summit meetings and a plethora of new structures and mechanisms designed to cope with post-Cold War Europe, the 52-member CSCE proved too unwieldy for effective action. In particular the central and eastern European states were discouraged by the fact that the CSCE merely monitored, rather than tried to curb, the wars erupting in Former Yugoslavia (FYU).

The only hope for an effective CSCE would be one led by a smaller concert of the major powers. In the early 1990s, the prime candidates for such a concert were the four members of the permanent UN Security

Common Security Series, Paper 16, Cambridge Mass., June 1988; Morten Kelstrup, Pierre Lemaitre, Elzbieta Tromer and Ole Waever, *The European Security Order Recast: Scenarios for the Post Cold War Era*, Pinter, London, 1990; Stephen van Evera, 'Primed for Peace: Europe after the Cold War', *International Security*, Vol. 15, No. 3, Winter 1990–1991; Adrian Hyde-Pryce, *European Security Beyond the Cold War*, Sage, London, 1991.

[27] Jane Perlez, 'Fearing Russia, Poland insists on NATO', *IHT*, 13 December 1993; Bruce George, 'NATO should offer the East Europeans more than partnership', *Wall Street Journal*, 15 December 1993; Eve-Ann Prentice, 'Alarmed Baltic nations see vote as threat', *The Times*, 14 December 1993; William Pfaff, 'NATO should be clear about eastern Europe', *IHT*, 20 December 1993; Sam Nunn, 'A Clear NATO Message To the Soviet Successors', *IHT*, 28 December 1993.

[28] Compare the two documents: North Atlantic Council, 'North Atlantic Cooperation Council Statement on Dialogue, Partnership and Cooperation', reprinted as an annex to *Atlantic News No. 2382*, 21 December 1991; 'Partnership for Peace: Invitation' and 'Partnership for Peace: Framework Document', both reprinted as annexes to *Atlantic News No.2587*, 12 January 1994. See also David Ottoway, 'Sowing uncertainty in Eastern Europe', *IHT*, 19 January 1994.

[29] On Yulu Kvitsinsky's attempt to proscribe the alliance possibilities for former WTO states, see Jane M. O. Sharp, 'Security Options for Central Europe in the 1990s', in Beverly Woodward, ed., *The Future of European Security*, University of California Press, 1992, pp. 54–78.

Council (P4) who are also CSCE participants: Russia, USA, UK and France.[30] Relations between the four were good compared with the recent past, with especially close collaboration between Moscow and Washington to strengthen the nuclear non-proliferation regime.[31] Perhaps most important for the effective functioning of a collective security system was the relatively high level of professionalism in the armed forces of all four powers. Finally, the manifestly superior economic and military capabilities of the USA, and the Clinton Administration rhetoric that supported multilateralism, suggested an American leadership role if the President would grasp it.

But the Clinton Administration showed no taste for leadership and little interest in Europe during his first year in office. Despite an inaugural speech in January 1993 in which the President said that the US would act with force 'not just to defend its interests, but when the will and conscience of the international community is defied', he squandered many opportunities to lead a collective action to curb genocide and land grabbing in the Balkans. In the interests of future European stability these actions should have been taken in close collaboration with Boris Yeltsin's Russia.[32] The best opportunity to do so would have been after Yeltsin emerged from the April 1993 referendum with what amounted to a public vote of confidence. Neither then nor since, however, did Bill Clinton focus seriously on the war in Bosnia.[33] There was thus little hope for an American-led CSCE concert, and even considerable apprehension in Europe that US would continue as an effective leader of the Atlantic alliance.

Nor did the west European powers appear capable of leadership, whether they were acting as individual countries or as members of NATO, the Western European Union or the European Union (EU). Their response to the wars in Yugoslavia showed that in terms of foreign policy

[30] In the 1990s Germany and Japan both showed interest in joining those with permanent seats on the UN Security Council but neither appeared ready to contribute military forces for peace enforcement actions as envisaged by Chapter VII of the UN Charter.

[31] On the need for US collaboration with Russia and other former Soviet Republics on nuclear non-proliferation, see Kurt M. Campbell, Ashton B. Carter, Steven E. Miller and Charles A. Zraket, *Soviet Nuclear Fission: Control of the Nuclear Arsenal in a Disintegrating Soviet Union*, CSIA Studies in International Security, Harvard University, November 1991; and Graham Allison, Ashton B. Carter, Steven E. Miller and Philip Zelikow, *Cooperative Denuclearization: From Pledges to Deeds*, January 1993.

[32] This case is argued more fully in Jane M. O. Sharp and Vladimir Baranovsky, 'For a NATO-Russian UN intervention to end the war in Bosnia', *IHT*, 26 February 1993.

[33] Randolph Ryan, 'Clinton's Bosnian Mess', *The Boston Globe*, 22 May 1993; Tony Barber, 'Wandering into Balkan blunderland', *Independent on Sunday*, 30 May 1993; James Baker, 'The President must restore America's role as world leader', *The Times*, 12 July 1993; Ian Brodie, 'President's men labour to forge Clinton doctrine', *The Times*, 27 August 1993; Adrian Karatnycky, 'America is turning inward', *IHT*, 24 August 1993; Martin Walker, 'Clinton aims to spread burden with new foreign policy', *Guardian*, 19 August 1993; Thomas Friedman, 'Clinton rebuffs Bosnian leaders in plea for help', *New York Times*, 9 September 1993; Jonathon Clarke, 'The conceptual poverty in US foreign policy', *The Atlantic Monthly*, September 1993; Elaine Sciolino, 'Clinton's lack of interest stymies his foreign policy triumverate', *IHT*, 9 November 1993.

they remained a group of independent nation states, notwithstanding the rhetoric about a Common Foreign and Security Policy (CFSP) and a European Security and Defence Identity (ESDI).[34]

Thus the third and most pessimistic scenario (European fragmentation) which seemed a far fetched possibility in the late 1980s, looked menacingly close in early 1994.[35] As was the case under the League of Nations in the 1930s, the indifference of the wealthy industrial western powers to the fate of their newly independent eastern cousins, was an ominous sign that Europe was heading towards fragmentation.

If the US is losing interest in Europe, and Russia is becoming an increasingly uncooperative and unreliable partner, west European leaders will have to grasp the nettle of pan-European leadership collectively or Germany will be forced to fill the leadership vacuum. This is an outcome nobody wants, least of all the current generation of German leaders, but this is where western appeasement is leading Europe in early 1994.

## The timing of outside intervention

There are few points in the normal cycle of conflict at which outside intervention can help to resolve differences between the parties: one of them is early, before opposing positions have hardened, another is late, when the belligerents have fought themselves to exhaustion.[36]

After political disputes erupt into armed conflict, outside mediators try to cool down the warring parties, negotiate a cease-fire and deploy UN peace-keepers to maintain the peace. In the best case peace is maintained and relations stabilised. But, as in Bosnia, cease fires often fail and conflict recurs. Sending in more passive peace-keepers at this stage is unlikely to be as useful as a military operation which disarms the warring factions and restores order. US General John Galvin, former Supreme Allied Commander Europe (SACEUR) testified to congressional committees in May 1993 that there were at least two points in 1991 when US action could, and should, have responded to Serb aggression against Croatia: the first was the bombing of Dubrovnik, the second was the bombing of Vukovar.[37] Emboldened by western acquiescence in the bombardment of Croatia, Serbia continued unchecked with its plans to absorb Bosnia.

If and when peace is restored in Bosnia, and we must recognise that Bosnia may be already lost, the international community and the parties on the ground should engage in a long-term process of 'peace building', as

[34] Simon Lunn, 'A reassessment of European Security' in Lunn *et al.*, *What is Security After the Cold War?*, Philip Morris Institute, Paris, December 1993, pp. 50–67.

[35] Paddy Ashdown, 'Europe's only federal ideal lies dying in the streets of Sarajevo', *The European*, 24–30 December 1993.

[36] Hugh Miall, *New Conflicts in Europe: Prevention and Resolution*, Oxford Research Group, Current Decisions Report, Oxford, 10 July 1992; see also Hugh Maill, *The Peacemakers: Peaceful Settlement of Disputes since 1945*, Macmillan, London, 1992.

[37] Galvin at congressional hearings cited by Anthony Lewis, 'Who really believes the Bosnians don't matter?', *IHT*, 11 January 1994.

proposed by Boutros Boutros-Ghali in his June 1992 report *Agenda for Peace*. This post-conflict consolidation phase is especially important in those former communist countries where civic society is weak and there is precious little social capital to draw on.[38]

Without peace-building activities to nurture civic structures and non-governmental networks that protect minority rights and build trust and inspire confidence throughout the domestic polity, the peace-making and peace-keeping operations may come to naught. The key to successful intervention is to follow up military operations, that impose order, with a civilian intervention to rebuild societies.

Seeing conflict in cyclical terms[39] helps to explain why Europeans were not much impressed with the Clinton Administration's 'lift and strike' proposals (i.e. to lift the arms embargo on Bosnia and to strike Serbian heavy artillery positions). Ineffective intervention is worse than no intervention at all, since it raises expectations and prolongs the conflict. Finally, to maintain peace mechanisms must be in place to allow the international community to engage in preventive diplomacy, to monitor and to defuse potentially explosive situations.

### *The failure of preventive diplomacy in post Cold War Europe*

Many of the smaller states in Europe, especially those that had been in the Soviet grip throughout the Cold War, viewed the CSCE summit meeting in Paris in 1990 as the peace conference to codify the end of the Cold War and hoped CSCE would provide the necessary mechanisms of preventive diplomacy in Europe. In Paris CSCE leaders re-affirmed the importance of human rights, the inviolability of borders, and proclaimed an end to adversarial relations between the NATO and the WTO.[40] Prospects for a cooperative pan European security system looked encouraging as the CSCE established a permanent secretariat in Prague, a Centre for the Prevention of Conflict (CPC) in Vienna, and an Office for Democratic Institutions and Human Rights (ODIHR) in Warsaw. In Helsinki in July 1992, CSCE created the position of High Commissioner for Minorities and in September of that year both the CSCE and the UN General Assembly expelled the Belgrade government on the basis of human rights violations. Nevertheless, while CSCE obviously recognised the protection of human rights within state borders as a fit subject for international controls, CSCE machinery was not used to good effect in Bosnia.

[38] On the concept of Social Capital, see Robert Putnam, *Making Democracy Work: civic traditions in modern Italy*, Princeton University Press, 1993; and 'The prosperous community', *The American Prospect*, Spring 1993, No. 13.

[39] The concept of a conflict cycle was developed at a conference on *The Lessons of Yugoslavia* in Spoleto, Umbria, in May 1993, jointly sponsored by the Centre for the Study of International Politics in Rome (CESPI), the British American Security Information Council (BASIC) and the Search for Common Ground, Washington D.C.

[40] *The Charter of Paris for a new Europe*, signed in Paris on 21 November 1990, is reprinted as Appendix 17B in The SIPRI Yearbook 1991, pp. 603–13.

Nor did Western leaders act on the intelligence they gathered in the Balkans in the late 1980s and early 1990s, despite clear warnings of trouble in former Yugoslavia. This was particularly surprising as the US knew of Milosevic's hunger for a Greater Serbia once he took power in 1987.[41]

As US Secretary of State James Baker made clear in an unfortunate speech in Belgrade in June 1991, the West saw Yugoslavia as the USSR in microcosm and wanted to maintain a unitary state as a model to deter the breakup of the USSR. This may explain (but is no excuse for) western passivity as Milosevic systematically persecuted the Albanian minority in Kosovo in the late 1980s, and bombarded Dubrovnik and other Croatian cities in late 1991.

Nor does it explain or excuse the inept diplomacy of the EC, in particular the recognition of Croatia in defiance of Robert Badinter's report condemning Croatian treatment of its Serbian minority.[42] Recognition of Croatia then triggered a referendum and subsequent declaration of independence by Bosnia-Hercegovina in early 1992, prompting (as Lord Carrington and others had predicted) the genocidal aggression by Serbia and Croatia as they proceeded to carve up Bosnia at the expense of the multi-ethnic communities there. Even after recognition of Bosnia the western powers passively tolerated Serbian bombardment of Sarajevo from April 1992 onwards and attacks on UN convoys from June 1992. A No-Fly zone was imposed in October 1992 with no attempt to enforce it until February 1994. Similarly, six areas of Bosnia were designated safe areas in late April but with no enforcement mechanisms.

The diplomatic and military interventions of governments under the auspices of the European Union and the Western European Union were no more productive than operations under the UN flag.[43] When Serbia invaded Croatia and Slovenia in June 1991, the European Community Troika of foreign ministers (Gianni de Michelis, Jacques Poos and Hans van den Broek) immediately went to Belgrade with a three point plan. Michelis told the press that the US had been informed rather than consulted, implying that the EC could handle the matter, and the Western European Union rather than NATO should undertake any necessary military action.

[41] Warren Zimmerman proposed more active intervention in Bosnia to the Clinton Administration during 1992 and 1993 and eventually resigned in January 1994; the fifth government official to resign in protest at US policy towards Bosnia since January 1993. AP 'Ex-US envoy quits in protest', *International Herald Tribune*, 7 January 1994; see also Edwin M. Yoder, 'A good man who shouldn't be lost', *IHT*, 19 January 1994.

[42] Conference pour la paix en Yugoslavia, Commission d'Arbitrage, Avis No. 5 Croatia, 11 January 1992 (The Badinter Commission).

[43] For different views: that the WEU made a useful contribution to the peace process in Bosnia, see John Roper, 'A wider range of tasks' in Roper, Nisihara, Otunnu and Schoettle, *Keeping the peace in the post-Cold War era*, The Trilateral Commission, Washington D.C., March, 1993, pp. 3–16; Willem Van Eekelen, 'WEU prepares the way for new missions', *NATO Review*, Vol. 41, No. 5, October 1993, pp. 19–23.

This was manifestly absurd, since the WEU had at that time neither forces nor a command structure at its disposal.[44] Rosalyn Higgins, a British international lawyer, believes this posturing by the EC, without any mandate, relevant experience or constitutional authority, was deeply damaging to the search for peace in former Yugoslavia, by encouraging the Serbian leadership to believe it had a free hand with the neighbouring republics.[45] After an embarrassing show of indecision over the Gulf Crisis in 1990 it was understandable for EC leaders to want to exert a more coherent front on Yugoslavia. But in the event they sacrificed the interests of peace in the region to their own desire to forge a semblance of foreign policy competence. The best form of preventive diplomacy in Europe would be for NATO to guarantee the borders of the former non Soviet WTO countries, even if the member states remain unwilling to take the former communist countries into the alliance as full members.[46]

## The Feasibility Criterion

The arguments against western involvement in a multilateral military intervention to save Bosnia from a Serbo-Croatian carve-up centred on the question of feasibility.[47] British defence officials were unwilling to allocate the necessary resources to mount an effective intervention operation, especially after the cutbacks agreed in July 1991.[48] British military officers also cited the problems of peace enforcement in Northern Ireland and Americans similarly cited the Vietnam quagmire as reasons not to become involved in open-ended commitments on the ground in Bosnia.

Other experienced military officers suggested, however, that an operation to restore order in Bosnia was feasible with a force of 60,000–75,000 men. In the UK for example, in parliamentary hearings and other forums, a former military attache in Belgrade, familiar with the capabilities of the former Yugoslav armies and with the terrain in Bosnia-Hercegovina, laid out eight separate military tasks.[49] A United Nations

[44] Steps were taken at the January 1994 NATO summit to provide WEU with access to NATO logistics for any future operations that WEU states may want to take without the US.

[45] Rosalyn Higgins, 'The new United Nations and former Yugoslavia', *International Affairs*, Vol. 69, No. 3, 1993, pp. 465–83.

[46] William Pfaff has made this case in a number of articles, see 'Invitation to war: the modernity of ancient hatreds', *Foreign Affairs*, Summer 1993; 'A partnership of anger and dashed expectations', *IHT*, 8–9 January 1994.

[47] Richard Falk makes a strong case against military intervention aimed at political restructuring in the target country while admitting that military intervention to oppose boundary changes can be effective. See 'Hard choices and tragic dilemmas', *The Nation*, 20 December 1993, pp. 755–64.

[48] The Ministry of Defence announced cutbacks in *Options for Change*, in July 1991. Some of the manpower cuts were modified in March 1993 in anticipation of future peace-keeping operations.

[49] Edward Cowan, *Military Intervention in Former Yugoslavia*, International Security Information Service Briefing 33, London, April 1993; see also 'Sarajevo could yet be saved', *The Independent*, 10 August 1993.

Transitional Authority (UNTA) to perform these tasks for Bosnia was proposed by the political parties in Bosnia as well as by several international lawyers and non-governmental organisations in 1992.[50]

Such a military intervention force could, in theory, have been mustered by the European countries, but in practice required American participation to make it credible to the warring factions on the ground. The Clinton Administration refused to send ground troops, however, except to police an agreed peace settlement and only then if they could serve under NATO rather than UN command. As there was no settlement Bosnia received only passive (and wholly inappropriate) UN Protection Forces (UNPROFOR). The US refused to contribute any ground force personnel to UNPROFOR, confining its aid to Bosnia to air-dropped supplies, much of which fell into Serbian military hands.

UNPROFOR, far from protecting victims of aggression, effectively supported Serbian and Croatian war aims at the expense of Bosnia. The disarray in UN operations during 1993 suggests that the UN is likely to mount effective military operations for many years, if ever, and that peace enforcement measures would best be left to a competent concert of nations capable of mounting and executing military operations for the common good.

## Lessons from UNPROFOR

Anyone familiar with the UNPROFOR operations in Croatia and Bosnia-Hercegovina will recognise that conditions there were wholly inappropriate for passive UN peace-keeping and humanitarian operations. Far from cooperating with the UN, Serb and Croat forces impeded UN operations from the beginning. Later, as the Bosnians increasingly felt betrayed by the UN, they too withheld cooperation. UN officials claim that if UN troops lose their impartiality towards belligerents UN peace-keeping operations will self-destruct.[51] But by striving to maintain impartiality in Bosnia, treating genocidal aggressors on the same level as the victims of such aggression, UN officials made a mockery of international law. Military tasks cannot be performed without good logistics, command, control communication and intelligence and properly equipped and trained manpower. The troops on the ground were not to blame for the inadequacies of UN operations, but their political masters certainly were, in particular the five governments who sit on the permanent UN Security Council. Far from choosing practicable mandates, these P-5 governments repeatedly passed resolutions without securing appropriate forces or adequate financing to execute them, thereby placing impossible demands on personnel in the field. Returning troops report that command and

[50] See for example, Zoran Pajic, 'UN Trusteeship can halt ethnic ghettoes', *Yugo-Fax*, No. 11, 7 May 1992; and 'The political aims of intervention', *Yugo-Fax*, No. 12, 29 June 1992.
[51] Cedric Thornberry, *Lessons of Yugoslavia*, op. cit.,

control arrangements were chaotic with, for example, Spaniards refusing to serve under British command and vice versa. In addition logistics were inadequate and many of the national contingents were ill-equipped and poorly trained. As for financial resources, even some of the P-5 consistently fell short of their allocated contributions to UN operations.[52]

The principal lesson from UNPROFOR is that traditional peace-keeping operations are not appropriate where the parties remain in conflict. When conditions are appropriate UN operations can be highly successful, as they were in Cambodia in the 1990s; but when rogue states commit genocide and attempt to change borders by force the P-5 governments should act as a collective security concert, recruiting others as necessary to mount effective military interventions to restore order, separate and disarm the warring factions and create conditions under which a settlement can be negotiated with appropriated authorities.

When parties to a conflict are still warring, and are unwilling to cooperate with the UN, traditional peace-keeping operations are more likely to exacerbate than help the situation. As in Yugoslavia, with such poor communication, command and control arrangements, the only way UN peace-keepers can operate is at the pleasure of the belligerents.[53] Thus, even when acting in good faith, peace-keepers deployed in war zones soon lose both the respect of the warring parties and the confidence of the civilian victims. The most vivid, and ironic, case of this syndrome was manifest in August 1993 when Bosnians besieged in Sarajevo expressed admiration for the masterly way in which their tormentor (the Serb commander General Mladic) persuaded the British and French commanders of UNPROFOR to place their own troops atop Mount Igman in order to deter the air strikes threatened by President Clinton.[54]

Despite many individual acts of heroism the net result of UNPROFOR was to undermine the credibility of the UN, whose forces proved so incapable, as well as the credibility of NATO, whose forces are manifestly capable, but whose governments proved unwilling to help in serious ways. Among the most shameful of the many failures of the US, France and Britain, all three of whom sit on the P-5 and maintain capable military forces, was neglect of the six areas designated 'Safe Areas' by numerous UN Security Council Resolutions beginning with No. 836 in late April 1993. In June 1993 UN Secretary General Boutros Boutros-Ghali said 34,000 troops were needed to guard Bihac, Gorazde, Sarajevo, Sebrenica, Tuzla and Zepa. Later, as it became clear that these troops would not be

---

[52] Enid C. B. Schoettle, 'Financing UN Peace-keeping' in John Roper, Masashi Nishihara, Olara Otunno and Enid C. B. Schoettle, *Keeping the Peace in the Post Cold War Era: Strengthening Multilateral Peacekeeping*, The Trilateral Commission, Washington D.C., March 1993, pp. 17–50.

[53] John Pomfret, 'UN Dilemma: Relieving Bosnian suffering prolongs the war', *IHT*, 25 November 1993.

[54] David Rieff, 'Doing the Bosnian Serbs' work for them', *IHT*, 12 August 1993; James Bone and Michael Evans, 'Washington orders UN to muzzle commanders', *The Times*, 19 August 1993.

51

forthcoming, UN officials claimed 7,500 troops and 50 military observers would be sufficient, but even these modest numbers were never mustered. In July, Barry Frewer, a Canadian UN official, admitted that no attempt was being made to implement the safe areas.[55]

Under pressure from the Clinton Administration, on 2 August 1993, NATO ministers agreed to bomb Serb forces if the latter did not end their strangulation of Sarajevo. A week later on 9 August the NATO ministers met again to clarify their collective position, saying it was essential the Serbs lift their siege of Sarajevo without delay, adding for emphasis 'There should be no doubt about the firm determination of NATO and its member nations to act against those responsible so that the resolutions of the UN Security Council are respected and the suffering brought to an end'. The Serbs continued to bombard Sarajevo for the rest of the year. NATO took no action, losing credibility as a serious military organisation with every Serb salvo. In October UNPROFOR troops were withdrawn from three of the six 'safe' areas, leaving the residents there more vulnerable than ever to Serbian and Croatian snipers through the winter.

At the turn of the year Britain, France and Canada, who provide the bulk of UNPROFOR manpower, recognising failure and still without any support on the ground from Washington, began to discuss pulling out of Bosnia, though French Foreign Minister Alain Juppe was obviously troubled about what impression this would give.[56] Hardly anyone in early 1994 expected the west to mount a rescue operation for Bosnia if the UN pulled out, but there were renewed calls to lift the arms embargo on Bosnia to allow for self defence. In the US, for example, a nonpartisan group, *The Action Council for Peace in the Balkans*, called for withdrawing UNPROFOR, lifting the arms embargo on Bosnia, and providing US air support to the Bosnia Army to carry out the protection of relief convoys.[57]

By January 1994 disillusionment with the UN was severe, not least among the troops sent to serve there. Both Belgian General Francis Briquemont and French General Jean Cot were withdrawn early from their UN commands in Bosnia because of their outspoken criticism of the UN. Briquemont denounced as pure hypocricy the tendency of the P-5 powers to pass resolutions without offering troops to execute them. He was especially critical of the refusal to follow through on the Safe Areas resolution. Cot was incensed by the refusal of the UN Secretary General to delegate authority for air strikes to him.

---

[55] Marcus Tanner, 'Un admits "safe areas" do not exist', *The Independent*, 29 July 1993.

[56] Ian Black, 'Owen warns of UN troop withdrawal: Canada to review its forces' participation in Bosnia', *Guardian*, 5 January 1994.

[57] Zalmay Khalizad, 'Europe's latest Bosnia plan is flawed', *The Wall Street Journal*, 3 December 1993; Anthony Lewis, 'For action on Bosnia: a double test', *IHT*, 8–9 January 1994.

## A sense of proportion and a sense of direction

Realists, especially in the US, argue that the decision not to enforce peace in Bosnia was prudent, indeed that those who urged a more forceful interventionist policy by the US were guilty of raising Bosnian expectations of rescue, prolonging the fighting on the ground, hampering the peace bargaining in Geneva, and undermining the deal that Bosnia was able to cut. They suggest that Bosnia was ill-served by the irresponsible rhetoric of the interventionists and should have agreed to an ethnic partition when it was first proposed by Peter Carrington in 1992.

In early 1994, surveying the collapse of the Geneva negotiations and the prospect of intensified conflict in Bosnia, such arguments carry weight. Fewer lives would have been lost if a settlement had been agreed earlier, especially if the US had come through with its share of an enforcement package. Without American leadership, however, Europe gave Bosnia the worst of all worlds: hundreds of thousands killed and wounded, and the destruction of one of the continent's more successful examples of an equitable multi-ethnic community. The west European powers also created enormous problems for their own future, unleashing an increasingly radicalised Muslim disapora, and setting an example to other rogue nations that might is right and genocide pays, because the major western powers are indifferent to the fate of their former communist cousins.

It could have been otherwise. A UN Transitional Authority incorporating a strong military and civilian presence, in place in early 1992 could have saved Bosnia. With a long-term commitment, the western powers could still separate and disarm the warring factions, restore order, train a multi-ethnic police force and remain in place until the multi-ethnic community had worked out a new *modus vivendi* with guaranteed rights for all national and religious groups. The foundations for success lay in the pre-war multi-ethnic republic of Bosnia-Hercegovina. Restoring Bosnia would require long-term civilian presence too, but it would be an investment in a Europe to be proud of. Moreover the costs of such an operation would be trivial compared to the costs that western nations now face in dealing with the instabilities that stem from policies of indifference and appeasement.

Clinton invoked a lack of consensus as an excuse not to act. Although the UN and the EC have been more active than either NATO or the CSCE in Yugoslavia, neither institution was being pressed by its member governments to act seriously. If the failure of UNPROFOR in Bosnia was due mainly to institutional chaos in New York, NATO's failure was a lack of will in the allied capitals, and the more ominous failing for the future of Europe.[58] NATO had the logistics, the manpower, the level of training and

---

[58] Jane M. O. Sharp, 'If not NATO, who?', *The Bulletin of the Atomic Scientists*, October 1992, pp. 29–32; Frederick Bonnart, 'We have the wherewithal but not the leadership', *IHT*, 3 November 1992.

the command, control communication and intelligence capability to restore order in Bosnia. Officials in Brussels conducted extensive planning in 1993 for the enforcement of a Bosnian peace settlement, but only in the context of an agreement signed by the belligerent powers.

At the summit in Brussels the NATO powers said their hands were tied unless strikes were requested by the UN Secretary General and approved by the Security Council, as if the three major NATO powers did not also sit on the P-5 and could not take the initiative themselves to generate a UN decision. The NATO powers had no intention of making air strikes (except to provide close air support to NATO troops serving with UNPROFOR) and with each articulation of an air strike threat the alliance looked more ridiculous.

NATO countries have always been successful at papering over differences and inadequacies, and President Clinton's summit pledge to keep 'about 100,000 troops' in Europe indefinitely, pumped a little life-blood into the alliance. NATO remains vital not only to deter outside aggression, but also to prevent war amongst its own members, and to deter the proliferation of more nuclear weapons in Europe. Nevertheless, it will be a miracle if the alliance survives the final collapse of Bosnia.

## Conclusion

The United Nations Security Council remains the most universally accepted authority, but the UN is unlikely in the near term to be capable of effective military operations. If Bosnia is any guide, the UN bureaucracy is many years away from coping with the logistics, command, control and intelligence required for a flexible military operation. Traditional, passive, UN peace-keeping operations will continue to perform a useful role in situations where a cease fire is in effect, but where the belligerents are still fighting, traditional peace-keeping risks doing more harm than good by effectively supporting the war aims of the strongest belligerent. When civil or interstate wars threaten to disrupt a region, multilateral intervention would better be initiated by a concert of militarily sophisticated powers, acting in accordance with Article 51, the principle of self defence. The P-5 could in theory serve as such a concert, but in practice this seems unlikely, not least because China is not in tune with the other four, and Russia appears to be moving steadily away from consensus with the NATO powers after the October 1993 elections.

With respect to what constitutes just cause for intervention, Bosnia may mark a turning point in public perception, from seeing intervention as intrusive and negative, to be avoided where possible, to a growing realisation that emancipatory military intervention could be a positive healing process in defence of human and minority rights. While the international community may be agnostic about which national groups merit more autonomy within the international system, it cannot be agnostic about the

54

means of achieving self-determination. Bosnia teaches that while borders may be re-negotiated and political units merged or separated, force must not be used to effect these changes. If Europe is to be equitable, secure and pluralistic, western governments must acquire the capability and exercise the will to stop bully states early in their rampages and halt the practice of land grabbing and of ethnic cleansing.

Even when the cause is just, governments temper their responsibility to act by weighing national interests against the public good. One of the main reasons Bosnia was destroyed was US reluctance to engage. Bosnian President Ali Izetbegovic was urged to hold out for a better deal in the Geneva talks, but suspicion grew in Europe, later confirmed by officials in Washington, that the Clinton Administration was unwilling to provide the 25,000 troops they had promised to police an agreed settlement. As a *Washington Post* editorial noted, just prior to the NATO summit in January 1994, the impression that the US would not do its share to supply peace-keeping troops was deeply troubling.

Bosnia showed what happens when the US remains in Europe, but will not lead. Europe simply dithers. Notwithstanding President Clinton's rhetorical commitment to leadership at the January 1994 NATO summit, there was no sign of US leadership in 1993 when it was sorely needed, and no reason to expect 1994 would be any different. The US role as western Europe's pacifier seems to have ended with the Clinton Administration. To maintain peace and stability in the post-Cold War system, the west European states must therefore now invest much more in their own armed forces, with all the attendant risks that increased military efforts could trigger new tensions.

With respect to the timing of military interventions, if intervention is called for, and is just, it had better come early rather than late. Serbian and Croation aggression could have been stopped. On every occasion when slight pressure was exerted on Serbia or Croatia their leaders backed down. Given the likelihood of conflicts erupting in many of the former communist countries, and the decreasing likelihood of US leadership, the European Union powers, as the Western European Union, must prepare credible rapid reaction forces, that can move early and efficiently to curb aggression that threatens the annihilation of national or religious minorities, grabs territory by force or in other ways destabilises the international system.[59]

---

[59] At the NATO summit in January 1994 NATO ministers proposed Combined Joint Task Forces (CJTF) both to nurture the concept of a European Security and Defence Identity (ESDI) and to promote cooperation and joint training with some of the former Communist countries who would participate actively in the Partnership for Peace. NATO summit communique *Declaration of the Heads of State*, Article 1. Brussels: Atlantic Document No. 83, 12 January 1994, *Atlantic News*.

# MILITARY INTERVENTION: DUTY AND PRUDENCE

## KEN BOOTH*

It has become a cliché of TV reporters, journalists and academics to liken the situation in Bosnia to a living hell. This is mistaken. Hell is for the truly evil. It is not a place to find people like Admira and Bosko. Sweethearts since their schooldays, Admira was a Muslim, and Bosko a Serb. They were in their mid-twenties when they were both clinically assassinated on 19 May 1993 as they crossed the lines during an official cease-fire in Sarajevo. Like many others in that once thriving and multicultural city, they did not believe until the last minute that the worst could happen. It is not clear who killed them,[1] but what their deaths show, yet again, is that innocent casualties are the first truth of war.

### The moral arena

We are morally engaged in the deaths of Admira and Bosko, whether we recognise it or not. It is naive and confused to deny that international politics is a moral arena, though a half-century of 'realist' thinking about the world has tried to suppress it. Ethics, as sets of ideas about how we should think and behave, infuse and inform every international event. Claiming that ethics should be kept 'out' is an ethical—and emotional— position, just as much (but not as intellectually tenable) as the position of those who accept that ethics and emotion are inseparable from politics. Recognition of this is important in cruel and complex civil/international wars, where every course taken, or not taken, will have unpredictable outcomes and unwanted consequences.

The last thing the suffering want is academics defining terms, but this is what is needed if policy is to avoid the extremes of legalist non-intervention, which tends to neglect the powerless, and international interventionism, which tends to neglect the powerful. The argument below will be based on the distinctions between rhetorical prudence and technical prudence, governmental obligation and human duty, and selfishness and self-interest. A case will be made against military intervention on the side of Bosnia, but for direct global engagement with the problems which Bosnia

* Ken Booth is Professor of International Politics at the University of Wales, Aberystwyth. He is presently working on two co-authored books: *The Security Dilemma: Anarchy, Society and Community in World Politics* and *Kant and International Relations*.

[1] Slavenka Drakulic, 'How mad war killed two star-cross'd lovers', *The Observer*, 10 October 1993.

exemplifies. In broad terms, the British government will be criticised for its failures in human duty, and the position of those advocating military intervention criticised on grounds of technical prudence.

When the British Foreign Minister—or the US President, or German Chancellor—talks about the 'international community' I want to respond like Gandhi, when he was asked what he thought about Western civilisation: 'I think it would be an excellent idea' he is supposed to have said. In G7-speak the phrase 'international community' belongs to the platitudes of a 'society of states' run by Western governments and a variety of local strongmen which bears an uncomfortable resemblance to a global protection racket. There is a sense of society among the countries of the liberal-democratic word, but precious little in their relations with those beyond. In the world's local neighbourhoods, governments and populations receive carrots or sticks from the powerful governments of the West depending upon the acceptability of their behaviour. As protection rackets go, this liberal-democratic/capitalist one is by no means the worst imaginable, but it is not a 'community' in the ethical sense of the term (as in the idea of human beings owing mutual respect and duties towards each other): it is only a community in the politically manipulative sense of this feel-good world, as in 'community charge'. The notion of 'international community' is hollow when used to describe a situation in which the powerful of the G7 prosper beyond historic dreams, while the weak in parts of Africa and elsewhere live utterly wretched lives. A cursory look at many governments in this international community will reveal its morality to be the diplomatic equivalent of honour among thieves. Furthermore, it is only an international community when Western governments want it to be. When they themselves have been roundly criticised across the world—as over the British government's position on sanctions against apartheid, or US intervention in Central America—we do not then hear talk of an international community, but only of a vociferous, ideological majority of countries in the UN General Assembly, with irresponsible voting power but no resources. It is in the context of this peculiar inter-governmental society or community that we should situate the idea of prudence as a diplomatic virtue.

'Prudence', like 'international community', is part of the discourse of global hegemony, the language of keeping things essentially as they are. When we consider prudence, therefore, selfishness needs to be distinguished from self-interest. Selfishness is behaviour in which one puts oneself first, without regard for the well-being of others. King Midas was selfish but not self-interested.[2] Selfishness treats others as means not ends, and is concerned with wants rather than needs. One cannot be selfish and unselfish at the same time. Self-interest, on the other hand, is part of being human, and a proper regard for oneself is not inconsistent with duty, since one can be self-interested and other-interested at the same time. This is

---

[2]  Martin Hollis, *Invitation to Philosophy*, Blackwell, Oxford, 1992, p. 129.

what love involves. A decent parent will be self-interested and other-interested. Parents will readily accept unconditional duties towards their children, but to carry them out to the full they need to be self-interested, maintaining themselves in good physical and psychological shape. There is also some requirement for a dutiful parent to be prudent—being able to handle practical matters, having good judgment, providing for future needs, and being careful about one's interests. A duty done imprudently may be a duty failed. This is *technical* prudence, within the context of an other-interested duty, in contrast to the *rhetorical* prudence which the political powers-that-be purport to be a diplomatic virtue. Prudence is a word which deserves to be pulled from its conceptual pedestal. Before an action takes place, prudence is indistinguishable from the discipline of rationality, while afterwards it simply becomes a label—'we acted prudently'—to excuse a failure or deepen a success. Furthermore, the cautious implications of the word can clash with other technical action-skills, such as seizing the moment. But most important of all, prudence without reference to other-interested behaviour is the opposite of virtuous: we presumably do not want prudent aggressors, or prudent rapists. What is virtuous is rational behaviour in the service of human duty, and this can sometimes be called technical prudence.

A foreign policy of selfishness consists of always putting one's own interests first, as individuals, as a government, as a Party and as a 'country'. Occasionally, costly actions are taken which are justified on the grounds, not so much of narrow national interest, but of upholding international law. The Falklands War and the Gulf War were of this type. When critics pointed to conflicts where international law has been flaunted but not opposed (quiescence in face of South Africa's brutal policy of destabilisation of the front-line states, Indonesia's violent take-over of East Timor, or Israel's invasion of Lebanon) the response was that just because a state cannot do good everywhere it does not mean that it cannot do good somewhere. Let us be clear about the meaning of 'good' here. What the British government (and others) did in the case of the Gulf War was to act *in accordance* with international law, not *out of respect for* it. It supported international law for selfish reasons, not out of principle. If its position on international law was a principled one—a matter of duty—then it would have seriously contemplated action in situations when its own interests were not directly involved. A duty consists of doing what you ought to do, whether you want to or not.

It is rarely in a government's power to do everything, but it is in a government's power to do something. Some actions have been in accordance with duty, but for the most part they have been actions to meet certain *obligations*—more specific commitments and constraints arising out of agreements and responsibilities, such as membership of the Security Council. So what we see is a form of sophisticated realism—Machiavelli with an English school accent. Humanitarian obligations are accepted—commitments to support human rights and the delegitimisation of racism for example—but these are imposed by responsibilities from outside and by pressure of opinion at home rather than from a sense of human duty. Those who speak for the government would obviously reject the charge of selfishness and indifference. The charge here is not that it does nothing, but that it does as little as it can get away with: this is not other-interested behaviour, but selfish behaviour which sometimes coincides with the interests of peoples elsewhere. The British government's attitude to its own weak—the 'undeserving poor'—does not suggest that it spends time agonising over powerless foreigners. This is confirmed by its attitude to the overseas aid budget, which already is the second lowest in Europe, and it will be at best frozen over the next three years.[3] When humanitarian concern is manifested, it seems to be TV cameras which focus the Cabinet's eyes. Britain's direct involvement in the Balkan crisis, like the earlier Kurdish crisis, was media-driven. The British government responded to pressures by its high-profile contribution to UNPROFOR. If UNPROFOR worked reasonably well, it would be a way of deflecting the criticism of those who said the government was 'doing nothing': if it failed, it could be used as an argument for showing the dangers of trying to do more (and, indeed, it would have demonstrated the government's prudence by its limited commitment). The record suggests that the government will act in such situations only when international or domestic opinion make inaction embarrassing.

The British government uses the rhetoric of prudence to cloak a conception of human duty which is stunted for a relatively wealthy and civilised country. In the case of the Balkan crisis, the government was justified in not advocating massive military intervention, but it made a number of diplomatic errors (such as the over-ready recognition of Croatia and the punitive arms embargo on Bosnia); furthermore, there have been no changes in its external policy to suggest that it has learned any lessons about what is required to reduce the risk of similar situations developing in future. Until Britain and other powerful countries accept a positive duty to common humanity, rather than merely a prudential obligation to statist norms, the development will be long delayed of that human community which alone will make a society of states worthy of the name. Human duty is a matter of long-term self-interest.

If the government's position in world affairs is lacking on grounds of human duty, it is on grounds of technical prudence that I want to separate my position from those the *Socialist Review* has characterised as 'B-52 liberals'. This group contains many individuals with whom I have no difference about our duties towards common humanity; but on this occasion I disagree with the prescription of those like Susan Sontag who went to Sarajevo to dramatise 'Waiting for Godot', in the shape of President Clinton and US air strikes. The military interventionists on this

---

[3] Polly Ghazi, 'Shrinking aid budget goes only to the telegenic', *Observer*, 22 August 1993.

occasion include people who on issue after issue over the past 30 years have cried that peace be given a chance. This time, they are arguing that we should have given bombing a chance.

## The case for military intervention

The proponents of intervention have based their case on five main arguments.

### i  *To maintain international order:*

One of the most consistent arguments in favour of intervention has been the claim that the 'international community' should have acted to defend the state of Bosnia. Failure to act to prevent its dismemberment will undermine international order. Parallels have been drawn between the Western failure to respond militarily to the present Balkan crisis and the appeasement of the 1930s. If aggression is left unchecked, it is argued, then international order is on a slippery slope towards a lawless world. The US/UN response to Saddam Hussein's invasion of Kuwait is brought out to show how international law can and should be upheld.

Such arguments are overdrawn and give too much significance to the Balkan imbroglio, though it goes without saying that it is preferable to have borders changed, and policies pursued, by peaceful rather than violent means. The argument is overdrawn because international order is more robust than is suggested. The post-war years have seen considerable aggression across borders by states such as Indonesia, Israel, South Africa, Turkey, the United States and the USSR—among others—and the edifice of order has remained in place. The key players know when and where the rules can be ignored, and which situations constitute the anomalies. Aggression by states acceptable to the major players, or by themselves, has not been seen as constituting a significant threat to international order. In contrast, those who have opposed the White House, for example, or who have broken the rules in strategic areas, have always had caused to worry, since aggression on their part will stimulate the *realpolitik* behind the US government's attitude to international law. In strategic terms Bosnia has been of minimal significance to the White House, while its significance to future international law and order was limited by a widespread belief (even among its foreign supporters) that Bosnia was not ready for self-government.[4] Furthermore, strangling struggling states at birth is less of a problem to the norms of international society than the disappearance of a mature member.

The condition of international society is unlikely to be significantly

---

[4]  Jane M. O. Sharp, *Bankrupt in the Balkans. British Policy in Bosnia*, IPPR, London, 1993, p. 12.

affected by what happens to Bosnia, though its partial dismemberment, which now looks certain, is obviously a cause for great concern for those who regret the triumph of crude power politics and the equating of ethnic nationalism and statehood. Too much can be made of its exemplary significance. The wars against the Galtieri dictatorship's invasion of the Falklands, and against Saddam Hussein's invasion of Kuwait, were supposed to show that aggression did not pay. But despite the literal force of these examples, there have been other attempts to change boundaries by force. The examples were not thought to be relevant. This will be the case in future, and would have been regardless of what had happened in Bosnia. This need not cause a surprise, since the connotation of the very word 'Balkan' attests to its historic function as a complex special case.

## ii  To respond to the moral imperative:

A strong body of Western opinion has argued that 'something should be done' because of their sense of moral outrage. We should not stand by, it is argued, while gross violations of human rights are taking place.

The horrors which have been taking place in former Yugoslavia are plain for all to see: ethnic cleansing, atrocities against civilians, crazed gunmen, widespread rape, and violence of a medieval rather than Clausewitzian character. It is a nightmare. But is this, in itself, a justification for military intervention? The proponents argue that it is, being sufficiently confident of making the necessary moral distinctions between the different causes, stories, forces and political identities to intrude an external military force to begin to sort it all out.

Comparisons have been made between the ethnic violence in former Yugoslavia and the holocaust, and between the West's 'futile gestures' and the complacency of the mid-1930s. These analogies can be dealt with relatively easily. While the moral sentiments they express are understandable, the comparisons are exaggerated. Serbia is not Nazi Germany, in power or ambition, while the argument that ethnic cleansing compares with the holocaust shows a distressing disregard of the latter's scale, systematic nature and scientific paraphernalia. Ethnic cleansing, which is an ugly phrase for an ugly concept, has not been entirely unknown in the post-war years. Nor have vicious civil wars. These points are not intended to minimise by one degree the nature of the atrocities taking place; they are meant to intrude a better sense of proportion.

Can we draw strategically practical moral lines through the Balkan imbroglio? I think not. For several decades most of us knew Yugoslavia only as package tourists, and understood little about its history or politics: now we risk being moral day-trippers in a region that lives in the historical present. The ghosts of the past do not exist in the wings, but in the front line. We rush to call groups 'aggressors', but would do better to recognise the sheer power of fear. A fear-driven explanation of what has happened

61

should make external powers less confident of being able to fight for peace.

The Serbs as a group have had the worst press, and some have deserved it. But the Serbs as a people suffered inhuman treatment at the hands of Croatia less than 50 years ago. In the present conflict the Bosnian Muslims have attracted Western sympathies, but little sympathy has been shown towards the 600,000 Serbs in Croatia—a country which was first given independence by Hitler and Mussolini (itself in part a reaction against Serb dominance of the South Slavs). Croatia in World War II conducted genocide against Serbs and Jews. In historic time, this mass murder was only yesterday, yet President Tudjman of today's Croatia adopted flags and uniforms and other symbols of the Fascist *Ustashe*, and a constitution which left the Serb minority feeling exposed. In such circumstances, it should not have taken much imagination on the part of observers to have guessed the psychological realities of the Serb populations coming under the sovereignty of the new Croatian state. Any uncertainties they may have felt as Yugoslavia disintegrated were quickly resolved by the certainty of historical fear. Tudjman's Croatia made war virtually inevitable. Bosnia-Hercegovina itself had been part of the World War II Fascist Croatian state.

On top of the contested truths of the past there are the contested truths of the present. The powerful but ultimately false story of Iraqi soldiers taking babies out of incubators (like German soldiers tossing up Belgian babies for bayonet practice in 1914) has been matched in the past two years by stories of massacres that do not seem to have happened, atrocities not committed by those widely reported to be guilty, casualty figures which have been roundly disputed (upwards and downwards), 'concentration camps' whose horrors have not always been substantiated, and 'rape camps' whose existence seems contentious. The truth is bad enough, but in such conflicts it is always distorted. War feeds on simplicity and propaganda, but the politics of stable peace require a feel for the complexities. These include the complexities of identity—'Serb', 'Croat', 'Muslim' and 'Bosnian'. War generates terrible stereotypes.

What we are witnessing in former Yugoslavia is people fighting not just the battles of their fathers and grandfathers, but also—for the middle-aged and older—the battles of their own childhoods and young adulthoods. Tito's Yugoslavia maintained order, but did not allow the old tribal enemies to purge themselves of the past in the democratic fashion, but admittedly different circumstances, of France and Germany after World War II. Nor was there any atonement. The experiment to build a Yugoslav identity failed, and many learned their ethnic history from heroic and paranoid songs and poetry. As a result, large numbers of people in the Balkans have their feet on embattled ground and their heads in the 19th century, or even earlier. But plenty of other people in that region have grown to political maturity, and are utterly distressed by what has happened. They—ethnically-tolerant 'ordinary' people, peace groups, mothers demonstrating in Belgrade, opposition politicians in all warring states, and cosmopolitan intellectuals—are caught up as victims on all sides.

Former Yugoslavia is a moral and political inferno, not a morality play. Its dynamics are made up of economic and constitutional problems and complexities, in addition to the more obvious ethno-national conflicts.[5] The region is inflamed by contradicting historical traumas, a sense on all sides of being victims of oppression (including genocide), the 'extra trauma of not being heard',[6] pressures for separatism, and ancient fears and modern ambitions. As if this was not enough, the rush of global events following the ending of the Cold War, a series of Western diplomatic mistakes, crass local politicians and anxious and potentially interfering neighbours produced a fast-moving situation where difficult questions were settled by tribal memories.

In the past, the peoples of former Yugoslavia lived together uneasily and sometimes treated each other viciously. Their histories have been written in blood. They have coexisted in prolonged peace when they have been dominated by local authoritarians or external imperial powers. The picture of moral and political complexity is not being advanced as an excuse for inaction, but as an argument for caution when comtemplating questions such as: how should we try to help, and how, and why?

*iii  To prevent the deterioration of relations with the Islamic world:*

One argument advanced for military intervention has been based on the worry that the failure to help Muslim-dominated Bosnia risks exacerbating relations between the (ostensibly Christian) West and the 'Islamic world'. Such inaction might confirm a widespread Muslim belief that the West is fundamentally hostile. One of the several consequences of this might be to radicalise parts of the Islamic world.

Since it seems likely that Western support of Bosnia will fall short of direct military intervention it could indeed have the consequences suggested. But like the 'Clash of Civilisations' thesis,[7] it over-simplifies the political coherence of both the West and the Muslim 'worlds'. The image among Muslims of aggressive 'Western' policies towards a range of Islamic countries in the distant and recent past is undeniable. But governments should not pursue a bad policy in the Balkans out of a bad conscience. One unwise policy cannot wipe the slate clean: wiser policies, elsewhere, can. Muslim 'radicals' could make something of the West's position on Bosnia, but they have plenty of other political ammunition.

[5]  See, *inter alia*, Hakan Wiberg, 'Societal security and the explosion of Yugoslavia', in Ole Waever *et al.*, *Identity, Migration and The New Security Agenda in Europe*, Pinter, London, 1993, pp. 93–109.

[6]  *Ibid.*, p. 99.

[7]  Samuel Huntington, 'The Clash of Civilisations', *Foreign Affairs*, Vol. 72(3), Summer 1993, pp. 22–49.

The Muslims in Bosnia are the weakest of the major belligerents in former Yugoslavia, and are therefore the ones who have suffered disproportionately. But they too have their warlords, and they too have played their part in the Serb trauma, being seen as willing anti-Serb accomplices of the Turkish and Austro-Hungarian Empires, and the *Ustashe*.[8]

It is desirable for Western governments to prevent any drift towards the polarisation of relations with Islamic countries, but this can best be done by reconsidering problems as they arise. It has also to be demonstrated that the 'anti-Muslim' image is justified by 'Western' behaviour.

### iv  To avoid setting a bad precedent for ethnic nationalism:

If the West-led UN did not intervene to protect national minorities in the Balkans, and the principle of multi-ethnic states represented by Bosnia, then this will send a signal to all those hyper-nationalists who might want to cleanse their own regions of undesirable minorities. The parallel with the 1930s is again made, when inaction arguably encouraged aggression.

Ethnic nationalism, without doubt, is a regressive force in world politics and one which should be delegitimised, but the exemplary significance of Bosnia can again be exaggerated. Local circumstances will be more telling than distant examples. In the territory of the former Soviet Union for example—where the fear of a bad precedent is worst—ethnic-nationalist struggles have already taken place. What matters most in the Caucasus and elsewhere is the likely response of Moscow, not UN HQ. Furthermore, so far at least, fears about instability and national upheaval in the former Soviet bloc have been greatly exaggerated. Indeed, an impressive degree of social tolerance has been shown across these huge stretches of territory, considering their enormous economic hardships and political and social dislocation. To date, the violence attendant upon the collapse of the Soviet empire has been rather limited when compared with that involved in the bloody decay of the British Empire, from the 1920s in India down to the present day in Northern Ireland.

Some ethnic-nationalist bullies, in some parts of the world, might be encouraged by the events in former Yugoslavia and the lack of external military intervention. Other people across the world are probably learning other lessons from the Bosnian precedent. What they see is that hyper-nationalism is not the way to run successful modern societies; the route to a better life does not lie through following the Balkan or Beirut models.

Finally we must consider the precedent that might have been set had the UN successfully intervened by force, and saved Bosnia at birth. If inaction might encourage bullies, might not intervention have encouraged the ambitions of separatist, sovereignty-seeking nationalists whose chances of achieving effective statehood was even less strong than that of Bosnia?

[8]  See Charles Lane and Theodore Stanger, 'Serbia's ghosts', *Time*, 19 April 1993.

64

*v To contain a threat to European peace:*

One of the strongest arguments in favour of military intervention has arisen from the fear that the Balkan conflict would otherwise spread into neighbouring countries, and then draw in a growing circle of belligerents. For some, Sarajevo in 1993 still echoes the warning shots of Sarajevo in 1914.

Without doubt, there remains a threat to international peace. Kosovo and Macedonia have been and remain powder-kegs, and Albania, Bulgaria, Greece and Turkey all have direct interests in what happens. A regional war still cannot be ruled out. There is no place for complacency, but there is some cause for hope. So far, the worst fears have not been justified, and the longer war is avoided the more cautioning voices can have a say. UNPROFOR has performed a useful task in drawing lines in the sand in a preventive fashion in Macedonia, and this may continue to be a deterrent. Other steps could also have been taken to deter external intervention, and indeed may have been behind the diplomatic scenes. Membership (or potential membership) of the EC and NATO can be used to discourage neighbouring states from getting drawn in.

There are continuing regional dangers, but it is hyperbole to argue that the whole peace of Europe might be threatened. Europe does not face an enemy with the power of Germany in 1939 and there is not the pattern of alliances as in 1914 which made that Balkan crisis so contagious. Furthermore, Western military intervention itself, expanding into a war against Serbia, could provoke disorder in Kosovo and Macedonia which might then draw in neighbouring countries as ambitious stabilisers, in the manner of the Syrian government in Lebanon.

## A Strategic Critique of Military Intervention

Whether or not one agrees with the political arguments above, there remains the issue of the utility of military intervention. In this section it will be shown that no decisive arguments have been advanced to demonstrate that military intervention satisfies the questions we should ask before committing troops, possibly indefinitely. Military intervention fails the test of technical prudence.

### Is there an achievable political settlement?

The historical truism of military intervention is that it is easier to send troops in than to get them out, leaving the country concerned in good political shape. Somalia is the latest reminder of this. When US Marines hit the beaches there in December 1992 it looked a relatively straightforward task (which was why it was chosen, as a farewell boost for President Bush and to deflect attention from Bosnia). The operation had a clear objective (to help the delivery of aid), an exit strategy, and a timetable. What could go wrong? Only six months later the UN/US forces had virtually become one of the warlord factions, women and children were being strafed, dead US soldiers were being dragged through the streets, and the UN had become the target of growing criticism. Even when 'it can't go wrong', it often does.

Somalia, a relatively straightforward case, is a warning for those who would inject external military force to stabilise complex distant conflicts. A workable post-military intervention political settlement has yet to be elaborated—a not infrequent outcome. Bosnia itself was not ready for self-government when it was recognised as a sovereign state. It lacked a history of self-rule and did not have a democratic political culture, and it faced divisions within and enemies outside its borders. As it quickly fell into civil war, could Bosnia have been put back together again by external powers, any more than Yugoslavia? One widely-discussed solution was a UN Trusteeship or Protectorate for Bosnia, following a military intervention and with a powerful and continuing military presence. But from the start the obstacles were manifold: the obvious problem of the so-called 'United Nations', which people are sometimes tempted to talk about as if it were significantly greater than a shifting coalition of governments; the warnings given by the difficulties faced by other countries in Eastern Europe, whose post-Communist reconstruction faces far fewer of the traumas suffered in the Balkans; the historic failure of outsiders to plant their own political ideas in the soil of different political cultures, such as the Soviet Union's attempts to Stalinize Eastern Europe, and Britain's attempts to West-minsterise its about-to-be-independent colonies; and the continuing arrogance of those in the West who believe that their own governments know best (particularly as it was the policies of some Western governments which had contributed to the downward spiral of events since 1991). The British government still does not have a political solution—only an acceptable level of violence—for Northern Ireland, nearly a quarter of a century after troops were sent in to keep the peace. Why should Bosnia be different? Some people are now tempted—justifiably—to look back with some nostalgia at the stability of the Tito years, but they overlook the brutality of the early years of his regime and his continuing authoritarian rule. It is undeniable that 'at least it was better than present horrors', but who can imagine any collection of UN officials and governments having the will, the legitimacy, the local knowledge, the authoritarian structure, the passion and the staying power of a Tito to hang in and create a viable polity?

One optimistic opinion about a UN Protectorate points to the reconstruction of West Germany after 1945. This is a fallacious analogy for a variety of reasons. Germany was a country with the social cohesion so violently absent in the Balkans. In 1945 Germany was utterly defeated and the victors had a clear run, occupying the country with continental-sized armies. Seeing Germany as the cause of two world wars, the Western powers had an intense interest that the 'German problem' did not arise again (and they were willing to keep their troops there indefinitely for the purpose). The West and Germany immediately faced the common 'Soviet threat' which soon came to overshadow that of Germany. Most Germans wanted a new start and rejected the past, whereas for key actors in the Balkans, it seems, the further back the political clock is turned the better. Finally, Germany had a political culture with traditions of liberalism and democracy on which the post-war order could be fashioned, and it had been one of the world's most successful capitalist economies. For all these reasons the post-war reconstruction of West Germany cannot serve as a model for thinking that the UN could reconstruct the Balkans.

It is arrogant on the part of those in the West to believe our governments can sort it out. Our governments have made serious diplomatic mistakes in the recent past, and there is no reason to suppose it would be different if they had the far more difficult task of actually running part of this combustible region. There may come a time when a relatively small number of peace-keepers will be generally acceptable, to monitor a general cease-fire and perhaps elections. That is one thing: sending in a peace-enforcement army to impose a cease-fire by force, and to police it indefinitely, is another matter entirely.

## Can military force deliver a solution?

One of the most surprising features of the pro-interventionist case has been the ease with which some individuals have developed amnesia about the use of force in the last thirty years of history, while remembering the previous thirty years only too well. In their instinct to 'do something', many people seem to have forgotten the limited utility of foreign forces in complex conflicts whose terrain features forests, mountains, cities and sanctuaries: Vietnam, Afghanistan, Beirut and Belfast. There is a dangerous over-confidence in military force in some quarters, which recent history does not support. For some the use of airpower in the Gulf War seems to have revived fundamentalist beliefs about bombing. True, UN/NATO airpower could pulverise Serbia into the past, as the US/UN bombed Iraq and the US bombed North Vietnam. But Saddam Hussein survives, and North Vietnam won. On a lesser scale, surgical strikes against local forces in Bosnia are unlikely to be politically decisive, and could be avoided to a significant degree, and in ways which would risk the spread of civilian damage. Small and mobile targets are inconvenient for the limited airstrike option.

The faith military interveners have placed in force in the last thirty years has invariably been a delusion. President Reagan himself made the point perfectly—though typically he did not intend to—when he described the intervention in Grenada in 1983 as 'our finest hour'. Against this, the alternative roll call includes the politically unsuccessful interventions into Vietnam, Afghanistan, Panama and Somalia. There are some things

67

external force can do, but is limited. Like their counterparts in the 1960s, military interveners today are invoking the Munich syndrome, while disregarding the fact that this emotion led Britain and the United States into their biggest foreign policy disasters of the post-war period: the military interventions into Suez and Vietnam respectively.

The charges of 'indifference' and 'spinelessness' levelled against those who would not send in the troops and bombers have therefore to be set against those who would learn the lessons of inter-war years too well, but those of the post-war years not well enough. Inaction might give a bad message, but so do 'Vietnams', 'Beiruts' and 'Afghanistans'. Military power is a blunt instrument, but it is sometimes unavoidable. When it is threatened, it is best if it has credibility; it must therefore be nurtured, which means using it sparingly. When it is used, it is best if it is deployed early; it must therefore be quickly reactive, which probably means conceiving it nationally rather than multinationally.

Some observers have advocated 'punishment' of 'the Serbs' by air-power. This has been argued on the grounds that it might stop the fighting, or at least show that there are costs to aggression, and that it would *encourager les autres*. This would be one of the worst options. Since precise targeting would be extremely difficult, 'punishment' would be no more than a form of state terrorism, comparable with that inflicted by the Reagan Administration from the *New Jersey* against Lebanese villages in 1983. This delivered up no political settlement, or terrorists, only civilian dead and injured and indefinite hostility. Such punishment is counter-productive. Furthermore, when humanitarian intervention merges into humanitarian punishment, we see it evolving into a secular Just War doctrine. And just as the Just War doctrine can justify anything,[9] so might humanitarian intervention justify anti-humanitarian behaviour. Not only is punishment unlikely to deliver a just political order, we should also think about what it does to *us*, as well as potential targets. As torture enters the torturer's psyche, likewise we should worry about the effects on the executors of feel-good punishment such as that evident in the Reagan years.

For those who believe that military intervention is necessary, but do not believe that bombing can be independently effective, discriminating or productive of amicable ethnic relations, there remains no alternative but to deploy large numbers of ground troops. The argument has recently appeared that Serb forces would quickly collapse in face of superior might, and that the old image was mistaken of the 'brave Yugoslavs' who in World War II pinned down large numbers of German and Italian forces, and who then deterred the Soviet Armed Forces from invading following Yugoslavia's defection from the Stalinist Soviet bloc. This is more wishful thinking. Twentieth century military history shows that fewer calamities

---

[9] Donald A. Wells, 'How Much Can the "Just War" Justify?', *The Journal of Philosophy*, Vol. 66(23), December 1969, pp. 819–29.

have been suffered by those who have paid their potential adversaries respect, than by those who have denigrated their ability and determination.

### Is there dependable domestic and international support?

Nobody believes that a ground force, once inserted to fight for peace and then manage the post-war reconstruction, could be withdrawn quickly. Success therefore requires steady and indefinite domestic and international support. There is no evidence from the past three years to suppose that such support would be forthcoming.

Attention on Bosnia in the West has been media-led, and it has risen and fallen. In the summer of 1993, briefly and microscopically, the British government encouraged the press to focus on poor little Irma from Sarajevo. A few months later people wondered: Irma who? Not only is public interest in democracies fickle, but no international consensus emerged when talk in the United States moved towards air strikes, and certainly no Western government rushed to offer large numbers of its own ground troops. Could we—whoever 'we' are—take casualties? Could deaths be kept to an 'acceptable' level? If not, what would be the reaction? Would intervention and occupation divide the societies and governments running the intervention—with their different sensibilities, loyalties and interests? And who would give the mission backbone? A good deal of easy talk has been directed at the United Nations, but that in practice means the United States, which never looked likely to risk getting embroiled in this particular conflict, except at the height of several thousand feet. The other contender as intervener has been the EC, which has been going through a delicate stage of its evolution. From early on it was evident that it was also unwilling to intervene massively. Without certain and long-term support, military intervention would be foolhardly and futile. Nobody has yet demonstrated that such support exists, or can be generated.

### Do we have the correct tactics and strategy for military intervention?

Even if the UN/NATO had an acceptable political settlement in view, and guaranteed long-term support, there would still be great difficulties in delivering the military foundations on which an eventual political settlement could be built. Unless wars are of the relatively straightforward conventional kind, as in Korea or the Gulf, and are clearly directed by one dominating power, then massive UN enforcement operations are problematic.

Fighting for peace in the Balkans would pose very different demands on troops than those for which they have been trained. It would not be a war like that envisaged for the Central Front, which was NATO's scenario for 40 years, or the set-piece Gulf War. And the larger and more mixed the international force, and the bigger the mission goals, the more there would

69

be scope for splits among the participating multinational forces, with their different training, languages, abilities and tactics. Again the experience in Somalia is telling. Even centrally-controlled US forces, with what seemed to be a clear and achievable mission, soon learned that those who fight clans and warlords tend to become warlords. The UN was not created to fight such wars, and nothing which has happened over nearly 50 years suggests that it has developed the ability to manage them.

The most effective military organisation to conduct a prolonged campaign in the Balkans would seem to be NATO, because of its history, skills and infrastructure. But what makes NATO impressive are not necessarily the attributes to bring a political settlement in a complex and unconventional conflict. Consider, for a moment, the idea of having sent Warsaw Pact troops to stop the fighting and to enforce peace in Northern Ireland in the early 1970s. Unfamiliar with the history and language of the region, and equipped and trained for a very different scenario, it is not obvious that a legitimate peace would have emerged when the forces left. A legitimate peace in such circumstances requires the protagonists to want one. It is not evident why NATO might do any better in the infinitely more politically complex and violent situation in Bosnia in the early 1990s than the Warsaw Pact might have done in the relatively simple and restrained circumstances of Northern Ireland in the early 1970s.

## Duties Beyond Military Intervention

It has been suggested that we are morally engaged with the problems of former Yugoslavia, that technical prudence warns against military intervention, and that there are human duties which go beyond government obligations. If this is the case, what should we think and do as simultaneous members of specific states and humankind in general?

### What principles should govern government policy in complex civil/international wars?

Governments are not yet bearers of global human duties, and many if not most people in the 'Culture of Contentment' would not want them to be.[10] Nobody should ever expect too much from governments, but in civilised countries citizens expect something. The following is an outline of the principles a government might follow in complex civil/international wars:

*Isolate the conflict.* It is desirable to stop wars spreading horizontally. This can be done by such tactics as sanctions, preventive deployment, and threats of withholding the privileges of membership in international organisations.

[10] The phrase 'culture of contentment' is from John Kenneth Galbraith, *The Culture of Contentment*, Sinclair-Stevenson Ltd, 1992.

70

*Support self defence.* The arms embargo has been justified on the grounds that it decreases the level of suffering, but the corollary of this is that the weakest (Bosnia) has suffered most. It is hardly the right of outsiders to determine the level of suffering a particular state is willing to endure to maintain its independence (think of the British attitude if the United States had refused lend-lease on such grounds in World War II). If an attacked state shows its determination to fight to protect itself, it is reasonable to supply the defensive means. But before this is done, calculations must be made about the dangers of embroilment in conflicts which have both civil and international components.

*Promote negotiations.* It is a judgment call between helping the vulnerable materially, and being in a position to act as a relatively impartial go-between or mediator. Nevertheless, outside powers should promote negotiations and seek settlement plans which recognise both power on the ground and civilised principles. At best the achievement of such a settlement might be long-term rather than immediate. Progressive elements within the warring camps must be given hope and shown concern. It is possible for intractable conflicts to be ameliorated, from within, over time, with the help of some external pressure, as recent events in the Middle East and South Africa show.

*Fulfil humanitarian obligations.* Even if the record shows that the present British government is unlikely to take the lead in the pursuit of humanitarian obligations, should we not expect it to do better than trail at the rear of supposedly civilised and rich countries? Whatever is done or not done about Bosnia, there are plenty of other situations where lives could be saved, with no risks, by the injection of relatively small amounts of money and technical expertise. And with the Cold War gone, there is now no excuse for quiescence on human rights issues.

*Recognise the limitations of military force.* Military intervention has proved itself a largely ineffective and sometimes counter-productive instrument in the post-war years. If a civil/international war cannot be prevented in the first place, it is probably better to keep out. Despite hopes being expressed about political 'early warning' and 'rapid reaction forces' for such conflicts, choosing the 'right' time for a military intervention is difficult. As a crisis builds up, natural caution will lead governments to stay their hands, because of costs and fears of inflaming the situation; after conflict erupts, it might then be too late.

*Learn lessons.* Mistakes have been made in the Yugoslavian imbroglio by outsiders and their international organisations. To learn from them it would be helpful not only for the relevant departments in Whitehall to conduct their own inquiries, but for the political parties to promote debate in Parliament. Publicity and discussion is one way to contemplate possible lessons. As it is, foreign affairs are largely sidelined by all parties in Britain. *Hansard* is not a source for learning about the world. But lessons can be learned from this experience about the diplomacy of recognition, keeping one's attention on combustible situations, the role of the UN, EC and

71

CSCE, and the attitudes of democracies towards the problems of world affairs.

## What are the lessons of Bosnia for 'domestic' politics?

Although the post-Tito break-up of Yugoslavia was long predicted, the speed and brutality of the last act came as a general surprise. In an interdependent world it is a mirror we should all hold up to our multicultural societies, since it shows their potential fragility. To reduce the risks of collapses into barbarism it is necessary to build up defences against intolerance, sexism, racism, fundamentalism, and hyper-nationalism. Overseas duties begin at home, both because civilised inter-personal relations are desirable in themselves, and because of the force of a good example.

There is an EC dimension to this. It is vital that the EC maintains its integrity as a multi-national, multi-ethnic community, committed to breaking down the old idea of autarkic sovereign states in the interests of peace and general prosperity. This should be borne in mind when considering calls for EC military intervention. Rebuilding the politics and economics of the Balkans is just the sort of strain the EC is not ready to take. A failed EC-led military intervention in a bloody Balkan war could have ripped the EC apart in a way comparable with the United States in Vietnam. Ultimately, the continued development of the EC as an internal security community and a non-military superpower will be more important for the evolution of global security than fighting for the 'sovereignty' of a desired but still-born state.

## What does Bosnia signify?

There are several situations around the world at the present time where the level of violence and the brutality is at least as great as in former Yugoslavia. But Angola and Azerbaijan, for example, have attracted nothing like the same amount of attention. It is worth considering the reasons why. The answer probably lies in a combination of media interest, relative proximity and political and cultural choice. As a relatively secure and relatively powerful state, military security has been the dominating post-war consideration for most British diplomats, soldiers, politicians and opinion formers. We have defined security in military terms and not in terms of the threat of hunger or the oppression of human rights. It has been estimated that as many as 40,000 children across the world die daily from disease and malnutrition—a figure which exceeds the annual average death toll in World War II.[11] The cost of saving many of those lives, as a result of the simplest medicines, has been compared with the non-

[11] Johan Galtung, 'Cultural Violence', *Journal of Peace Research*, Vol. 27(3), 1990, pp. 291–305; and 'Peace', p. 688 in Joel Krieger, ed., *The Oxford Companion to Politics of the World*, Oxford University Press, 1993.

purchase of twenty advanced fighters. Sending troops into Bosnia and creating a more equitable global economic system are not mutually exclusive, but if we want to maximise the saving of life, prudently, then giving attention to suffering children is the most efficient and effective way to do it.

Why do we prioritise arenas in world affairs made for military heroes as opposed to those for nurses? It cannot be anything to do with the level of need of the victims, as the figures above bear out. It must therefore have to do with a militarised and masculinised ethos, which also leaves global power where it is. In contrast, dealing with the starving—overcoming 'structural violence'—makes us ask uncomfortable questions about our own society, our wealth and the global economic system we help run through the G7.

## What sort of UN do we want?

The Bosnian crisis raises serious questions about the UN. The standard view of the organisation is that its growth was blocked during the Cold War by superpower rivalry, but that possibilities of a 'New World Order' opened up in the late 1980s, including something called 'collective security'. The Gulf War was seen as its first test, and victory. A successful UN is generally seen as one in which the major powers will be in agreement, and able to act in concert to enforce peace and stability.

The common-sense view of the UN just presented is based on the adage: 'When the UN is democratic it is ineffective, but when it is effective it is not democratic.' What this implies is that the UN was no more than an ineffective 'talking shop' as a result of the massive expansion of the General Assembly following the increase of Third World members after the mid-1950s. In contrast, when the United States dominated (as at the time of the Korean and Gulf Wars) the UN was able to act effectively. But this adage is based on a fundamental misconception. In historical terms it can be argued that the UN was effective when it was democratic. Global talking shops should not be denigrated. Their goods are ideas. During the ostensibly ineffective/democratic period, the UN in fact did work of world-historical significance, as a legitimiser of norms.[12] The historic forces of racism and colonialism were globally delegitimised, while the idea of economic development was legitimised. The UN played a role as one of the sites of a global debate about human rights, and put on the agenda notions such as 'the common heritage of mankind' and the 'new international economic order'. In comparison with such norm-development, the enforcement actions to prevent South Korea becoming communist or to eject Iraq from Kuwait seem relatively minor in world-historical significance.

[12] Inis L. Claude, *The Changing United Nations*, Random House, New York, 1967, pp. 73–103.

If the UN remains dominated by the Western states then it may never become an 'international community' in any sense other than G7-speak. For the UN to develop as an arm of a genuine international community it must be more representative, and this means giving more attention to its norm-creating roles than to the fixation with putting teeth into the Military Staff Committee and Chapter VII. A UN which is simply an arm of the leaders of the global protection racket mentioned earlier can more or less maintain order, but on past experience cannot deliver either justice or community—the bases of an international society worth its name. The historical record suggests that this must be built from the bottom up, by societies, not states.

## What are our duties?

We are simultaneously members of the British state and the human race. Both positions create duties and obligations. If we want to create a genuine international community—one which is more than inter-governmental rhetoric—then it is necessary that it be pursued from bottom up. Further, by the middle of the next century Britain will represent only a small portion of a 'West' which may itself be struggling as a result of shifts in the global balance of physical and cultural power. If this is the case, deepening the ideas and institutions of human community is in the self-interest of the British. The idea of common humanity, seeing humankind as the ultimate community of all communities, already takes this as a duty. Thus, for the 21st century, the universalist moral policy is also the rational policy. Duty and prudence converge.

In policy terms this means strategies at two levels for individuals. The first, at the inter-state level, involves seeking to encourage British govern-ments to act as 'local agents of the world common good'.[13] This means trying to shift British external policy from a policy of selfishness to self-interest. This will be difficult to achieve not only because of governmental dispositions but also because of the attitudes represented by the 'culture of contentment' in the population at large. Consumerist and individualist ideals do not encourage other-regarding attitudes towards the world at large. The government bears some responsibility for this, in idealising the politics of selfishness at home and only taking a lead with public opinion on foreign policy issues when it and the 'international community' deem it 'prudent'. The 'society of states' has in part to be worked through, but it cannot be relied upon to deliver order and justice until it is more expressive of a sense of world community. The second strategy involves foreign policy from below, through the building of global civil society. The latter entails supporting the development of those non-governmental organisations which attempt to delegitimise those very ideas and practices

---

[13] The phrase is Hedley Bull's: 'Order and Justice in International Relations', *Hagey Lectures*, University of Waterloo, Waterloo Ont, 1983, pp. 11–12, 14.

which have been so evident in former Yugoslavia, attempt to relieve suffering wherever it is found, and attempt to build the infrastructure of emancipation. The values of such a global civil society in essence are non-violence, human rights, economic justice, ecological sustainability and humane government. As presently conceived and propagated these are values which are generally seen to be *from* the West, but they are not values *of* the West since they can be traced to universal traditions and resonate in all cultures. These two strategies just sketched engage with Bosnia, but reject military intervention. Sometimes, children get caught in fires caused by their drunken and careless parents downstairs. In such circumstances there is no duty to send in the firefighters at great risk to their own lives, if it is believed that the innocent cannot be saved. The main duties are to limit the spread of damage, learn lessons, and to try to make sure it does not happen again.

Many thousands of innocent people have been killed and are suffering in former Yugoslavia. Sending in the fighter-bombers and cohorts of unready troops over an indefinite number of years could not have guaranteed—even at an early stage—that a stable, tolerant and multi-ethnic state would be created in a region charged with fear and over-flowing with guns. A few ring-leaders might have been killed, captured and tried, but probably not their ultimate handlers; at best the violence might have been kept to more acceptable levels until the peace enforcers with-drew. But ultimately the peoples of the region themselves have to decide to coexist. If 70 years of Yugoslavia could not achieve it, could 5 or 10 years of the UN/NATO?

We are morally engaged with the problems of former Yugoslavia, but have to accept that we cannot 'solve' them there, at this time. What the situation illustrates is that the G7 international community will remain an empirical sham until it is infused by the world order values and universalist solidarities of global civil society. Creating this requires that individuals make some commitment, however limited, to the growing global network of human rights organisations, development bodies, peace movements, feminist organisations, environmental and indigenous peoples' protection groups. If this is accepted as a duty, the lives of Admira and Bosko, and all the others, will not have been entirely wasted.

# DISENGAGEMENT BY STEALTH: THE EMERGING GAP BETWEEN AMERICA'S RHETORIC AND THE REALITY OF FUTURE EUROPEAN CONFLICTS

THOMAS HALVERSON*

> Using military force makes sense as a policy where the stakes warrant, where and when force can be effective, where no other policies are likely to prove effective, where its application can be limited in scope and time, and where the potential benefits justify the potential costs and sacrifice.—George Bush, 5 January 1993

THIS prescription represents the core American attitude to the use of military force. Yet this conceptual map provides no specific advice for navigating Europe's post-Cold War security threats. How will America decide when the stakes warrant, where military force will be effective and its use limited in nature and time? These are the essential questions America must answer when considering future military interventions in Europe. This paper argues that strongly-held strategic principles and political priorities constrain the use of American military power, and despite continuing rhetorical pledges to uphold old and new European security commitments, the fact that emerging security problems will not threaten vital U.S. interests means that the probability of American military intervention on the grounds in European conflicts will be remote. This argument proceeds in three stages: (1) an exploration of America's post-Cold War security options; (2) analysis of government policy concerning the definition of U.S. interests, emerging threats, appropriate force postures, and the use of American military power; (3) an examination of evidence from the Gulf War, Somalia, the former Yugoslavia and Latin America.

## A Definition of Intervention

Intervention can mean mild economic coercion up to full-scale invasions of foreign lands. This paper employs a high-threshold definition of intervention. There will clearly be considerable U.S. participation in the

* Thomas Halverson is a lecturer in International Relations at Keele University. He writes regularly on issues in American foreign and security policy.

76

evolution of European security policy. American ground troops, naval and air forces will remain in Europe for the foreseeable future. Those forces will perform various missions, such as: disaster relief, humanitarian assistance, limited air and naval combat, and perhaps peace-keeping functions. This paper accepts that this sort of intervention will occur regularly, as it is relatively low-risk and cheap in terms of casualties. Intervention, for this analysis, is defined as the injection of ground forces in a European conflict where combatants are opposed to a U.S. presence; ground combat, in the commonly understood sense. The key question is whether, when, why and how to expect America to intervene on the ground in Europe in the future.

## America's Freedom to Choose

Much has been written about the implications of the Cold War's demise. Despite initial optimism, few now believe the future will bring a 'new world order' of international cooperation and peace based on collective security and the rule of law. Rather, conflict is becoming more common and intractable. Yet the continuity of official rhetoric defining American interests masks the magnitude of Washington's freedom to choose. The debate about America's policy choices is extensive. Some believe America should seize the 'unipolar moment' and seek to protect and deploy its international primacy to shape aggressively an international environment conducive to United State's interests.[1] Others support selective disengagement from existing commitments to concentrate on fundamental domestic, economic and social weaknesses. A slender consensus seems to remain, though, behind a broadly internationalist foreign and security policy. The argument turns on the principles which should underlie it and the most appropriate means of execution. The first debate splits broadly between 'realists' who believe America should remain internationalist to promote and defend America's global interests, and others who believe that particular principles such as promoting democracy or human rights should be the guide.[2] Spurred by humanitarian operations in Iraq, former Yugoslavia and Somalia, some analysts advocate a doctrine of 'humanitarian intervention' driven by moral or humanitarian impulses.[3] The

[1] Charles Krauthammer, 'The Unipolar Moment', *Foreign Affairs, America and the World 1990/91*, Vol. 70, No. 1; Samuel P. Huntington, 'Why International Primacy Matters', *International Security*, Vol. 17, No. 4, Spring 1991.

[2] Huntington argues strongly, for example, that American interests, broadly defined, are best protected in a world where the United States retains its current position of primacy. Huntington, 'Why International Primacy Matters'. Arguments for making the promotion of democracy a central principle are exemplified by: Larry Diamond, 'Promoting Democracy', *Foreign Policy*, Summer 1992, No. 87, pp. 25–46; Morton Halperin, 'Guaranteeing Democracy', *Foreign Policy*, Summer 1993, No. 93, pp. 105–22.

[3] See Stephen John Stedman, 'The New Interventionists', *Foreign Affairs, America and the World 1992/93*, Vol. 72, No. 1.

second debate involves two parts, (1) whether American interests should be protected by unilateral actions, through collective defence and security arrangements or through a reinvigorated United Nations; (2) what role should military force play in support of American foreign policy.[4]

Although there are structural changes in the international political system which makes today different from similar historical transition points, a return to a traditional policy of minimised international security responsibility is available to America. Why, without any serious military rivals and no imperative like the containment of a clear and present Soviet threat, should the U.S. retain forward deployed global power projection capabilities? No ready imperative exists to motivate continued American forward strategy.[5] The freedom to choose between engagement or withdrawal therefore exists comparable to that of 1815, 1898 and 1945.[6] To sustain a continued forward military strategy in Europe requires a new and persuasive rationale for the American people. A public mood demanding domestic action propelled Bill Clinton to the White House promising to correct America's internal weaknesses and vulnerabilities. Nevertheless, America is integrated more comprehensively into the world than ever before. Economic, political, cultural and historical interdependence with Europe explain the official rejection of isolationism. Bush and Clinton have navigated around these choices seeking to sustain internationalist policies; how have they reacted to this strategic debate?

## Groping for New Principles

The United States government has responded to radically changed circumstances by clinging broadly to past policy guidelines. What has changed is the nature of the threat and appropriate response. In early 1992 new defence planning guidance revealing the fundamental logic behind U.S. global strategy was leaked.[7] For Europe, the document reflected the Cold War imperative: prevent the emergence of a rival hegemony in Eurasia. Although subsequently redrafted with more restrained ambitions, this fundamental U.S. interest surely remains.[8]

---

[4] Doug Bandow, for example argues that collective security is less useful to the United States after the Cold War, Doug Bandow, 'Avoiding War', *Foreign Policy*, Winter 1992–93, No. 89, pp. 157–74. Edward Luck argues that the United States should invest more resources in a reinvigorated UN, Edward C. Luck, 'Making Peace', *Foreign Policy*, Winter 1992–93, No. 89, pp. 137–55.

[5] For an interesting articulation of how America should stop the continental expansion of interest definitions and military commitments see Christopher Layne and Benjamin Schwartz, 'American Hegemony—Without an Enemy', *Foreign Policy*, No. 92, Fall 1993, pp. 5–23.

[6] Samuel P. Huntington, 'America's Changing Strategic Interests', *Survival*, January/February 1991, Vol. XXXIII, No. 1, p. 7.

[7] *International Herald Tribune*, 9 March 1992.

[8] *International Herald Tribune*, 25 May 1992. The *National Security Strategy of the United States, January 1993*, Washington: The White House, states the interest as 'ensuring that no hostile power is able to dominate or control a region critical to our interests', p. 3.

American political and economic interests are best protected by minimising conflict, retaining the benefits of allied security decision-making through NATO, maximising open and cooperative economic relations, assisting the transition of Eastern Europe and the former Soviet Union to liberal political and economic systems, and convincing her major European allies to carry a growing portion of the political/military burden in protecting these shared interests. This much has changed little from Bush to Clinton and represents the bedrock consensus of American interests in Europe.[9] The Clinton administration is more interesting when redefining the threats to those interests.

### The Threat Debate

Bereft of a handy threat to rationalise its existing force posture, the Pentagon fashioned a new one based on concepts rather than capabilities. Chaos and instability, nationalism and tribalism are the new enemies. Potential aggressors, the Pentagon believes, learned from the Gulf that America cannot be defeated by conventional military power and will choose instead to employ low intensity conflicts and indirect warfare.[10] Stability and the peaceful evolution of reform processes within the CIS also became vital interests.[11] Fundamentally, the Pentagon believes the real threat we now face is that of the unknown and the uncertain. The threat is instability and being unprepared to handle a crisis or war that no one predicted or expected.[12] Exactly why these indistinct threats require a forward deployed force posture of Cold War proportions remains unclear. Yet these conclusions were not repudiated, merely refined and improved, by the Clinton administration.

Four 'pillars' make up the Clinton threat definition. They are (1) nuclear proliferation and loss of control of existing nuclear weapons; (2) regional, ethnic and religious conflict; (3) risk of reversal of reform in Russia/CIS; (4) American economic security.[13] Obviously numbers 2 and 3 apply most directly to questions of intervention in Europe. What is instructive about

[9] See *National Security Strategy of the United States*, p. 3. For an introduction to the attitudes of the Clinton administration see Thomas Halverson, 'The Clinton Administration: Foreign and Defence Policy Priorities', *Brassey's Defence Yearbook 1993*, Brassey's, London, 1993, pp. 380–96; the administration's security thinking is set out by Secretary of State Christopher in 'Towards a NATO Summit', *NATO Review*, August 1993.

[10] See the speech of James R. Locher III, assistant secretary of defense for special operations and low-intensity conflict, 'Military Strength Remains Ultimate U.S. Trump Card', 5 November 1992, *Defense Issues*, Vol. 7, No. 59.

[11] 'Our number-one foreign priority today', according to the *National Security Strategy of the United States*, p. 6.

[12] 'The Changing Strategic Environment', Based on Chapters 1 and 2 of the 1992 *Joint Military Net Assessment*, in *Defence '92*, November/December 1992, p. 8.

[13] See Frank Wisner, 'Wisner Warns of Nuclear Proliferation Danger', *European Wireless File News Alert*, 5 March 1993; Department of Defense News Briefing on the Fiscal Year 1994 Defense budget, 27 March 1993; Remarks by Les Aspin, Secretary of Defense, to the VFW National Convention, Dallas Texas, 23 August 1993.

the Bush and Clinton threat definitions is their unifying theme: they are systemic in nature. By their nature all but number 4 are unspecific and do not directly or uniquely threaten vital American interests. They are as much threats to the international system of sovereign states or Europe generally as threats to critical American interests. Why should the United States pay a higher proportional price in blood and resources to protect international public goods such as sovereign European borders, human and ethnic rights than European countries more directly threatened? Are any of these threats potential grounds for intervention?

There is little prospect that nuclear dangers from within CIS will ever motivate intervention. Even if a major conflict occurred in the region, there is almost no conceivable nuclear problem which would motivate intervention with conventional forces. Nor is intervention relevant to the problems of reform within Russia/CIS. That leaves only regional, ethnic and/or religious conflicts. Here the threat is apparent and most easily construed as threatening U.S. interests. These threats usually emerge as in the former Yugoslavia: tensions within weak states driving self-determination leading to civil war in circumstances of intermingled ethnic populations and mismatched boundaries. Traditional cross-border aggression will be rare, the real threats—which the international community is least capable of handling—will derive from fragmentation of weak and unstable states with irresolvable political tensions devolving into violence. America will rarely understand the regional history or political dynamics and will not practise decisive preventive diplomacy or take much interest until the violence is underway; at which point there is little that can be done. The international community is being reminded that it has no ready solution to intractable conflicts where the participants are determined to fight. Besides, in the more remote areas of Europe where these conflicts are most likely the United States either has no interests vital enough to fight to protect or has more important interests—good relations with Russia, for example—best protected by resisting aggressive regional political or military intervention. Although regrettable, violent border changes and ethnic cleansing will just not in themselves be either readily soluble or dangerous enough to motivate American intervention. Even if vital interests were at stake it is hard to see how intervention would be a useful antidote. We are left to conclude that official definitions of threats to U.S. interests in Europe fail to provide sufficient justification for intervention. More persuasive arguments are needed to convincingly justify large existing force structures, let alone any potential intervention in a regional/ethnic European conflict.

## Force Posture and Institutional Framework

Arguments over force size and posture are often surrogates for disagreements over definitions of interest and the best means to defend them. Criticism of current American threat and interest formulations has been meagre. Undue energy has instead been expended arguing about the Pentagon's comprehensive 'bottom-up' review, the intricacies of NATO's new posture, institutional 'architectures' and troop levels in Europe. Force posture conclusions deriving from the Clinton Administration's six-month 'bottom-up' review indicate that America views the Gulf War as an appropriate planning scenario for future regional was. America must retain, according to the Pentagon, the capabilities to fight two such regional wars simultaneously. The emphasis will be to capitalise increasingly on the technical advantages in information and data processing, intelligence, communications and weapons systems which the Gulf War demonstrated effectively. Use of this 'force multiplying' technical edge, and an increasing reliance on air power and sophisticated weapons are hoped to become, where possible, substitutes to putting infantry in danger. More mobility will also be a central element of future U.S. defence posture, including the use of former strategic nuclear airpower for global conventional bombing capabilities. The main worry with these changes is whether they are appropriate for the context of future European interventions. Most emerging conflicts in Europe will be in political and geographical circumstances where ground troops are the most appropriate weapons and America's technical emphasis will either be ineffective or only useful as an adjunct to the humble infantryman.

These emerging trends in U.S. forces should be analysed carefully in Europe where they will increasingly cause problems for allies who already depend enormously on American intelligence, combat support, logistics and air power. How exactly will this European dependence on various U.S. capabilities be resolved if American constraints on intervention become more stringent? These problems will be a continual source of discussion and tension in future as American policy on the use of its capabilities in conjunction with European allies will often determine whether any serious European intervention is possible. Europeans may find the U.S. arguing for a sort of military 'comparative advantage', whereby the U.S. provides these unique critical capabilities towards a joint objective while allies are expected to provide the necessary ground troops. Obviously such a scenario to reduce American ground force risks at the expense of European allies would be controversial at best. Such tensions were experienced in former Yugoslavia and demonstrated already a problem which will re-emerge.

Much debate about U.S. force posture in Europe devolves into whether the troop numbers should be 150,000 or something less, rather than an analysis of what interests would ever be vital enough to justify the use of American ground forces.[14] In reality, the most salient purposes of U.S. forces in Europe have less to do with preparation for intervention against emerging threats than to cement the cooperation and coordination of

[14] See Don M. Snider, 'US Military Forces in Europe: How Long can We Go?', *Survival*, Vol. 34, No. 4, Winter 1992–93, pp. 24–39.

defence policy among the major allies. Washington also values its forward presence in Europe as a staging post for military action further afield; for example, in the Middle East. Given the diverse political functions of America's European forces and that intervention will be highly unlikely given U.S. interests and the nature of the threats, the appropriate force size for Europe is debatable. About 100,000 troops seems enough for the Clinton administration, down from 150,000 under Bush. Yet the exact force posture will not be decisive in questions of intervention, unless existing forces are completely inappropriate for the crisis at hand. The central issue is when they will ever be used.

As to the security framework, NATO will continue to be the vehicle for America's European security policy. Although increasingly under question, NATO retains support in the United States because it is the organisation where America wields most influence and it provides a framework for defence cooperation which prevents a fracturing of the allies. NATO's retention, for example, is valued highly throughout Europe because it allows the continued subordination of the Bundeswehr to an alliance framework and prevents the renationalisation of defence policy. Exactly how to handle relationships with central and East-European countries will remain problematic, despite the 'partnership for peace' and other recent initiatives designed to associate the Poles, Hungarians, Czechs and Slovaks closer with NATO. NATO's touted transformation and cooperation with the East are inadequate substitutes for the rights and responsibilities of full membership which these countries want. Few in the West are keen to provoke Russian sensitivities or provide security insurance to clients who live in a dangerous and unstable neighbourbood. Essentially the problem is a failure to operationalise exactly how NATO can 'project stability' in to the East. Given that the sources of instability derive primarily from ethnic, social and economic tensions occurring within weak and fractured political structures and governments, how can NATO solve what are at root domestic problems requiring home-made solutions? Revived Russian assertiveness toward the former Soviet republics and East-Central Europe is also worrying. Neither America nor Europe has carefully thought through the security choices necessary if the region is to escape a concerted drive for a revived Russian sphere of influence. Enthusiasm for NATO revitalisation tells us little about American attitudes toward intervention. NATO will be used as a vehicle for intervention if Washington's interests are thus served. Alliance organisational structure will not predict when or how that will happen. For this answer we must understand the factors which influence American decisions to intervene.

## When and How to Use Force

What are the criteria the United States will apply to decisions about when, why and how to intervene in future European conflicts? A heavy legacy from the past influences the answers of today's leaders. Vietnam casts a long shadow on the debate, but there are other recent salient experiences. In the wake of the Beirut disaster, where 241 United States Marines and naval personnel were killed by a suicide bomber, a reappraisal of the purposes and methods of intervention was undertaken. Vietnam and the difficulties of peace-keeping amidst a civil war in Lebanon led Secretary of Defense Weinberger to derive six principles, or 'tests' which should be applied when deciding to commit U.S. conventional military forces to combat.

(1) forces should not be committed unless vital interests are at stake;
(2) if forces are committed, the U.S. must provide sufficient numbers and support to win. If the country is unwilling to do so then forces should not be committed;
(3) any intervention requires clearly defined political and military objectives;
(4) the relationship between objectives and force size must be constantly reassessed and adjusted if necessary;
(5) before forces are committed the government should have a reasonable assurance of domestic political support from the public and Congress. This support requires candour from the government in making clear why vital interests are threatened, 'and by the use of American military forces, we can achieve a clear, worthy goal'.
(6) commitment of U.S. forces should be a last resort—'only after diplomatic, political, economic and other efforts have been made to protect' vital interests.[15]

These significant constraints on the use of U.S. military power outlived the Reagan administration.

Since the 1986 Goldwater-Nichols military reform legislation, the Chairman of the Joint Chiefs of Staff has been the primary military adviser to the President. The man who was Weinberger's military assistant during and after Beirut, General Colin Powell, was Chairman of the Chiefs from 1989–1993. During that time the influence of the Weinberger logic was demonstrated repeatedly. Although chairman Powell criticised those who would use a fixed set of rules or criteria for the use of force, his formulation represented as significant a constraint on the use of military power as Weinberger's. Relevant considerations before using force include:

Is the political objective we seek to achieve important, clearly defined and under-stood? Have all other nonviolent policy means failed? Will military force achieve the objective? At what cost? Have the gains and risks been analyzed? How might the situation we seek to alter, once it is altered by force, develop further and what might be the consequence? . . . When the political objective is important, clearly defined and understood, when the risks are acceptable, and when the use of force can be effectively combined with diplomatic and economic policies, then clear and unambiguous objectives must be given to the armed forces. These objectives must be firmly linked with the political objectives.[16]

[15] Caspar Weinberger, 'U.S. Defense Strategy', *Foreign Affairs*, Spring 1986, pp. 686–7.
[16] Colin L. Powell, 'U.S. Forces: Challenges Ahead', *Foreign Affairs*, Winter 1992/93, Vol. 71, No. 5, p. 38.

Once a decision to intervene has been made, overwhelming force is the preferred means. This too, has been made clear in word and deed in recent years. According, for example, to the *1992 Joint Military Net Assessment*:

> Once a decision for military action has been made, half-measures and confused objectives can extract a severe price in the form of protracted conflict, causing needless waste of lives and resources, a divided nation at home and defeat. Therefore an essential element of our strategy is the ability to rapidly assemble and apply *decisive force* to overwhelm our adversaries and thereby terminate conflicts swiftly with minimum loss of life.[17] (emphasis added)

The wisdom and influence of this logic in the White House became evident following President Bush's decision to intervene in Somalia, when the President moved the argument on when and where to use American military power forward.

In words the United States may regret, Bush explained the deployment of troops to Somalia by arguing that America must shoulder such responsibilities because of her sheer diplomatic and military preeminence in the post-Cold War world:

> In taking this action I want to emphasize that I understand the United States alone cannot right the world's wrongs. But we also know that some crises in the world cannot be resolved without American involvement, that American action is often necessary as a catalyst for broader involvement of the community of nations. Only the United States has the global reach to place a large security force on the ground in such a distant place quickly and efficiently and thus save thousands of innocents from death.[18]

This prescription sits uneasily with the logic of Weinberger and Powell; it is, given international conditions, a recipe for global intervention. Applied consistently, it would relax significantly the Weinberger-Powell constraints. In essence it dictates intervention, not because it is in U.S. interests, but because it is morally necessary and only America can do it. Perhaps fearful of allowing so expansive a definition to stand, Bush subsequently rearticulated the Weinberger-Powell constraints. On January 5 1993, Bush presented the more circumspect logic which opened this paper. He identified the key criteria for intervention: that the mission be clearly defined and its success achieveable.[19] In walking back from his Somalia defence he argued that leadership does not mean unilateral or universalism. 'We need not respond by ourselves to each and every outrage of violence. The fact that America can act does not mean that it must. A nation's sense of idealism need not be at odds with its interests,

---

[17] 'The Changing Strategic Environment', p. 11.
[18] Address to the Nation on the Situation in Somalia, 4 December 1992.
[19] Remarks at Texas A&M University in College Station, Texas, 15 December 1992.

nor does principle displace prudence.' Moving from the general to the specific, Bush clarified the Somalia decision:

> The United States should not stand by with so many lives at stake and when a limited deployment of U.S. forces, buttressed by the forces of other countries and acting under the full authority of the United Nations, could make an immediate and dramatic difference, and do so without excessive levels of risk and cost . . . In every case involving the use of force, it will be essential to have a clear and achievable mission, a realistic plan for accomplishing the mission, and criteria no less realistic for withdrawing U.S. forces once the mission is complete.[20]

Despite the apparent aberration of Somalia, President Bush left Bill Clinton a restrictive attitude regarding the use of ground troops, heavily influenced by the powerful constraints represented by the Weinberger and Powell principles, and quietly but powerfully supported by National Security Adviser Brent Scowcroft in the White House.[21]

Bill Clinton the candidate differentiated himself from Bush by criticising his 'coddling of dictators' and timidity in supporting democracy and self-determination; not least in the former Yugoslavia. Yet Clinton's priorities are domestic economic regeneration and he clearly fears foreign adventures might squander valuable political capital. Clinton professes continued internationalism and moral 'leadership' although with an enhanced reliance on multilateral diplomacy, collective security and a lightening of American global responsibilities. Nevertheless, there is extreme sensitivity when it comes to admitting the latter desire publicly. Protestations of continued leadership aside, the nature of the emerging European and international system and American domestic priorities mean that overall the U.S. will act less forcefully, less often, and rely whenever possible on the assistance of allies and international institutions in its foreign policy.

As for the use of force, Clinton has never presented a carefully reasoned concept. Asked before the election when the use of American forces would be justified, he said: 'When our vital interests are at stake, when there is a clear, sharply defined objective that is achievable at acceptable costs, and when you are sure you can build the support here at home.'[22] Given the nature of European threats discussed earlier, it is hard to envision a circumstance in which these criteria could be met. Few European conflicts will threaten vital U.S. interests, sharply defined objectives will be rare, costs and prospects for success will be indeterminate and domestic political support will be shallow at best. Particularly

[20] Remarks at the United States Military Academy in West Point, 5 January 1993.

[21] Brent Scowcroft, 'America: The Mission Is New Leadership for a New Deterrence', *International Herald Tribune*, 5 July 1993.

[22] Quoted in Halverson, 'The Clinton Administration: Foreign and Defence Policy Priorities', p. 384.

if the President refrains from expending valuable political capital to build support; a prospect guaranteed to vitiate success on the more important domestic agenda. Overall, the Clinton administration's formulation and enunciation for evaluating possible intervention does not constitute a persuasive strategy.[23] As a result Powell's constraints and criteria continue to dominate the debate, though the views of the new Chairman of the Joint Chiefs, General John Shalikashvili, will influence strongly its evolution.

President Bush argued after the Gulf War that Vietnam had finally been laid to rest: America had regained her military confidence. Not so, the lingering ghosts of Vietnam, Beirut and now Somalia are not apparitions, but continuing constraints. The Clinton administration accepts the argument that U.S. forces, when used, should be employed with decisive force and only with full public support—the commonly perceived weaknesses of the Vietnam strategy. Extreme political sensitivies regarding casualties is one residual effect of Vietnam which explains the obvious predilection for the use of air power first and exclusively in nearly all circumstances. A combination of increasing air power effectiveness and political unwillingness to accept casualties in pursuit of limited objectives creates the frequent and militarily unsound resort to air power as a substitute for ground troops rather than as a necessary complement. This desire to use air instead of ground force often determines the point at which further intervention is ruled out; which explains the high-threshold definition employed in this paper. Motivated by political necessity America's predilection for airpower solutions is often responsible for military and diplomatic failures in places like Bosnia and Somalia where a willingness to employ ground troops might have proved decisive in preventing further escalation and fighting. The use of ground forces as a last resort can thus sometimes be counterproductive; last resort should not necessarily always mean after all other measures have failed. Political constraints such as the unwillingness to accept casualties in pursuit of limited objectives are likely to increase steadily. Even after strenuous exertions to garner public support for the use of force against a clearly defined threat in the Gulf, President Bush only squeaked his authorisation through the Congress. Polls have continually shown a deep ambivalence to intervene in the Yugoslav civil war. Public attitudes will remain sceptical of European interventions unless a clear and persuasive rationale is provided by the President. Any future intervention must also have support from a wary Congress.[24] Changes of administration aside, foreign policy practitioners realise that a failed intervention will inevitably erode continued support for an internationalist foreign and defence policy,

[23] See the series of speeches made by high-ranking administration officials in September 1993: UN Ambassador Madeleine Albright, 24 September 1993, National Security Adviser Anthony Lake, 22 September 1993, Secretary of State Warren Christopher 20 September 1993.
[24] See the conditions laid out by House Speaker Thomas Foley for Bosnia, *International Herald Tribune*, 10 May 1993.

creating the very result they seek to avoid. Initial reactions to Somalia already bear this out.[25]

If the argument that these constraints will keep America from intervening in future messy, ethnic nationalist conflicts in Europe is correct, surely the response is to support a robust menu of preventive diplomacy and peace-keeping regimes so that such disputes can be smothered by concerted international action before they deteriorate into regional wars? In theory, yes. Peace-making and peace-keeping capabilities are planned as important elements of future American capabilities. This emphasis, deriving from the recent reinvigoration of the United Nations' role, began under President Bush who announced plans in September 1992 to enhance America's peace-keeping capabilities. Combat, engineering and logistical units were to receive special training; United States lift, logistics, communications and intelligence assets would be made available to the U.N. Other areas of American expertise would be mobilised to support U.N. activities. A line item was established in the Pentagon budget in 1993 for peace-keeping; $398 million was set aside by the Clinton administration for peace-keeping, humanitarian and disaster relief so that such activities would no longer consume military operations and maintenance funds. Actual new initiatives, though, are far less ambitious than the initial Clinton administration rhetoric suggested.[26] They do not support Butros Ghali's call for a standing U.N. army, nor do they countenance earmarking specific American units or capabilities for use with the U.N. Instead a list of capabilities that America might contribute 'on a case-by-case basis' will be assembled and assistance provided to improve currently inadequate peace-keeping headquarters in New York.[27] Plans aside, serious tensions exist regarding the difference between peace-keeping and peace-making and when an American troop presence will be appropriate in ethnic or regional European disputes. To date, peace-keeping participation has been limited to policing agreements reached between warring sides who are exhausted and ready to cease hostilities. Extreme reluctance exists when discussions turn to U.N. activities where deployments would be in conditions of ongoing violence, where warring sides do not all agree on the desirability of a UN presence, and the commitment is not limited in time. Speaking to the UN General Assembly, President Clinton indicated what America would want to know before agreeing to participate in new peace-keeping missions:

Is there a real threat to international peace? Does the proposed mission have clear objectives? Can an end point be identified for those who will be asked to

---

[25] Rick Atkinson, 'Guns Ready, U.S. Forces Prepare to Quite Somalia', *International Herald Tribune*, 9 December 1993.

[26] See the comments of U.S. Ambassador the United Nations Madeleine Albright, 'Peace-keeping: A Critical U.N. Interest', *USIS Official Text*, 21 June 1993; *International Herald Tribune*, 19–20 June 1993.

[27] *International Herald Tribune*, 6 August 1993.

participate? How much will the mission cost? The United Nations simply cannot become engaged in every one of the world's conflicts. If the American people are to say yes to U.N. peace-keeping, the United Nations must know when to say no.[28]

Command and control will also be a problem; although U.S. troops were subordinated to U.N. command for the first time in Somalia, this precedent met with deep scepticism and the Pentagon insists on retaining the right to end its participation unilaterally and take whatever actions it deems necessary to protect its troops, including disobeying U.N. orders.[29]

## Weighing the Evidence

American policy in future European conflicts will be shaped by the lessons of past and present experiences. Policy plans and government intentions rarely correspond to actual crisis decisions taken in real life. Will the carefully crafted intervention criteria outlined above survive the conflicting demands of America's leadership designs and moral precepts, when faced with the dichotomies of confused and ambiguous political-military choices which will present themselves in the future? The answer will depend on the attitudes and experiences of America's leaders, and partly on how they are influenced by the disparate recent formative experiences of the Gulf War, Yugoslavia, Somalia and Latin America.

### The Gulf

Two elements of the Gulf experience were most salient for this analysis: the characteristics of the dispute, and the method of American intervention. The Gulf crisis threatened vital, easily understood American interests. As a traditional cross-border invasion, the task of intervention— destroying a conventional army and ejecting its remnants from Kuwait— was easily identified, and success measurable. Costs were manageable given international support. Most important, success was certain; the result was never in doubt, only the amount of exertion required. Finally, the geography and physical characteristics of the theatre of combat were conducive to American weapons and doctrine. Few would dispute that the conflict played to traditional American military preferences and strengths.

Contrary to Gulf war optimists' conclusions, the experience was more a historical anachronism than a foretaste of the post-Cold War world— particularly for Europe. Acts of such bold aggression which palpably

[28] See the remarks of Madeleine Albright before the National War College, 24 September 1993.
[29] *International Herald Tribune*, 6 August 1993; Robert C. Byrd, 'Don't Blindly Follow the U.N. Lead', *International Herald Tribune*, 21–22 August 1993; Jeane Kirkpatrick, 'Clinton Does Have a Clear Foreign Policy: Just Ask Butros Ghali', *International Herald Tribune*, 28–9 August 1993.

threaten American interests are extremely rare. Although they need only happen once, a reoccurrence in Europe is unlikely. Rather than building up credibility which will deter threats to U.S. interests worldwide, the Gulf experience demonstrated that even when United States interests are seriously threatened the American public and Congress will barely countenance intervention to protect them. Aggressors did not learn that they cannot prevail over American forces in conventional combat. They learned that American fights well under certain circumstances, but that it you do not threaten U.S. interests egregiously and live in a geographic environment not conducive to American military capabilities and doctrine, then aggression can still pay. To the White House and Pentagon, the Gulf reinforced their belief in the wisdom of their restrictive intervention criteria. However inappropriate, the Gulf also drove the force planning conclusions of the Clinton administration's bottom-up review. The problem is that the emerging post-Cold War European security threats are as different from the Gulf as night from day.

## Somalia

The Somalia intervention eroded American enthusiasm for humanitarian U.N. interventionism within failed states. After an optimistic start and public support, Somalia went rapidly sour. With Somalia, President Bush allowed morality to loosen the constraints on the use of American military power. As a result, American and allied troops stumbled into potholes which would have been avoided if the government's own logic had been applied—though thousands of Somalis would have died. The Pentagon and CIA both correctly feared a Somali quagmire but were overridden by the White House and State Department.[30] Among Somalia's lessons was the realisation that TV had become increasingly influential in setting the political agenda. Starvation and vicious civil wars were occurring simultaneously in several other African countries, but there were no cameras to record the mangled figures and dying babies. Despite serious deficiences in experience and knowledge of conditions in Somalia, America resolved that 'something should be done' to relieve the unfolding tragedy. Securing food distribution seemed simple enough at the start, but the operation violated two of the government's own tests for successful intervention. No vital interests were at stake and there was no clear strategy for measuring success and quitting. By intervening, the U.S. and then the U.N. became politically responsible for Somalia: how do you shed such responsibility in a country with no government, without allowing the return of the pre-intervention conditions? What began as a mission limited in time and scope metamorphosed into a U.N. mandate to take over the administration of a collapsed state and create democracy in its place. Only one day of combat with 28 American deaths was needed to destroy America's will to

---

[30] *International Herald Tribune*, 7 December 1993.

fulfil these ambitions, precipitating a nearly immediate declaration to withdraw within six months.[31] The experience has shown how gratitude for international assistance can turn into hostility against a foreign occupation force. Somalia became a long term commitment where America's predilection for air power proved inappropriate, with American and U.N. troops increasingly unable to distinguish combatants from civilians. The desire induced by sensitivity to casualties to substitute air for ground power was demonstrated comprehensively in Somalia, where a disorganised and unsophisticated force shattered U.S. resolve by killing and capturing only a few U.S. soldiers, a lesson that was not missed in other parts of the world. Despite the post-Cold War need for long-term U.N. deployment in circumstances of instability and civil conflict, America's Somalia experience make repeat performances in Europe and elsewhere unlikely.

*Yugoslavia*

It has been in the former Yugoslavia where the gap between actual European threats and America's willingness to intervene is most stark. Initially, Washington viewed the Yugoslav problem through the prism of Soviet politics. Worried about the precedents of supporting self-determination within a polyglot federation, President Bush opposed unilateral attempts at independence. He feared the precedent would aggravate Mikhail Gorbachev's enormous secessionist problems. For prudent reasons of self-interest and to support the EC's growing foreign policy ambitions, Washington remained in the background to allow Europe room to solve the problem. This attitude shaped policy until the collapse of the Soviet Union in December 1991.

The Bush administration's reluctance to intervene also represented a belief that Yugoslav violence was beyond the power of outside powers to control and represented renewed historical tensions against which the application of force would be inappropriate and unsuccessful short of massive use. The fighting was seen as the direct result of the uncoordinated independence declarations avoidable only by negotiated separation with guarantees of pluralism and protection for minorities. Although the potential for escalation was far less than in the past, its prevention was effectively the only interest which motivated any American thought about intervention in the early months.

From a basic lack of interest in the conflict flowed the specific policies which emerged as the conflict worsened. Instead of leading the formation of an international intervention coalition and seeking legitimacy for the use of force from the United Nations, Washington left the initiative to the EC and U.N. In response to the growing humanitarian consequences of

---

[31] Madeleine K. Albright, 'Good Work in Progress in Somalia', *International Herald Tribune*, 11 August 1993.

war the United States was willing only to alleviate the suffering of the victims. Not until after the separation of Yugoslavia was officially recognised and the war moved to Bosnia did the conflict become serious enough to motivate a debate about intervention. In response, the administration clarified its analysis of the interests at stake, if only to have a more persuasive rationale for not intervening. As long as a peace process, Serbian election, or some handy excuse existed, intervention was resisted.

Aside from moral considerations, two basic interests were at stake for the United States in the former Yugoslavia: conflict containment and protecting international principles. As the war intensified, it began to threaten regional stability. Although there was serious disagreement among the Western allies about the causes of the conflict, the principles which any peace should codify, and the means to implement it, few disagreed about the need to contain the conflicts within the boundaries of the former Yugoslavia. For Washington, that was the most important interest at stake. If the conflict could not be smothered, Washington's primary interest was to keep it from splitting the cohesion of the great powers which was seen as the key to global peace.

Of course Washington shared the general interest that dangerous precedents should not be allowed to emerge from the Yugoslav case. Potential aggressors should not get the impression that the politics of nationalism, separatism, ethnic cleansing and the movement of borders by conquest would be allowed in post-Cold War Europe.[32] Clearly these principles are vital to the peaceful functioning of the international political system. However, the U.S. government saw no reason why it should intervene and pay disproportionately to protect these principles when they seemed logically more salient in this case to her European allies. In some cases (Somalia) Washington did demonstrate a willingness to act as catalyst, pay disproportionately and tolerate free riders, but only when the prospective costs—particularly in terms of casualties—were low and the prospects for success high. Despite the steady growth of the danger caused by the Balkan war, it never threatened United States interests enough to intervene in the fighting.

This conclusion explains U.S. policy. President Clinton equivocated between an initial aggressive determination that something must be done and an acceptance that the consequences of aggression will have to be tolerated. After receiving no international support for his threats to employ air power with air strikes against Serbia and arm Bosnian government forces, President Clinton lost interest in Bosnia until early 1994. American hesitation, and reluctance until February 1994 even to use the air power deployed from August 1992 to enforce the No-fly Zone, demonstrate that the Balkans never became a serious enough threat to

[32] For the administration's logic see U.S. Congress, Senate, *Situation in Bosnia and Appropriate U.S. and Western Responses*, Hearing before the Committee on Armed Services United States Senate, One Hundred Second Congress, Second Session, 11 August 1992.

loosen the constraints on the use of ground forces. Perhaps more would have been done, but for the inability of the major European powers (Britain, France, Germany, Russia) to agree either on the principles or the interests which should be protected, or joint military actions in their defence. The Pentagon and the State Department consistently opposed the use of American ground forces except for peace-keepers after a stable peace was established.[33] Not only were too few interests at stake, but the characteristics of the war were not conducive to U.S. strategy, and risks of casualties was high. Poor terrain, civil war dynamics, and inadequately defined objectives comprehensively rejected the Balkans as a target of intervention: it reminded the Pentagon of the Lebanese civil war. Military reservations might have been overruled for political reasons, but not without agreed multilateral action by the allies. Military and political constraints reinforced each other. Even the reluctantly expressed willingness to participate in a multilateral NATO–U.N. peace-keeping force to implement a peace plan was only possible if it was a 'fair settlement, generally and freely entered into by the Bosnian government'. U.S. forces would only participate if fighting had ceased, all sides to the conflict had to fully support the plan and broad Congressional and public support was essential.[34] Under no circumstances was Washington willing to act unilaterally or interject ground forces between warring parties. Indeed, as Secretary of State Christopher admitted on 21 July 1993, 'The United States is doing all it can consistent with our national interest'.[35]

Although each case will be different, the Yugoslav experience represents the sort of European war likely to emerge in coming years. From it emerges a paradox: regional conflicts of this sort will never engage vital U.S. interests unless or until they become a serious threat, but because of casualty sensitivities and the combat characteristics, the more they escalate and threaten U.S. interests, the less amenable they are to successful resolutions by military intervention. Here, then, is the lesson of Yugoslavia for the United States. Despite the rhetorical commitment to participate fully in the resolution of European security problems in the 1990s, America judged the case for intervention on its merits. Yugoslavia failed to trigger intervention beyond limited air power, peace-keeping and humanitarian activities. Where in East or Central Europe would a different conclusion be reached?

## Latin America

America's security attitudes toward post-Cold War Latin America provide few guides to European policy. Active interventions in the region

---

[33] See the conditions for the use of force outlined by Warren Christopher, *International Herald Tribune*, 28 April 1993.

[34] Press conference with Italian Prime Minister Ciampi, 17 September 1993; see also Clinton's remarks at his meeting with Bosnian President Izetbegovic, 8 September 1993.

[35] *International Herald Tribune*, 22 July 1993.

during the Cold War, such as Grenada, often derived from superpower competition. Yet, even during the confrontational 1980s, America was unwilling to take large risks to intervene directly, for example to overthrow the government of Nicaragua. But in 1989 Panama was invaded for reasons exclusive of superpower competition. Without Cuban and Soviet influence as justification, other American reasons for intervention will emerge, for example drugs. Nevertheless, diplomatic and domestic political costs will increasingly constrain intervention. Nearly all Latin American governments are now democracies, however weak, and the threat has evolved from insurgency and civil wars to narco-trafficking. Although drug problems absorb increasingly large U.S. military assets and assistance, they are not in themselves an intervention trigger. Intervention may occur periodically but only when strong interests dictate—Panama's historical dependence on the U.S. and America's strategic interests in the canal and Southern Command headquarters are unique in the region— and where overwhelming force is expected to keep casualties minimal. Beyond Panama there is almost nowhere that would warrant the costs of intervention, as Haiti has recently demonstrated. America's past and future Latin American policies will tell little about Europe. In Latin America the U.S. makes intervention decisions largely alone; there is nothing like the institutional structures and powerful regional allies and potential rivals which make European diplomacy more complicated.

## Conclusion

The analysis of this paper demonstrates that, despite official U.S. enthusiasm for multilaterialism, peace-keeping and robust involvement in European security after the Cold War's end, intervention will be constrained by both political considerations and military logic. These factors will proscribe the use of American ground forces to limited circumstances in order to avoid possible quagmires, casualties and failure. Unfortunately, the nature of emerging European security threats mean that few will be serious enough for significant American ground forces to be employed. Although Washington may be willing to participate in circumscribed peace-keeping roles and employ air and naval forces for limited objectives, the likelihood of intervention on the ground is remote. These conclusions are supported by the patterns of recent American military experience. Over time we can expect America's case by case behaviour to progressively erode its commitment and profile to a central role in resolving the European conflicts which are already emerging.

# THE BRITISH DEBATE ABOUT INTERVENTION IN EUROPEAN CONFLICTS

## PHILIP TOWLE*

DURING the last 20 years British armed forces have been involved on a significant scale in five types of campaign: unilateral anti-guerrilla operations (Northern Ireland since 1969), UN peace-keeping (Cyprus since 1974), unilateral intervention (the Falklands in 1982), multilateral intervention (Beirut in 1982–4, Kuwait in 1991) and humanitarian intervention (UN operations in Bosnia in 1992–3). As far as the general public is concerned, the highly publicised successes in the Falklands and Kuwait have tended to obscure the much more ambiguous results in Northern Ireland and Cyprus, and given a false impression of the efficacy of conventional military power. Popular opinion has not caught up with the change from the traditional order in which civilians were vulnerable to enemy attack and armed forces were strong, to one in which conventional armed forces are sometimes far easier to defeat than the peoples they are supposed to protect.

The clamour for intervention is motivated in many cases both by the assumption that force can be effective and by emotion: anger against the Argentines in 1982 for seizing British territory; against the Iraqis in 1991 for their mistreatment of Kuwaitis and of foreign hostages; against the Serbs in 1992–3 for their attacks on the Bosnian Moslems. Christian–Humanist traditions set the standards by which foreign affairs are judged, causing and justifying this anger.

Because of their once-commanding international position, both the general British public and the political establishment have less resistance to letting their anger push them into action and thus become involved in foreign crises more readily than most smaller countries. Their image of Britain unconsciously and unquestionably assumes its right to be a major actor on the international stage. British power has declined slowly rather than being shattered by some catastrophic defeat, as happened in most countries of similar size. That is not to deny that Britain suffered major humiliations at Singapore in 1941 and Suez in 1956, but these were avenged in the first case and gradually forgotten in the second. Thus the tradition of intervention, or of behaving like a Great Power, has been unbroken. Moreover, Britain and the Old Commonwealth countries were

* Dr Towle is Deputy Director, Centre for International Studies, University of Cambridge.

94

founder members of the existing international order, and feel an interest in defending that order at whose creation they were present.

British governments and commentators are also becoming increasingly sensitive about the threat to their permanent seat on the UN Security Council. The United States now argues that Japan and Germany should have similar seats. Some of the large Third World countries are also contenders. If Britain and France were removed, others could join without the Council becoming too large. The British government may feel that it has to be more active in peace-keeping and other international activities to offset its economic weakness and to confirm its status. Thus the 1993 Defence White Paper justified Britain's extensive involvement in UN peace-keeping on the grounds that such involvement was expected of a permanent member of the Security Council.[1]

If tradition, experience and national pride make it easy in certain respects for British people to countenance many types of intervention, within the political establishment they inhibit involvement in the sort of conflicts which are now breaking out in the former Soviet Empire. For centuries British power has been ineffective in the heartland of Europe.[2] Today, even if the development of airpower has changed some of the geostrategic factors involved, there is an instinctive reluctance within the government and armed forces to become too deeply involved in Central and Eastern Europe, a reluctance reinforced by experience of the limitations both of counter-insurgency and of peace-keeping operations. These feelings have been difficult to articulate effectively because the government does not want to admit its impotence, to dismiss peace-keeping operations altogether, or to spread unwarranted despair over its longest running struggle—the guerrilla war against the IRA in Northern Ireland.

## British Interests in Central and Eastern Europe

It has become a cliché that Central and Eastern Europe are likely to suffer from instability over the coming decades. This assumption is based not only on this region's history in the Inter-War period and on the numerous frontier and minority disputes between the states there, but also on the fact that instability is almost inevitable after the collapse of empires. While empires are in the ascendant they freeze history, once they disappear old rivalries reassert themselves—between Hindus and Moslems in South Asia, between Turks and Greeks in Cyprus, between Vietnamese and Cambodians in IndoChina. Post-imperial instability can take the form of conflict between states, of civil war, insurgency and military coups within

---

[1] *Defending Our Future: Statement on Defence Estimates 1993*, Cm 2270, HMSO, London, 1993, p. 48.
[2] Admiral Sir Herbert Richmond, *Statesmen and Seapower*, Clarendon Press, Oxford, 1947, p. 338.

an individual state or of some combination of these. It can take decades before the unrest subsides and a new equilibrium is established. How far, if at all, outside intervention can help establish such an equilibrium, or reduce the suffering whilst it is achieved, is basic to the debate, although rarely examined with much care. The general public and the media take a more optimistic view of the benefits of outside intervention than the government and armed forces.

Ways of achieving stability are controversial: what is clear is that Britain has five major interests in seeing such stability established in the former Soviet Empire. First, and most obviously, British nationals are directly at risk when unrest breaks out. Tourists, businessmen and others may be trapped by fighting. This is, of course, true in any part of the world, but the numbers threatened in Eastern Europe are growing rapidly. Secondly, Eastern Europe is the area with by far the greatest potential for economic growth in the continent presenting major opportunities for industries and finance houses. But, thirdly, if that growth fails to materialise, East European expectations are completely thwarted and unrest occurs, dictatorial and threatening governments may appear again in the region. There are fears that floods of refugees and illegal immigrants may pour into Western Europe, encouraging the growth of right-wing extremism. Fourthly, weapons released by governments in Eastern Europe find their way to West European terrorists, including the IRA, or to governments elsewhere which are hostile to Western interests. It is now alleged that even radioactive material is beginning to be smuggled out of the former Soviet Empire. Lastly, and potentially equally serious, any fighting in Eastern Europe which destroyed nuclear power stations or chemical factories would threaten the whole continent. This threat the civil disaster at the Chernobyl nuclear power station on 26 April 1986 made very clear.

Significantly, the government has made no concerted effort to underline these interests. This may be partly because some of them are so obvious that they need no emphasis and partly a tribute to the way in which public debates in Britain about intervention have to be carried on in terms of ethics rather than interest; indeed 'interest' is often considered a term of abuse by left-wing critics. In any case, the tide of interventionist feelings is already strong enough without adding to it. On the other hand, the failure to articulate British interests has led critics of government policy in Bosnia to argue that whereas Britain acted against Iraq in the Kuwaiti crisis purely because of its interests in oil, its failure to act more decisively in Bosnia can therefore be explained by the absence of material interests there. In fact, despite Western dependence upon Middle East oil, it is possible to argue that Britain's interests in stability in Eastern Europe are quite as great as its interests in the Middle East. Britain is itself largely self-sufficient in oil and, if its economy cannot be insulated from turbulence in oil prices, neither can its security be insulated from events to the east.

96

## Public Opinion

The British public and governments have frequently been prepared to use their armed forces in battles waged far from Britain itself. The public gave staunch support to operations to regain the Falklands in 1982 and to UN action to expel the Iraqis from Kuwait a decade later. On both occasions the use of force was opposed only by a small and largely middle-class minority.[3] The debate was largely about whether first the Argentines and then the Iraqis could be persuaded to retreat without force actually being used or whether fighting would break out. There were subsidiary and much more specialised debates about whether successful military operations were possible, but the public largely saw the issues in moral and emotional terms. Nor is this situation novel. In 1914 and again in 1939 it was the House of Commons, reflecting public opinion, which in emotionally charged debates called for a declaration of war on Germany.[4] The military implications of such traumatic decisions were only dimly perceived by the majority of MPs.

The public are today very much more aware of the full enormity of what is happening in various parts of the world than was the case in the past. When India was partitioned at independence hundreds of thousands died in communal violence. People read about this in their papers but it had no discernible impact on the popularity of the government which had agreed to partition the sub-continent. It is inconceivable that this would have been the case had the public seen the full extent of the tragedy on their television screens. Today governments are blamed for sins of omission as much as for sins of commission.[5] Here the unbroken tradition of intervention abroad is very important. If something is happening, however far away, which people deplore, there is pressure in Britain for the government to act. This is a phenomenon which is so obvious to the British people that it goes unremarked; and it is only when people from different political cultures, such as the Japanese, comment on it that it is actually examined. Calls for intervention in Bosnia, Kurdistan, Somalia and elsewhere stem from the power of the media to excite public opinion. Massacres and the deliberate starvation of cities are regarded as intolerable because it is now possible to see what they really mean rather than to consider them as

[3] On the Falklands see Philip Towle, 'War and Western values: Britain and the Falklands Conflict', *Oughtopia*, Kyung Hee University, Seoul, December 1983. On the Gulf War see 'Three in five back military action in Gulf', *The Times*, 17 November 1990. Compare opinion in the United States, *Time*, 20 August 1990, p. 10 and 10 December 1990, p. 41.

[4] Viscount Grey of Fallodon, *Twenty Five Years*, Volume 2, Hodder and Stoughton, London, 1925, p. 15 *passim*. L. S. Amery, *My Political Life*, Vol. 2, Hutchinson, London, 1953, p. 21 and Vol. 3, 1955, p. 324. D. C. Watt, *How War Came*, Mandarin, London, 1990, p. 579 *passim*.

[5] Maggie O'Kane, 'Giving thanks for little Irma', *Guardian*, 10 August 1993; George Kenney, 'American policy "borders on complicity in Balkan War of genocide"', *Guardian*, 17 August 1993.

abstractions. Public pressure may be particularly strong when bloodshed occurs in areas which resemble Britain or which are familiar to British holiday makers.

## The Debate within the Armed Forces

Over the last 300 years, British forces have been fairly constantly involved in warfare far from their own shores, in America, Asia and Africa. Less frequently they have been drawn into great wars on the European continent to prevent first Spain, then France, Germany and the USSR from gaining hegemony. There is no significant British tradition of peace-keeping or attempting to damp down minor conflicts within Europe itself. Although British forces in the 1920s did carry out this function in Upper Silesia, on the Rhine and in the Soviet Union, this was a painful exception.[6] Historically Britain has lacked the power and the will to assist with the maintenance of order in Europe.

In the 18th and 19th centuries, British forces were designed to keep order within the British Empire and to dominate the oceans. *Now for the first time in modern history Britain is faced with preparing its armed forces for conflict when it has neither an imminent threat from a major continental power nor an empire to police.* Thus many would argue that, given British interests in seeing stability established in Eastern and Central Europe, British armed forces could make a useful contribution by participating in UN, CSCE or other peace-keeping operations in the area. Such a commitment would give them a raison d'etre and help to justify defence expenditure in the face of Treasury pressures for cuts. Yet the armed forces have not generally looked on this prospect with enthusiasm. In part this is because of the absence of any tradition of operating in that region. Concentration on peace-keeping in Eastern Europe might also render the armed forces less capable of responding effectively to a revived threat from Moscow or to attacks from the Middle East and elsewhere. Traditional UN peace-keeping methods require infantry and lightly armoured soldiers with their logistical back-up. They do not require sophisticated fighter aircraft, heavy tanks or artillery, to say nothing of surface warships.

The balance between the three Services is determined in large measure by the operations in which they are expected to participate. Thus inter-Service rivalries influence attitudes to peace-keeping, as to any other military activity. The Soviet Empire collapsed in 1989 and the British government announced the 'Options for Change' policy for the armed forces the following July.[7] Cuts fell most heavily on the army as it was no

---

[6] D. G. Williamson, *The British in Germany 1918–1930*, Berg, New York, 1991.
[7] Compare the *Statement on Defence Estimates 1988*, Cm 344–1, HMSO, 1988 with *Statement on Defence Estimates 1990*, Cm 1022–1, HMSO, 1990.

longer necessary to prepare for a massive Warsaw Pact tank drive across Northern Europe. However, the growth in UN peace-keeping operations led to a reconsideration. By 1992 Britain had become the second largest contributor to such operations with forces in Cyprus, Western Sahara, Iraq-Kuwait, Cambodia and in the territories of the former Yugoslavia.[8] The result was a partial reversal of the decision to amalgamate some of the infantry regiments and yet further cuts in the number of frigates and submarines in the Royal Navy and of interceptor aircraft in the RAF. 55 infantry battalions in 1990 were to be reduced to 38 under 'Options for Change' but this figure was subsequently increased to 40. On the other hand the decision to reduce armoured regiments from 13 to eight was confirmed, while the Tornado F3 force was reduced from 122 to 100 and the frigate force from 44 to about 35. This left Britain with a smaller naval escort force than Russia, the US, China and Japan.[9] Inevitably the RAF and the Navy watched the debate on peace-keeping with an eye to the further reductions in their capabilities which might result from increased commitments in Eastern Europe.

## The Debate over Bosnia

The clash between public and media, with their high assessment of the efficacy of force, and the majority of the political and military establishment came to a head over Bosnia in 1992 and 1993. The public was in favour not just of humanitarian aid to Bosnia, which the government and armed forces provided, but of military intervention to impose peace on the combatants (peace enforcement). Members of the Muslim minority in Britain argued that the government's failure to use force to protect the Bosnian Muslims from Serb attacks was the consequence of the anti-Muslim feeling rampant in Britain. Yet the popular majority in favour of enforcement demonstrates clearly that anti-Muslim feelings played no part in the debate. What was particularly curious (and a marked reflection of the irrelevance of distance in the modern world and of religious considerations in mainland Britain) was the contrast between the majority in favour of enforcement in Bosnia and the majority in favour of withdrawal from Northern Ireland. A typical public opinion poll in October 1991, for example, showed that 61 per cent of Britons were in favour of the withdrawal of British troops from the province.[10]

The political parties were deeply divided on the Bosnian issue, but the Labour and Liberal Democratic parties, as well as the Thatcherite Tories, eventually came out in favour of peace enforcement. The Left was divided between the non pacifists, who took a highly moralistic view of

8 See note 1 *supra*.
9 *Loc. cit.*, Annex A, p. 89.
10 'Troop withdrawals from Ulster "backed by 61% of Britons"', *The Times*, 25 October 1991.

international affairs and thus called for massive intervention in Bosnia, and those, like Bruce Kent, the former chairman of CND, who placed their priority on the avoidance of war. The interventionist Right led by Margaret Thatcher stressed the importance of avoiding appeasement of aggression. Here guilt over the Munich agreement continued to play its part. Thatcherite Tories and foreign critics of British policy saw it following the traditions of Chamberlain and Halifax. It seems likely, in fact, that the Thatcherites would have been the only group single-minded enough to insist on intervention had they been in office and able to impose their view on the armed forces.[11]

The serious press was generally in favour of peace enforcement though not without serious divisions and doubts. *The Times'* leaders stridently advocated this policy, though they were vague about what actions they wanted the government to take and, ironically, they also backed large-scale defence cuts. Many of the paper's columnists, led by Simon Jenkins, were as hostile to enforcement as the editorials were in favour. The *Daily Telegraph* called for 'all or nothing' and argued that, if Western governments were not going to support peace enforcement, it was better to make this perfectly clear. Some of its columnists, such as Robert Fox, argued for greater involvement and its Defence Editor, the distinguished military historian, John Keegan, contended that there were two realistic courses of action which would be 'worthwhile'; to bomb Belgrade with precision guided munitions in the way that Baghdad had been attacked in the Gulf War, or to send an air assault division to attack the Serbs besieging Sarajevo and to kill as many as possible.[12]

*Guardian* leaders were also generally in favour of enforcement with many more troops sent under the UN banner to impose peace though, like *The Times*, it was generally unspecific about how this was to be achieved. Its columnists, Maggie O'Kane, Tihomir Loza and Martin Woollacott called for enforcement and it also published articles by Paddy Ashdown, the Liberal Democrat leader, and George Kenney, formerly with the State Department, who strongly advocated greater use of force. Edward Pearce sounded one of the few dissenting notes. *The Independent* bitterly attacked Western appeasement and devoted its front page on two occasions to the names of the members of the public who wanted to impose peace on the Serbs. It published letters by Sir Anthony Duff, the former Deputy Secretary in the Cabinet Office, by David Alton MP, Michael Meacher and others in favour of greater use of force.[13]

[11] See the very useful summary of various points of view in 'Should we use force in Bosnia?', *The Times*, 20 April 1993.
[12] 'Spotlight on Milosevic', *The Times*, 1 May 1993; Simon Jenkins, 'The war the West avoided', *The Times*, 9 June 1993; 'All or nothing', *Telegraph*, 4 August 1993; John Keegan, 'Only a short sharp shock will end their defiance', *Telegraph*, 10 August 1993; Robert Fox, 'The West's last chance to prevent a winter tragedy', *Telegraph*, 25 August 1993.
[13] 'Enough is enough', *Guardian*, 4 August 1993; Tihomir Loza, 'Shut down the shooting galleries', *Guardian*, 6 August 1993; Martin Woollacott, 'The West's empty hand',

Governmental opposition to peace enforcement in Bosnia did not stem from the sort of deep political divisions which had helped to stop British intervention in the Spanish Civil War in the late 1930s. There was relatively little disagreement about the ethical and political issues involved. The Serbs had their defenders who pointed to the atrocities committed by the Croats in the Second World War and the unfairness of the frontiers drawn up by Tito. But these were in a minority. The media suggested and the majority of the public accepted the view that most of the murders, rapes and tortures had been carried out by Serbs. This simplified picture was threatened by reports of Muslim massacres and refugee camps in September 1993, so the anti-Serb line temporarily wavered.[14]

Why then did the official line on Bosnia appear so hesitant? The government permitted Britain to become heavily involved in humanitarian intervention with troops running supplies to starving civilians, trying to mediate between combatants and evacuating some of the wounded. But these operations were carried out with the agreement of the combatants. Opposition to going beyond these measures and to peace enforcement was partly based on military considerations about the type and disposition of forces already engaged. Thin skinned armoured vehicles spread along narrow roads and dispersed in the countryside were highly vulnerable if the Serbs or Croats made a determined attack upon them. This was a difficult point to explain to the general public and certainly the government failed to convince the public of the difference between forces used in humanitarian intervention and in enforcement. Yet the attempt to explain to the British public that the armed forces in Bosnia were highly vulnerable weakened their deterrent effect against Serbian forces.

British officials were influenced, not only by these military considerations, but also by the experience of guerrilla warfare and of UN peace-keeping. Britain gave independence to its colonies in the period after 1945, very largely because of the power of Third World peoples to deny European armies the ability to maintain imperial rule at acceptable cost. Britain had been defeated by anti-colonial guerrillas in Palestine, Cyprus and Aden. Where it had been successful, as in Malaya and Kenya, it had been favoured by circumstances, not least the absence of external assistance to the rebels and the fact that they belonged predominantly to specific ethnic groups. But the British army still had to struggle in Malaya for more than a decade to beat the insurgents. Above all the experience of the previous quarter century of trying to damp down sectarian violence in

---

*Guardian*, 2 August 1993 and 'Commentary',*Guardian*, 8 September 1993; Paddy Ashdown, 'The ghost of Europe's future', *Guardian*, 5 August 1993; 'The folly of betraying Bosnia', *Independent*, 26 July 1993; 'Sarajevo: Action Now!', *Independent*, 1 October 1993; Sir Antony Duff letters to the *Independent*, 26 August and 3 September 1993.

[14] For a defence of the Serb position see Nora Beloff's letter to *The Times*, 8 July 1993. For criticism of Moslem behaviour see 'Muslims accused of slaughtering Croat villages', *The Times*, 16 September 1993.

Northern Ireland made the British government and armed forces deeply hostile to pressure to involve them in similar religious and ethnic feuds in Bosnia.[15] They had no illusions, Serbia's conventional armed forces could be swept aside by any of the NATO nations within a matter of hours, guerrillas could also be defeated in the very long run; but the costs could be high. The Yugoslavs had shown their capacity for guerrilla warfare in the Second World War and they had been trained for 40 years by Tito's regime to fight in the same way if the country were invaded by NATO or the Warsaw Pact.[16]

Thus the majority of officers, serving and retired, who commented on the war in Bosnia, was sceptical of enforcement. General Sir John Akehurst, Admiral of the Fleet Lord Lewin, and others took the majority view. Of course it is an exaggeration to say that this was a universal view amongst the military. There was a minority, including very experienced officers such as General Sir Anthony Farrar-Hockley, who disagreed and it was unfair to argue, as Lord Hailsham did, that the argument was entirely between the armchair strategists and moralists on one side and those with military experience on the other.[17] But there has been no open division amongst the military of the type seen in America between those who believe that air power alone might be effective and those who see air attacks on Serbian positions in Bosnia as simply the first stage in an ever-widening war. There may be RAF officers who believe in the potential efficacy of air power on its own in Bosnia, but they have not played any major part in the public debate and British experience has been that air power has to be used very carefully if it is to play a constructive role in anti-guerrilla operations.[18] John Keegan and others raised the possibility of air strikes against Belgrade, but the suggestion evoked little apparent enthusiasm, not least because of the certainty that some civilians would be killed inadvertently and because of the difficulty of deciding on a subsequent strategy if the Serbs still refused to obey UN commands.

It may indeed be that US emphasis on air attacks consciously or unconsciously reinforced British reluctance to become involved in an American-led campaign against Serbia. Those taking the crucial decisions had come of age in the 1960s when the predominant image was of US air operations in Vietnam. In any case American advocates of air power failed to explain what the next step would be if air attacks on Serb artillery failed to produce decisive results. The assessment that the American armed forces were incapable of waging low key operations was reinforced by the failure of the hostage rescue mission in Iran and by calamitous attempts at

---

[15] Desmond Hamill, *Pig in the Middle*, Methuen, London, 1986.
[16] For Yugoslav resistance in the Second World War see Fitzroy Maclean, *Eastern Approaches*, Four Square, London, 1965; Milovan Djilas, *Wartime: With Tito and the Partisans*, Secker and Warburg, London, 1980.
[17] See note 11 *supra*.
[18] Philip Towle, *Pilots and Rebels: The Use of Airpower in Unconventional Warfare*, Brasseys, London, 1989.

peace enforcement in Beirut and Somalia. Nothing was more likely to produce a 'U turn' in public opinion than media coverage of heavily armed helicopters firing their weapons in densely populated areas and causing the deaths of women and children.

Attitudes towards the UN and towards peace-keeping were also important in shaping policy. Those, like Lord Chalfont, who believed that the UN was exceeding its role by interfering in the internal affairs of states, were critical of intervention. Others, like Sir Anthony Parsons, the former British Ambassador at the UN, were mainly concerned that the world body would lose authority if its actions proved ineffective.[19] For a brief period after the end of the Cold War there was an euphoric tendency to believe that peace-keeping was the answer to the problems in Cambodia, Angola, Bosnia and elsewhere. Yet British experience with multi-national peace-keeping was no happier than with anti-guerrilla operations.

For almost 20 years British forces had been helping to separate Turks from Greeks in Cyprus and so prevent them attacking each other. Yet there was still no end to the dispute. British participation in the military intervention in Beirut from December 1982 to February 1984 had been even more ineffective and humiliating. British experience was that, even when it prevented violence, peace-keeping did not solve the underlying political disputes, any more than imperialism had done in the past. Indeed what is peace-keeping, but imperialism with a multinational and human-itarian face? Its effect is to protect people from the need to reconcile their differences. It may save human lives in the short run but, unless the warring factions grow closer together, the whole process may ultimately be in vain. As the Foreign Secretary, Douglas Hurd, argued in June 1993, 'who runs the place when the blue helmets have gone? If the UN is involved we have to be in a position to answer that'.[20]

Moreover one side or even both in the dispute may come to hate the peace-keeper. British troops were initially welcomed in Northern Ireland in the first stage of the current troubles there. Within a short time they were perceived by many in the Catholic community as their enemies.[21] Very often it is the stronger side which resents the peace-keepers because they stand in its way and prevent outright victory. In other circumstances the very presence of the military and their efforts to rout out those whom they regard as trouble makers set them at cross purposes with the local community.

Thus many in the Services fear that any force sent to Bosnia, which went beyond the provision of humanitarian aid, would become embroiled in interminable disputes with the different warring factions. The

[19] For Sir Anthony Parson's view see note 11 *supra*. For a summary of the UN's problems see James Bone, 'When in trouble blame the UN', *The Times*, 17 August 1993.

[20] For British actions in Beirut see Robert Fisk, *Pity the Nation. Lebanon at War*, Andre Deutsch, London, 1990, pp. 472 and 534. For comments by Douglas Hurd on UN peace-keeping see *The Times*, 18 June 1993.

[21] See note 15 *supra*.

super-imposition of incompetent UN control and the intrusion of journalists ready to publicise any mistakes would only exacerbate the situation. Consequently the British government was not prepared to go beyond humanitarian intervention, despite pressure from the United States, from the media and public and from the two main British opposition parties. What it failed to do was to convince the majority of British people that its policy was a sensible deduction from past experience and tradition. It also took much of the blame in the German, French and America media for the failure to bring peace to Bosnia.[22] In political terms this might not have mattered too much to Mr Major's government since elections are not won or lost over foreign policy. But the government's moderation over Bosnia reinforced its image of weakness and incompetence and thus did have important political implications.

## Conclusion

The willingness of the British public to countenance intervention has helped the government and armed forces when there was a consensus between the establishment and the general public that such involvement was desirable. This was true of the Falklands and Gulf Wars. Frictions arise when the public and media push strongly for intervention on humanitarian grounds and when the government and armed forces doubt the wisdom of such a course of action. The debate about intervention in Bosnia was damaging to the armed forces and to the government because they failed to achieve a national consensus that humanitarian intervention to run supplies to besieged civilians was all that could be attempted. The government was accused of appeasement and vacillation. The armed forces were criticised for interference in the political domain and for abetting government weakness.[23]

Because instability will occur in Eastern Europe for many years and much of the consequent suffering will appear on Western televisions, British governments are going to have to work very hard to convince the public of the limitations on the ability of outsiders to reduce the damage. The public has to be persuaded that the decision to employ armed forces should be determined not only by the justice of the cause but also by their likely efficacy. Humanitarian intervention can only marginally reduce the suffering. Peace-keeping is only effective: (1) when the parties to a conflict are geographically and spatially separated so that the peace-keepers can be interposed between them; (2) when the parties are themselves in favour

---

[22] 'A strangled threat', *The Times*, 11 August 1993; William Piaff, 'Sarajevo: Great Powers play out tragedy again', *International Herald Tribune*, 15 August 1993; Peter Riddell, 'The price Britain will pay', *The Times*, 23 August 1992; 'Clinton attacks UK and France over Bosnia war', *The Times*, 18 October 1993.
[23] 'Nato soldiers should leave politics to politicians', *The Times*, 29 April 1993; Roger Boyes, 'Now for a short sharp war', *The Times*, 7 May 1993 and *Guardian*, 12 August 1993.

of the peace-keepers' presence; (3) when the parties see that peace-keeping is only a temporary phase and that they must negotiate a political solution with their enemies; (4) when there is, therefore, minimal danger that those intervening will become bogged down in a bloody and unpopular guerrilla war. There are circumstances when enforcement may be practical and necessary—when the North Koreans invaded the South or when Iraq invaded Kuwait. But in both those cases the aggression was clear, the forces were spatially separated and thus the fighting was primarily conventional. Even then the Korean War became increasingly unpopular because of its duration and ferocity. It is a salutary reminder that it is far easier to intervene, to become embroiled, than it is to extricate forces without humiliation and demoralisation.

# THE DEBATE IN FRANCE OVER MILITARY INTERVENTION IN EUROPE

## JOLYON HOWORTH*

SINCE 1990, the strategic establishment and intelligentsia in France has talked of little else than the necessity of a fundamental review of security and defence policy and programming. The literature on the subject is super-abundant. The 'debate' actually predated the fall of the Berlin Wall by several years as defence circles strove to nudge France's strategic doctrine and force structures imperceptibly away from their stereotyped Gaullist moorings and towards greater practical cooperation with the construction of a 'European Pillar' within the Atlantic Alliance.[1] The lessons of the Gulf War, of the Yugoslav conflict and of considerable French involvement in UN peace-keeping and humanitarian operations in various parts of the globe have, since 1991, underpinned what has become a wide-ranging reflection on the role of France in the post-Wall world. Like all such debates in France, the discussion has been informed by abstract and theoretical considerations in which history, politics, ethics, statecraft, philosophy and the vast issue of national self-perception have shared centre-stage with more strictly diplomatic, military and strategic considerations. In 1992, a transitional military programme law (*loi de programmation militaire*—LPM) covering the period 1992–1994 came into effect. This replaced the projected, and traditional, five year planning period.[2] In parallel, a succession of restructuring measures specifically focused on the army, and culminating in the plans known as *Armée de terre 1997*, have aimed to transform that service from an instrument structured for East-West confrontation into a force capable of

* Jolyon Howorth is Professor of French Civilisation and Jean Monnet Professor of European Political Union, University of Bath.

[1] See, on this, Philip H. Gordon, *A Certain Idea of France. French Security Policy and the Gaullist Legacy*, Princeton University Press, 1993, esp. chapters 6 & 7. Also Jolyon Howorth, 'France and the Defence of Europe: redefining continental security', in Mairi Maclean and Jolyon Howorth (eds), *Europeans on Europe: transnational visions of a new continent*, Macmillan, London, 1992.

[2] Assemblée Nationale, *Projet de Loi de Programmation relatif à l'équipement militaire et aux effectifs de la défense pour les années 1992–1994*, No. 2877, 15 pp. (1992). This short document was then the subject of a 965 page parliamentary report: Assemblée Nationale, *Rapport fait au nom de la commission de la défense nationale et des forces armées sur le projet de loi de programmation (No. 2877) relatif à l'équipement militaire et aux effectifs de la défense pour les années 1992–1994*, No. 2935 (2 volumes, 1992). Hereafter, this *Rapport* will be cited as Boucheron, after the name of its author, Jean-Michel Boucheron, then president of the parliamentary defence commission.

permanent 'adaptation to a multiplicity of risks'. Throughout most of 1993, a top-level commission conducted investigations into French military planning with a view to producing, for the first time since 1972, an overall defence White Paper (*Livre Blanc*), published in March 1994. At the heart of most of this reflection and debate has been the question of military intervention.[3]

For France in particular, this represents a fundamental revision of her traditional security thinking. For a quarter of a century, strategic doctrine stressed nuclear deterrence as the ultimate guarantee that the armed forces would not in fact be called upon to serve in a shooting war. The gradual realisation that real combat intervention is likely to become the main activity of the future armed forces has led to an agonising reappraisal of many basic tenets of French strategic posture, including the validity of conscription, the appropriateness of command structures, the adequacy of logistics, the structure of relations with allies, and even the relevance of nuclear doctrine. In what follows, my aim if threefold. First, to rehearse the evolution of official thinking on force restructuring for intervention and its relationship to broader issues of strategic review. Second, to analyse the debate on the Bosnian crisis with a view to drawing out the lessons which may have been learned in Paris. Finally, to examine the extent to which institutional, doctrinal and programmatic shifts appear to be suggesting the bases of a discernible current French approach to the overall question of European security.

## Programmatic restructuring and military intervention

It was the 1991 Gulf War which forced France's political and military leaders to face up squarely to a problem which most had long been aware of: the parlous state of her conventional forces, for thirty years progressively starved of resources in favour of the nuclear deterrent.[4] Tactical lessons drawn concerned, overwhelmingly, inadequate operational or protection equipment on most of the weapons systems deployed in the Gulf. Strategic lessons were of five main types.[5] First, France's almost total operational dependence on American intelligence facilities. Second, the need for allied coordination and interoperability. These lessons concern

---

[3] Boucheron, p. 239. On 27 May 1993, these plans from the previous government were endorsed with no perceptible changes by the new defence minister François Léotard: Ministère de la Défense, *Propos sur la Défense*, Vol. 34, Mai 1993, pp. 164–72. Also, Assemblée Nationale, *Rapport d'Information sur la politique militaire de la France et son financement*, No. 415, 2 July 1993, *Livre Blanc sur la Défense*, Documentation Française, Paris, 1994.

[4] David S. Yost, *France and the Persian Gulf War: Political-Military Lessons Learned*, Naval Postgraduate Institute, Monterey, Ca, 1992; Jolyon Howorth, 'French Policy in the Conflict', in Alex Danchev, ed., *International Perspectives on the Gulf War*, Macmillan, London, 1994, pp. 175–200; Gordon, *op. cit.*, pp. 178–83.

[5] Boucheron, pp. 111–25.

France's perception of her relations with her allies, which we shall examine in the final part of this chapter. Third, the importance of 'smart' weapons, an issue which concerns the specific nature of the Gulf War. Fourth, the need for professionalisation of fighting units. Fifth, the importance of force projection and logistics. It is these latter two lessons which have served as the basis for reflections on intervention. The first point to note here can be dealt with almost parenthetically. It concerns a very recent discernible shift in nuclear doctrine. Virtually every paper on France's future defences (including the 1992–1994 LPM) begins with a re-assertion of the primacy of the nuclear 'deterrent'. However, with the change of government in March 1993, there was increasingly open and widespread talk of adapting nuclear weapons *for use* in surgical strikes against potential or actual threats from (Third World) countries considered capable of 'state terrorism'.[6] Apart from this—highly significant— exception, 'force projections' implies conventional units and is the central feature of current defence thinking.

The LPM outlines two new structures for force projection, which are fleshed out in the Boucheron report. The first is conceived 'within the framework of a general balance of forces in Europe' and involves 'procurement of the means necessary for crisis prevention or for the conduct of limited peace-reinforcement operations, or even for engaging alongside our allies in wider conflicts'. The Eurocorps is designated as the 'key element' of these missions. The second is a similar structure destined for 'Overseas' deployment which may or may not be used in conjunction with allies. Each of these formations will be under the operational command of a new inter-service general staff, the European one based explicitly on interoperability and allied planning. The entire armed forces are being restructured along 'organic' and 'operational' lines. At the first level, the army, air force and navy will henceforth embrace 'organic

---

[6] Prior to 1993, this ideas was the preserve of a tiny and heterogeneous group of individuals. The concept of a 'deterrence of the weak by the strong' was first launched by François de Rose, 'La dissuasion du fort au faible', *Le Monde*, 9 November 1990, and the surgical strike notion later rehearsed by 'Ewen Faudon' (pseud.), 'La Guerre avec l'Irak et la progammation militaire française", *Libération*, 27 February 1991, and Jean-Louis Gergorin, 'Deterrence in the post-Cold War Era', *Adelphi Paper* 266, London, IISS, 1992, p. 12. In 1993, however, it ceased to be a minority opinion and was taken up (with nuances) by establishment commentators as diverse as Paul-Marie de la Gorce, 'Une réflexion nouvelle sur la politique de défense', *Défense Nationale*, January 1993, p. 13), François Heisbourg and Pierre Lellouche, 'Maastricht ou Sarajevo?', *Le Monde*, 17 June 1993, General Charles-Georges Fricaud-Chagnaud, 'L'histoire après la "fin de l'histoire"', *Défense Nationale*, November 1993, p. 54 and defence minister François Léotard, 'L'effort de défense: une volonté politique', *Défense Nationale*, October 1993, p. 14. Most recently, a report by the vice-president of the parliamentary defence commission Jacques Baumel has recommended that France shift to a 'nuclear use strategy', Assemblée Nationale, *Avis présenté au nom de la commission de défense nationale*, Tome IV, *Dissuasion Nucléaire*, No. 583, 7 October 1993, *Le Monde*'s defence correspondent, Jacques Isnard, claims that both the United States and Russia are heading in the same direction, 'La dissuasion se cherche des nouvelles règles du jeu', *Le Monde*, 6 November 1993, p. 12.

groupings' or 'force reservoirs'[7] from which will be drawn, on a pick-and-mix basis, the appropriate forces for any given assignment. These will be drawn up and commanded by three inter-service command structures: Europe; Overseas; and Special Operations. Beyond that, precise details are hard to obtain and the framers of the law have taken care not to make any of the fundamental choices which will one day have to be made: as between allied interoperability and a more international division of labour; as between concentration on Europe and on 'Overseas'; as between crisis management and high intensity conflicts; as between a professional army and a mixture of professionals and conscripts. In theory, the new arrangement will allow for all or any of these options (Boucheron, p. 240).

Highly placed sources in Paris stress that both the existing LPM and the new White Paper lack any real political vision or dynamic and in effect amount to a fudged compromise between existing programmes (and their attendant culture) and the inchoate demands and constraints of the post-Cold War world. Most authors and spokespersons recognise that, for the moment, there are no clear answers to any of the major questions being asked.[8] By culture, France prefers to engage in abstract questioning and conceptualisation *prior to* making pragmatic changes. It was essentially this feature which caused the final squabbles between Paris and NATO from the spring of 1990 (the Key Largo meeting between Bush and Mitterrand) to the autumn of 1992 (Pierre Joxe's 'New Strategy' colloquium): for the French, it made little sense to restructure NATO and to devise a new military doctrine *before* reaching agreement on the political and strategic objectives of the alliance in the new world 'order'.[9] Therefore, the debate still rages in France over the precise identity of the new 'risks' which confront Europe and over the best way of reacting to them. Some see the future risks as essentially non-military or 'a-military' to the extent that the Gulf War itself has demonstrated to any would-be aggressor the utter futility of taking on a Western military machine which is arguably fifty years ahead of the field. Over and above problems arising from state terrorism and the arms trade, this view argues, the main risks to

[7] These are: *Army*: (1) Corps blindé mécanisé; (2) Force d'Action Rapide; (3) Eurocorps. *Navy*: (1) Force d'Action navale; (2) Groupe d'action sous-marine; (3) Force de guerre des mines/aviation embarquée; (4) Aviation patrouille maritime. *Airforce*: (1) FATAC; (2) Force de défense aérienne et spatiale; (3) Transport aérien militaire (Boucheron, pp. 233–4).

[8] François Fillon's parliamentary defence commission's verdict on the plans for the army were highly critical, arguing that the Defence Ministry was still unable to decide between the past and the future: Assemblée Nationale, *Avis présenté au nom de la commission de la défense nationale et des forces armées. Défense. Forcese terrestres*, No. 2258 (1991), p. 9. Interviews in Paris in November 1993 with several consultants to the White Paper Commission confirm this judgement.

[9] This is made clear in France's '9 Points' at the NATO summit in Rome in November 1991, and in President Mitterrand's press conference after the summit. Texts in *La Politique Etrangère de la France*, November–December 1991, pp. 17–21.

security now derive from demographic explosion and migration, from environmental problems such as lack of water and inadequate health care, but also from the new Mafias and from religious fundamentalism.[10] For others, Bosnia has shown that military intervention on the part of 'the West' is going to become the new order of the day.

For such interventionists, the most urgent political decision to be taken concerns the recruitment base of France's armed forces. It is ironic that the current debate on conscription was sparked in the late eighties through a combination of detente, demographic decline, and a growing sense that military service was largely a waste of time. Apart from the occasional incursion into Africa, the armed forces had little to do. Today's continuation of that debate takes place in totally different circumstances. Since 1991, the armed forces have been at full stretch in most of the hot spots of the globe. At the end of 1992, of the 60,000 UN troops deployed throughout the world, 10,000 were French—by far the largest single contribution. The political decision to accept such a disproportionate share of the burden has much to do with France's self-perception as a major power and as a permanent member of the Security Council, features which are invariably stressed in official explanations of the country's role.[11] But the growing call on France's combat manpower (which has in practice meant that a small number of elite troops have been almost permanently mobilised in different theatres for years on end) has led to a generalised review of conscription. There is effective unanimity in favour of the notion that the armed forces need to be professionalised, and that the system of national service needs a radical overhaul. But the political decision to opt for a *purely* professional army has been impeded by two non-military considerations. The most sensitive is the historico-cultural equation, dating back to the *levée en masse* in 1792, between citizenship in the Republic and military service. The most hotly-disputed is the financial cost of replacing the conscript army with a purely professional force. To some extent, these quarrels merge into one another as those in favour of maintaining conscription for ideological reasons inflate the projected cost of abandoning it, while those in favour of a professional army tend to minimise the cost.[12] While the politicians squabble over principle, the

[10] Admiral Guy Labouérie, 'Des menaces nouvelles?', *Défense Nationale*, April 1993, p. 75.

[11] This theme runs like a leit-motif through most official statements on France's entitlement to a permanent seat. Typical in this respect is Alain Juppé's response to a journalist's question about a permanent seat for Germany: 'The states which wish to be permanent members must assume the obligations such membership involves, including participation in peace-keeping operations.' Interview in *La Croix*, 26 August 1993.

[12] Thus the Gaullist François Fillon, one of the main advocates of a professional army, in a parliamentary report (*Avis*, f/n 8, pp. 92–3), calculated the extra costs at between six and seven thousand million francs a year over a probable five year period. The previous year, in the parliamentary debate, he had put the figure at only five thousand million. He had been obliged to revise the sum upwards because of the counter claims of the Socialist Party's François Hollande, who is in favour of retaining conscription, and who estimated the cost of a professional army at nearer to twelve or thirteen thousand million francs per year.

soldiers disagree largely on detailed practicalities, the main bone of contention being the realistic prospect of attracting, each year, the necessary numbers of professional recruits (20–30,000). A growing consensus among the military elite favours a professional army core of 100,000 to 120,000 men backed up by around 50,000 long-term (2 to 3 years) service volunteers.[13] At the same time, it is believed that the precise balance between professionals and long-term recruits will depend crucially on a much-needed *political* decision as to the numbers of combat troops to be kept permanently mobilised for immediate intervention anywhere in the world.[14] Some believe that France should aim to have available for immediate deployment up to 75,000 professional soldiers[15] and there is a general feeling that the aim of whatever restructuring takes place should be for Paris to be in a position, in the event of a major conflict such as the Gulf War, to deploy around 50,000 troops, while, in the context of operations such as Bosnia, she should be in a position to send at least one further division without having to borrow from other commitments. In short, the military is happy (at least on paper) to be much more professional and much more interventionist. It remains to be seen whether the politicians are prepared to foot the bill. However, although the main inter-service structure scheduled for 1994 to which I referred earlier is explicitly earmarked for intervention *in Europe*, the debate over Bosnia does not make it easy to see quite how, where or under what circumstances this new professional intervention force would actually be deployed.

## The debate over intervention in Bosnia

The French debate over intervention in Bosnia is instructive in two respects. First, unlike in most countries, it has been a very lively, wide-ranging and public debate, involving scores of participants. Second, it has been characterised by periods of intense public and political pressure *in favour of* military intervention, if necessary by France acting on her own. Moreover, within the relevant international bodies, France has generally

---

Assemblée Nationale, *Rapport fait au nom de la commission des finances, de l'économie générale et du plan sur le projet de loi des finances pour 1992*, No. 2255, Annexe 39, Défense (1991), pp. 15–22.

[13] Throughout 1993, the quasi-official defence monthly, *Défense Nationale*, carried a regular article on this issue, with all main protagonists opting for some form of 'armée mixte': Maurice Schmitt, 'Armée de métier ou armée mixte?' (April, pp. 9–18); Henri Paris, 'Armée de métier ou de conscription?' (May, pp. 89–96); François Valentin, 'Armée de conscription ou armée professionnelle?' (June, pp. 9–15). See also the proposal on civilian service by Philippe Ricalens, 'Le Service national: une nécessité sociale' (February, pp. 91–102) and the highly negative response by Henri Vieux, 'Service national: retour à la nécessité' (July, pp. 59–77).

[14] This is the conclusion of former Chief of the General Staff Maurice Schmitt in *op. cit.*, p. 16.

[15] Valentin, *op. cit.*, p. 11.

exerted the greatest and most constant pressure for military involvement of one sort or another. At the same time, the French government has consistently held back from autonomous action and has insisted on situating the French military contribution within the contexts of the international community, under the aegis of the United Nations. At one level, the debate has come full circle from beginnings which appeared highly interventionist, to a kind of conclusion which implies that, short of sending perhaps 500,000 troops, there is really nothing more that can be done to save the Yugoslavs from themselves. However, in addition to the strictly military dimensions of the debate (to which I shall return shortly), there are a number of other features of it which are worth recording.

One has to do with the presidential monopoly of foreign and defence policy: the so-called *domaine réservé*. The very duration of François Mitterrand's tenancy at the Elysée and the continuous accretion of (increasingly accident-prone) presidential control over diplomacy and security issues, has had two consequences. First, opposition statements on foreign and security policy often assume an 'internal political' dimension in that they are informed as much by a desire to score points against the President as by any lingering desire to generate a coherent alternative policy. For this reason, challenges to the 'official line' are often more formal than substantive, more conjunctural than sustained. Second, in large part because of executive stranglehold over security issues, voices are beginning to question presidential control in a situation where actual military intervention (as opposed to nuclear stalemate) is leading to loss of life. Political control over intervention, the argument goes, now requires a type of 'War Powers Act' with parliamentary veto.[16]

Another complicating feature of the debate is the important role of historical reference. The first element of this is the alliance between France and Serbia during two world wars, a factor frequently cited by both the *Elysée* and the *Quai* as being of fundamental significance. The second is the experience of the 1930s and the memory of Spain, Munich and appeasement, references frequently made by a wide variety of commentators, mainly interventionists. This historical dimension also embraces a more complex politico-cultural phenomenon peculiar to France. That is the permanent 'Franco-French' debate about the very nature of the Republic which dates back to discussions within the Convention in the 1790s. Put simply, it is a debate between, on the one hand, those for whom the Republic signifies the indivisibility of the central state as the guarantor of both legitimacy and stability, and, on the other hand, those for whom the institution has more to do with citizenship and with the

[16] See, on this, my chapter, 'The President's special role in Foreign and Defence Policy', in J. E. S. Hayward (ed.), *De Gaulle to Mitterrand: Presidential Power in France*, Hurst, London, 1992, pp. 150–89. Also, Charles-Georges Fricaud-Chagnaud, 'Gestion des crises et démocratie', *Défense Nationale*, February 1993; and Jacques Isnard, 'La stratégie du soldat de plomb', *Le Monde*, 26 December 1992.

complex relationship between the individual and the collectivity, based on self-determination.

A third noteworthy feature is the chronological aspect of the French debate. There have been three main periods of intense pressure for military intervention. Pressure first mounted in summer 1991, when many authoritative voices argued in favour of immediate intervention in order to nip the conflict in the bud. Indeed, throughout the entire process, interventionists have argued that, since intervention is inevitable sooner or later, it had better be sooner, indeed as soon as possible. This approach led to the 19 September 1991 Franco-German proposal to the European Council meeting that the United Nations should be asked to authorise a peace-keeping force, failing which the WEU should send one.[17] In the event, what was actually proposed to the UN was a much more modest initiative intended merely to protect EC 'observers'. Thus ended the first serious skirmish in favour of military intervention, originally informed by several factors. First, an unstated assumption that such an operation would be relatively simple, the more so in that such force restructuring as had recently taken place in France was predicated precisely on the demands of such a situation. Second, a clearly articulated feeling that this was a European problem which the Europeans were quite capable of handling. Third, a vague sense that the Gulf War had provided a model for the functioning of the 'new world order' which was more or less universally applicable. But by the autumn of 1991, all three of those assumptions had already proven to be false.

The pressure then died down for almost a year, re-emerging in August 1992 on revelations of the existence of Serbian 'concentration camps'. This time, emotion and an unexpiated sense of historical trauma led to a barrage of demands for military intervention. The pressure was complicated by the Maastricht referendum and the impassioned debate over the future of Europe which became indissoluble from the various positions taken up by the many participants in the intervention debate. These discussions posed both political-constitutional questions (loose confederation or tighter federation) and moral/ideological or even metaphysical questions (were the Europeans, now wallowing in the peace and prosperity of a civilised democratic system, no longer actually willing *to die* to defend that system?). 'The fate of Europe is being decided in Bosnia' was a frequent leit-motif. As early as 6 December 1991, a number of leading intellectuals had appealed in *Le Monde* for the EC leaders to shift

---

[17] The proposal was first mentioned in François Mitterrand's Berlin press conference during a state visit to the FRG on 19 September. See *La Politique étrangère de la France*, September–October 1991, p. 57. It appears that Helmut Kohl was prevailed upon to support the idea in exchange for French concessions on the creation of the Eurocorps but he only did so secure in the knowledge that John Major would veto the idea. In 'Les Plans de l'état-major français', *Libération*, 20 September 1991, it was claimed that plans had been drawn up to send in as many as 10,000 French troops, mobilisable in 15 days. I was reliably informed in April 1992 by sources close to defence minister Pierre Joxe, that such plans had been on the drawing boards for almost two years.

the venue for their Maastricht summit and to convene the meeting in Dubrovnik! The pressure for intervention in the summer of 1992 came close to embracing a consensus across the political class[18] and it was only silenced on 13 August 1992 by a firm presidential *nyet* in an interview in *Sud Ouest*. The pressure mounted once again in December 1992 in response both to the emotional prospects of Christmas in a besieged Sarajevo and (at a more serious political level) to the re-election of Slobodan Milosevic as Serbian President, a result which effectively dashed the hopes of those many commentators who had mistakenly believed the political opposition to the Serb leader to be greater than it in fact was. The Geneva/New York peace talks and the Vance/Owen plan succeeded temporarily in dowsing this third burst of enthusiasm for military intervention. However, around Easter 1993, and thereafter in a sporadic and increasingly unconvincing fashion, the ongoing martyrdom of Sarajevo and generalised revulsion at what was clearly perceived as Western connivance in Serbian territorial conquest led to continuing demands from by now predictable quarters for military intervention.

In order to make sense of the debate, one must distinguish between the various constituencies involved in it. There have been five distinct sets of actors: (1) politicians, (2) the press, (3) intellectuals, (4) military officers and (5) church leaders. One feature of these distinctions is that, while each category has used somewhat different arguments, it is almost impossible to divide them into clear 'camps'. Politicians from virtually right across the spectrum have been passionately committed to intervention, while others, again from right across the spectrum, have been equally passionately opposed. The same has been true of military officers. Intellectuals tend to have divided themselves into those pleading a particular cause (Serbian, Croatian, anti-communist, humanitarian, or whatever) and those seeking a complex and extremely elusive global solution. The press, rather astonishingly, has been largely at sea, confining itself to regular lamentations about how dreadful the situation is. Church leaders have attempted above all to maintain ecumenical unity, but everybody has been aware that, not far beneath the surface, has lain the sensitive issue of Croatian Catholicism and the memory of the Ustashe period. Significantly, only the National Front as an organisation has taken an overtly pro-Croatian stance.

In the early months of the crisis, the official line of the French government involved two parallel sets of contradictions. First, on the one hand, respect for the integrity of the Yugoslav federal state, on the other hand recognition of the right to self-determination.[19] Second, on the one hand, a

---

[18] In favour of some form of military intervention were leading politicians from across the entire political spectrum: Bernard Stasi, Brice Lalonde, Jacques Delors, Jacques Chirac, Charles Millon, Laurent Fabius, Philippe de Villers, Alain Lamassoure and Nicolas Sarkozy. Only the Communist Party was officially opposed.

[19] Roland Dumas, Point de Presse, The Hague, 8 July 1991 in *La Politique Etrangère de la France*, July–August 1991, p. 9. On the distinction between the two interpretations of *the state* involved in these contradictory positions, see Dominique David, 'L'Europe des Douze

114

desire for Europe as a whole to 'make' policy on the Yugoslav crisis while, on the other, agitating firmly for that policy to be *French* (basically pro-Serb). After September 1991, however, French diplomacy stuck rigidly to a coherent official line. The United Nations (rather than the EC or WEU as such) should be pushed constantly and relentlessly into taking proper control of the Yugoslav situation. This would mean ever greater military intervention but such intervention was to be exclusively concerned with monitoring cease-fires, supervising demilitarisation and protecting humanitarian convoys, all under the aegis of the United Nations. There would be no question of an independent or unilateral French military initiative, but France was prepared—indeed willing—to take the lion's share of UN peace-keeping on the ground. Europe and the UN should not be 'bounced' by Washington into taking erratic or precipitate action beyond that agreed in New York and Geneva. Responsibility for the fighting should be attributed equally to all sides (although Mitterrand was eventually led to accept that Serbia was the main aggressor). In short, responsibility for solving the Yugoslav crisis was placed firmly in the hands of the 'international community' via the United Nations, the majority of whose 'active' resolutions on the Yugoslav situation were prompted by French diplomacy.[20]

One concept which is central to the French position is that of *le droit d'ingérence* (the right of intervention), the constant reference being UN Resolution 688 (5 April 1991) which had authorised operations inside Iraq to protect the Kurds. The most energetic advocate of *ingérence* has been France's mercurical former Humanitarian Affairs Minister, Bernard Kouchner, whose arguments were essentially moral and political. For him, *le droit d'ingérence* was 'a great and powerful idea, [a] new political concept for the century wich will soon open, [the] conquest of the world community [and the victory] of negotiation over massacre'. Such intervention, he added, would have a necessary and salutary effect throughout the whole of Eastern Europe. This approach was supported by *Le Monde*'s seasoned international affairs expert, André Fontaine, who argued that the Kurdish precedent had opened the door to intervention by the international community in the internal affairs of sovereign states.[21] After the passing of progressive UN resolutions in favour of humanitarian assistance, followed by decisions to implement such activities by force (especially the General Assembly's Resolution 47/121 of 18 December 1992),

---

et la Yougoslavie', *Le Trimestre du Monde*, No. 24, 1993/IV, pp. 129–38. These interpretations correspond to the two views of the Republic noted earlier.

[20] There have been approximately fifty UN resolutions on former Yugoslavia since Resolution 713 on 25 September 1991 (which pronounced an arms embargo and demanded a cease-fire). A large majority of these have been sponsored by France. See on this, Jean-Marc Coicaud, 'L'ONU et l'ex-Yougoslavie: actions et auteurs', in *Le Trimestre du monde*, No. 24, 1993/IV, pp. 89–122.

[21] Bernard Kouchner, 'Devoir d'Assistance', *Le Monde*, 20 September 1991. André Fontaine, 'L'Ingérence', *Ibid.*, 6 July 1991.

both Roland Dumas and François Mitterrand insisted that a milestone had been reached in international law which would have fundamental repercussions in the future.[22]

The intellectuals (always a vociferous group in any major French debate) tended to espouse more limited politico-moral arguments. Most were in favour of military intervention, but often for quite different reasons. Leading the pack were men like Alain Finkielkraut and Milan Kundera, who interpreted the recognition of Slovenia and Croatia as *de facto* acceptance of the existing borders which should subsequently be guaranteed by the 'international community'.[23] Others, such as Bernard-Henri Lévy, Pascal Bruckner and André Glucksmann took the high moral ground and argued for intervention on largely humanitarian principles,[24] while more sophisticated political thinkers such as Edgar Morin, Edgard Pisani and Paul-Marie de la Gorce highlighted the complex political dimension of the problem created by frontiers, minorities and refugees.[25] Still others, such as Maurice Duverger, argued for intervention in order *to restore* the integrity of the Yugoslav federal state.[26] There was an exceptionally high—and sustained—level of intellectual mobilisation through petitions, demonstrations, concerts and other special events and the contribution of many dozens of intellectuals was no doubt significant in posing the terms of the debate and in keeping it at the forefront of public awareness.

The role of politicians was no less visible, but considerably less sustained. Virtually every leading politician in France took up a position, usually in favour of military intervention and usually during one or both of the two moments of intense public agitation (summer and Christmas 1992). In the early days, when it seemed Europe might show a lead, the main interventionists were almost exclusively from the centre-liberal Giscardian parties, men who had either been (Jean-François Deniau, Jean François-Poncet) or were about to become (Alain Lamassoure) foreign

[22] Dumas, interview with *Paris Match*, 7 January 1993; Mitterrand, interview with *Le Monde*, 9 February 1993. Bernard Kouchner, since leaving the government in March 1993, has devoted all of his activities, via his *Association pour l'Action Humanitaire*, to agitating for the future development of the notion of *droit d'ingérence*. Interviews with author in Oxford (October 1993) and Paris (December 1993).

[23] Milan Kundera, 'Il faut sauver la Slovénie', *Le Monde*, 4 July 1991, p. 4; Alain Finkielkraut, interview in *ibid.*, 9 July 1991, p. 2. Finkielkraut was enormously active, writing articles in the main newspapers at an astonishing rate, and eventually expounding his overall pro-Croat philosophy in a book, *Comment peut-on être croate?*, Gallimard, Paris, 1992.

[24] Interview with Bernard-Henri Lévy, *Le Monde*, 5 January 1993; André Glucksmann, 'Une philosophie de concierge', *Figaro*, 29 June 1992; Pascal Bruckner, 'Il faudra bien intervenir', *Figaro*, 10 August 1992.

[25] Edgar Morin, 'L'Agonie yougoslave' and 'Le circuit infernal', *Le Monde*, 6 & 7 February 1992; Edgard Pisani, Edgar Morin and Félix Guattari, *Le Monde*, 10 June 1992; Paul-Marie de la Gorce interview in *Dialogue*, Vol. 2/5 March 1993.

[26] Maurice Duverger, 'Le Virus de la fragmentation', *Le Monde*, 27 December 1991. Similar arguments are to be found in Michel Foucher, 'Fragments d'Europe', *Le Monde*, 13 July 1991, p. 2.

ministers. It is notable that, with the exception of Deniau (for whom Yugoslavia became a late-life crusade), these actors became more discreet, as the European option faded, giving way to party heavyweights such as Giscard himself, Simone Veil and Raymond Barre, who adopted a position indistinguishable from that of the government, in which the United Nations was given the main role, the over-simplistic but seemingly ubiquitous analogy with the Gulf War was taken to task and intervention as such was seen as a highly sensitive and complex issue.[27] This was not the case for a presidential aspirant such as Jacques Chirac, who clearly saw his function as that of an interventionist gadfly, constantly calling the government in general (and Mitterrand in particular) to task for their timidity and lack of imagination, but nevertheless avoiding specific proposals.[28] But the politicians tended mainly to act as a barometer of public opinion, itself largely stimulated by the media and the intellectuals, although the degree of support for military intervention among senior establishment figures was very considerable and certainly much higher than in any other country.[29]

This raises the question as to what extent French military intervention, either alone or in alliance with others, was ever a realistic prospect. The military as such were comparative latecomers to the debate, the assumption among defence analysts until early 1992 being that the silence

[27] Alain Lamassoure *et al.*, 'SOS Yougoslavie', *Figaro*, 14 August 1991; Jean-François Deniau, 'L'Europe doit montrer la voie', *ibid.*, 27 August 1991; Deniau, 'Avant qu'il ne soit trop tard . . .', *Figaro*, 23 June 1992. François-Poncet interview on *Radio Monte Carlo* in *Le Monde*, 30 June 1992, p. 5. Simone Veil interview in *Figaro*, 18 August 1992. Her arguments castigating the Gulf analogy had been marshalled several days earlier by Michel Tatu in an important piece in *Le Monde*, 'L'improbable "Tempête des Balkans"', 14 August 1992. Valéry Giscard d'Estaing, 17 August interview with RTL quoted in *Libération*, 18 August 1992. See on the impact of Maastricht on the Yugoslav debate, Patrick Jarreau, 'Un débat alimenté par la guerre', *Le Monde*, 21 August 1992.

[28] Jacques Chirac, 'Devant le massacre, la démission del'Europe', *Figaro*, 1 June 1992; Jacques Chirac, 'Refuser d'intervenir, c'est se rendre complice', *Figaro*, 14 August 1992.

[29] Throughout 1992, most (particularly the more 'responsible' voices such as Chirac or Fabius), confined themselves to demanding air strikes on Serb artillery batteries around Sarajevo and explicitly ruled out any ground operations. Others, with far less political credibility or strategic sense (Millon, de Villers) went much further, urging strikes on Serbia itself and even a ground war. Millon, who repeatedly stressed the Gulf analogy, went so far as to say that, as a politician, he did not have to consider the risks involved: they were for the military men to deal with: 'On ne peut plus se contenter de se donner bonne conscience', *Libération*, 12 August 1992. Editorials joined the chorus for a French-led military intervention. See, for example, Jean-Michel Helvig, 'Avant qu'il ne soit trop tard', *Libération*, 12 August 1992, but note the continuing hand-wringing of *Le Monde* in its first editorial on 'Purification ethnique', 7 August 1992. On 9 January 1993, *Le Monde* reported that almost every leading politician in France, with the exception of Simone Veil and Jean-Pierre Chevènement (to whom *Figaro* on 13 January added Charles Pasqua and Pierre Messmer), was in favour of active military intervention. Even the Green Party, which had steadfastly denounced the Gulf War, put out a policy statement in favour of intervention. Many called for the lifting of the arms embargo and for a veritable policy of arming the Bosnian Muslims. The most complete analysis of the politicians' positions is in *Figaro*, 13 January 1993, 'Le débat sur une intervention française'.

of 'la grande muette' should be taken as a rejection of any military option. This seemed to be confirmed in May 1992 when one of the first to speak out, General Philippe Morillon, who had been appointed as the deputy commander of UNPROFOR, ruled out any prospect of a 'military solution' on the ground, arguing that 'the confrontations in Sarajevo are between bands of madman with no political control'. He explained that the whole of Yugoslavia was one vast arsenal, especially in the countryside and that no military solution imposed from outside was even conceivable.[30] Such a prospect was nevertheless implicitly floated in a speech in London on 22 May 1992, when James Baker hinted at NATO being sent in to relieve Sarajevo. On 4 June, Klaus Kinkel, speaking to WEU, insisted that such a prospect could not be ruled out. On the French side, however, despite constant governmental pressure on the UN to do more, the military establishment seemed opposed to intervention. Nevertheless, *Libération*, on 27–28 June reported that the *Force d'Action Rapide* had been put on 'Cobra alert', a degree of mobilisation which allowed deployment within 24 hours. The paper claimed that a regiment of 1,000 men drawn from the 9th Marine Infantry Division was ready to secure Sarajevo airport very rapidly and then move down the road to pacify the city. This was clearly connected with Mitterrand's dramatic flight to Sarajevo on 28 June. On 2 July, *Le Figaro* claimed that the French Ministry of Defence had prepared three battle plans: (a) a 'warning shot' commando attack on Serb units around Sarajevo; (b) a 10,000 strong force to take over the entire Sarajevo theatre; (c) in conjunction with the UN, 100,000 troops to pacify the whole of Yugoslavia (a figure which *Figaro* estimated to be 50—70 per cent short of the real requirement).

Two events in early August 1992 led to the most intensive debate ever on intervention—before or since. The first was a report by Lothar Rühl in *Die Welt* to the effect that the French *état-major* had decided that Serb artillery could be taken out relatively easily and with little collateral damage.[31] Ministry of Defence and Quai denials, later reinforced by personal denials from both Mitterrand and Dumas, were unconvincing and Paris was abuzz with rumours about an imminent unilateral French initiative. Then, secondly, came the revelations about the 'concentration camps'. The ensuing public and political demand for 'intervention' brought onto the stage the retired but not inactive generals. Former Chief of the General Staff, MEP and self-styled potential presidential candidate Jeannou Lacaze argued that a WEU task force should go in and take out Serbian military installations using air and naval power. If WEU was not prepared to do this, the general argued, then France should go it alone: 'Whether Europeans or French, military intervention is now absolutely necessary.'[32] This approach was reinforced by maverick General Etienne

[30] Interview with General Morillon, *Le Monde*, 19 May 1992, p. 3.

[31] See *Die Welt*, 3 August 1992 and reports on the article in *Le Monde* and *Libération*, 5 August 1992.

[32] Gen. Lacaze, 'Il faut intervenir', *Figaro*, 6 August 1992.

Copel who claimed that a surgical strike taking out all Serb artillery around Sarajevo was extremely simple: the military personnel itching to do the job, he claimed, were simply 'waiting for the order'.[33]

Former Chief of the General Staff Maurice Schmitt was recalled from vacation to offer an official refutation, using *The Military Balance* to argue that the former Yugoslav army was bigger and better equipped than that of France and that any intervention would have to meet three conditions: (a) that all the most important military powers should be involved; (b) that none should be allowed to be exempted by constitutional niceties; (c) that it be clearly understood that there would be many casualties.[34] But it took the vigorous line adopted by Mitterrand himself in his interview in *Sud-Ouest* on 13 August to blow the whistle on this second campaign. From September to December 1992, the occasional lone voice would be raised proposing some version of military pressure on Serbia (usually preceded by an ultimatum), which would then be indirectly countered by a senior military authority demonstrating the practical impossibility of intervention.[35]

Around Christmas 1992, the debate on military involvement began to shift focus, becoming much more active among military officers themselves. This was presaged by a comment from a so-far relatively silent source, Chief of the General Staff Admiral Lanxade who, in a radio interview on 8 December, publicly expressed exasperation at the 'no-win situation' in which French troops in UNPROFOR2 now found themselves and hinted darkly at the prospect of massive military intervention.[36] His concerns had in fact been first raised over a month earlier when he asked Defence Minister Pierre Joxe to arrange an interministerial meeting at the *Elysée* during which the government was made fully aware of the almost impossible mission troops were being asked to carry out.[37] Only one day

[33] Etienne Copel, 'Lâcheté!', *Figaro*, 10 August 1992.

[34] Interview with *Antenne 2* reported in *Le Monde*, 12 August 1992. In a more substantial article in *Figaro*, a week later, 'Les Risques d'une intervention militaire', 19 August 1992, Schmitt went into great detail to explain the military difficulties of intervention, insisting that such an action would unleash a general Balkan War. A similar military line was taken by Jacques Baumel's defence information letter, *Défense et Sécurité*, 19 August 1992, although a year later, this same publication was to argue that France had sold out to German pressures by refusing to intervene (No. 42–43 nouvelle série, 17–24 June 1993, 'La Vérité sort du puits').

[35] Interventionists included an *Académicien* and journalist like Bertrand Poirot-Delpech, 'Mourir pour Sarajevo', *Le Monde*, 23 December 1992; politicians such as the Socialist Party's international affairs secretary Gérard Fuchs, 'Pour une intervention en Bosnie Herzégovine', *ibid.*, 22 November 1992, p. 5; and intellectuals such as Pascal Bruckner, 'L'Europe de l'Obscénité', *ibid.*, 22 October 1992. 'Non-interventionist' responses were from Admiral Lanxade, *Cols Bleus*, 20 November 1992 and in *Le Monde*, 22 November 1992 and General Morillon, *Le Monde*, 5 December 1992.

[36] 'I hope we shall not have to go as far as intervention in Bosnia, but we are now on the verge of taking stronger constraining measures in order to ensure that sanctions are complied with', *Europe 1*, 8 December 1992.

[37] See report on this 21 October 1992 meeting in Claire Tréan and Yves Heller, 'Impuissance et Fatalisme', *Le Monde*, 4 November 1992.

after his radio interview, Lanxade raised the military temperature several degrees by stating that 'The situation is getting so bad that we are going to have to choose: either we employ force, or we withdraw'. He conjured up a major air offensive to enforce sanctions, pleaded for the despatch of massive troop reinforcements to Kosovo and Macedonia and estimated that Bosnia could be entirely surrounded by Western troops within fifteen days.[38] The seriousness of Lanxade's statement can be judged by the fact that it elicited an immediate (and quite unprecedented) press communiqué from the *Elysée* insisting that the Admiral was speaking as an individual and not as Chief of the General Staff. There can be no doubt that a rift had appeared between the President and his most trusted military confidant, based on Lanxade's frustration at Mitterrand's continued refusal to entertain anything approaching military action against Serbia. Lanxade's comments must be seen in their proper context: that of the ongoing discussions within the UN and NATO about enforcement of the no-fly-zone (nfz) and about the ability of UN troops to retaliate if under fire. On both of these, political France, strongly supported by Britain, was dragging its heels while the US was pushing for tougher measures. Admiral Lanxade clearly appears to have been aiming to put maximum pressure on the international bodies to authorise the military procedures which would allow the troops to do the job they had actually been sent to do. Otherwise, he could no longer acquiesce in what amounted to sending troops overseas as sitting ducks with inadequate orders to defend themselves. The politics of intervention in Yugoslavia had clearly come into direct conflict with the military dimension. Authoritative articles began to appear, explaining the necessity, in the event of enforcement of the nfz, of restructuring and especially regrouping of the ground troops so as to render them effectively combat-operational. Detailed analyses of the military situation were also put forward by various generals and admirals, debunking the previously cautious 'official' line (Yugoslav army alleged to be 'stronger' than the French) and arguing that military intervention was not only morally necessary but also militarily simple.[39] By the end of 1992, there seemed to be a growing consensus among credible senior officers in favour of large scale military intervention. Once again, a quasi-consensus formed among leading politicians in support of such a course.[40]

[38] Reports on his dramatic statements in *Le Monde*, 11 December 1992, p. 5 & *Libération*, 10 December 1992, p. 5.
[39] General Michel Fennebresque, 'L'Europe face au drame bosniaque', *Figaro*, 30 November 1992 and especially Admiral Antoine Sanguinetti, 'Une dossier militaire qui frise l'"intox"', *Le Monde Diplomatique*, January 1993.
[40] A bipartisan appeal in *Le Monde*, 22 August 1992 by Julien Dray (PS) and Charles Millon (UDF) was followed by a huge rally that same day in the *Mutalité* at which politicians from all parties spoke in favour of intervention. The following day, Chirac, Sarkozy (RPR) and Barrot (UDC) reiterated these calls while Cambadélis (PS) demanded the recall of parliament in order to vote on military intervenion. Opinion polls showed anything from 68% to 76% of those questioned to be in favour of air strikes against Serbia. Respectable

At the beginning of January 1993, the French government, in response partly to public pressure and partly to a new, more bellicose, discourse out of Washington, abandoned its 18 month policy of excluding any military action against Serbia and crossed the 'interventionist' Rubicon—at least at the level of discourse.[41] But all the signs suggest that there was an element of irrationality in this shift. So fraught had the situation become, and so tense were the various actors involved that when, on 9 January 1993, the Bosnian deputy Prime Minister Hakija Turajlic was shot by a Serb sniper while sitting under UN protection in a jeep in Sarajevo, even the urbane Roland Dumas appeared to crack, announcing, the following day, that France was now prepared to go in—alone, if necessary—to liberate the camps.[42] Since then, the 'debate' has largely stagnated. The arguments have been exhausted, the impasse seems total. The level of frustration has been extremely high, which accounts in large part for the way in which an individual general, Philippe Morillon, who took a personal stance in Srebrenica in mid-March 1993 in order to force through relief convoys, was turned overnight into a national hero. But despite the flag-waving over Morillon's stand, France has come to recognise that, alone, there is very little that she can do. By the summer of 1993, that was being stated explicitly by the new government.[43]

## France and her allies

The main lesson which seems to have been learned from the Yugoslav situation, in addition to the force restructuring and projection plans analysed earlier, concerns France's relations with her allies. The most important legacy of 'Gaullism', contrary to the received wisdom which continues to stress French independence and particularism, is the un-remitting French quest, ever since 1944, for an interdependent, integrated and self-standing *European* security entity which, while closely allied to the United States in a restructured Atlantic Alliance, would nevertheless be capable of acting, within the European theatre or wherever Europe's

---

military experts such as Jacques Baumel and Jean-Michel Boucheron actually called for the bombing of Belgrade. On Christmas Day, Michel Rocard, hitherto noticeably silent, came out in favour of intervention and various articles appeared in the press analysing this veritable consensus within the political class.

[41] Claire Tréan, 'La France "prendra sa part à une action contre l'aviation serbe on Bosnie', *Le Monde*, 29 December 1992. Tréan interpreted this decision as a highly significant turning-point.

[42] Dumas' remarks in *La Politique Etrangére de la France*, January–February 1993, pp. 21–8, esp. pp. 23–4. Analysis of these remarks by Jean-Pierre Langellier in *Le Monde*, 12 January 1993 and *International Herald Tribune*, 11 January 1993.

[43] In an extremely forthright statement to Parliament on 21 April 1992, the new foreign minister, Alain Juppé, effectively excluded any serious military option as totally out of the question: *La Politique Etrangére de la France*, March–April 1993, p. 120. That has remained the position ever since.

121

vital interests appeared to be under threat, with relative autonomy from Washington. In other words, for much greater balance between the two sides of the Atlantic.[44] This has been the underlying objective of all France's recent attempts to revitalise WEU, and it was, as I have indicated earlier, at the heart of the sometimes petty squabbles between Washington and Paris in 1990 and 1991. It is the Bosnian crisis which has brought France to a much more realistic appreciation both of the strategic subtleties and of the timescale involved in any such restructuring of the existing alliances.

France's priority remains the constitution of that elusive European security entity which she hopes will emerge from WEU. In the early months of the Yugoslav crisis, there appears to have been a solid belief in Paris that the situation could be managed politically by the EC and, if necessary, militarily, by WEU. That illusion lasted no more than three months. Thereafter, the constant insistence that the *United Nations* be regarded as the appropriate forum for establishing policy on Yugoslavia reflects a strong commitment to the principle of international order supported by the totality of the 'international community'—and not simply imposed by one superpower. However, France recognises that, in the post-Cold War world, the 'rules of the game' which might one day apply to the management of a UN-imposed international order, are unclear and still need to be established.[45] Therefore, the French government has, since 1992, pursued a twin-track approach involving long-term promotion of WEU while engaging in (possibly short-term) immediate rapprochement with NATO.

The promotion of WEU needs little further elaboration. Paris was four-square behind the Petersburg Declaration of June 1992, which outlined the political and military ambitions of the European security institutions. These were explicitly stated as being of three types: 'humanitarian and rescue tasks; peace-keeping tasks; tasks of combat forces in crisis management, including peace-making'.[46] Such ambitions, as we have seen, echo totally the aims of current French military planning. Central to this European security identity (at least in French thinking) is the French/German/Belgian Eurocorps, which was officially installed in its Strasbourg HQ on 5 November 1993. Whatever the eventual status of a still hypothetical European army, it is noteworthy that the Eurocorps itself expresses the sorts of compromises and strategic shifts which Paris is now

[44] This was argued by Stanley Hoffmann as long ago as the 1960s and is best encapsulated in his chapter 'De Gaulle's Foreign Policy: the Stage and the Play, the Power and the Glory', in his *Decline or Renewal: France since the 1930s*, Viking, New York, 1974. It is the main thesis of my forthcoming book, *France and European Security: Independence and Integration 1944–1994*, Oxford University Press. See also, Frédéric Bozo, 'A French View', in Richard Davy (ed.), *European Detente: a reappraisal*, Sage/RIAA, London, 1992.

[45] On this problem, see Frédéric Bozo, 'Organisations de sécurité et insécurité en Europe', *Politique Etrangère*, 1992/3, pp. 450–1.

[46] The text of the Petersberg Declaration is in *Letter from the Assembly*, Newsletter of the WEU, No. 12, July 1992, pp. 12–15.

prepared to engage in. For the Eurocorps was explicitly designated in May 1992 as coming under the joint command both of WEU and of NATO.[47] This was the first time since 1966 that French forces had agreed to be part of the integrated command structure of the Alliance.

This shift in the direction of NATO is, at least in part, a direct result of France's experiences in Bosnia. Although Paris has continued to insist that, for reasons of international legitimacy, the political decisions about Bosnia should be taken by the Security Council, she has also, for reasons of efficiency, come to accept that only NATO has the operational command structure to allow those political decisions to be implemented. This became increasingly clear throughout 1992, but it was the debate about enforcement of the no-fly-zone in December 1992 that crystallised matters. Several authoritative voices in France argued that any air campaign would have to be coordinated by a single command structure and that that structure could only be NATO (i.e. American).[48] Roland Dumas himself, on the occasion of the NATO meeting in Brussels on 17 December 1992, all but announced France's de facto reintegration into the military command structure.[49] It was the new government of Edouard Balladur which decided, in April 1993, that henceforth France would resume its seat with full deliberative status on NATO's military committee, explicitly in order to be able to participate fully in future discussions and decisions on military intervention.[50] This French participation has, in its turn, severed the Gordian knot which was preventing NATO and Washington from giving their blessing to the ambitions of the European Union and of WEU. The North Atlantic Council meeting in January 1994 led both to an enthusiastic endorsement of the 'European Security and Defence Identity' (ESDI) and, subsequently, to a Franco-American breakthrough when NATO issued the long-awaited ultimatum to Serbia on Sarajevo. All of the lessons France seemed to have learned through the Bosnian crisis finally appeared to have been instrumental in unblocking a number of inter-related—and long-standing—diplomatic and military problems[51]

[47] See the official statements of Chancellor Kohl and François Mitterrand in *La Politique Etrangère de la France*, May–June 1992, pp. 70–2, and the analysis by Henri de Bresson and Claire Tréan, 'Paris et Bonn protestent de leur fidélité à l'OTAN', *Le Monde*, 22 May 1992.
[48] See the important articles by Jacques Isnard, 'Quel commandement unique et quels ordres?', *Le Monde*, 17 December 1992, and 'L'appel des Nations Unies à l'OTAN est la consécration des moyens américains', *ibid.*, 18 December 1992. See also the 16 January 1993 interview in *La Croix* with Col. Besse, the French commander in Bihac, who felt that military intervention had become unavoidable, but that only the Americans could organise it.
[49] *La Politique Etrangère de la France*, November–December 1992, pp. 218–20.
[50] This was 'revealed' with absolute discretion, not by any formal ministerial statement, but by a journalist: Jacques Isnard, 'La France siège désormais avec voix délibérative au comité militaire de l'OTAN', *Le Monde*, 14 May 1993, p. 5.
[51] *Le Monde*, 4 December 1993, p. 7. See the enthusiastic remarks about NATO-WEU cooperation by the French foreign minister Alain Juppé, in Quai d'Orsay, *Bulletin d'Information*, 223/93 3 December 1993, pp. 9–11. Author's interview with General Jean Paul Pelisson, head of French delegation to NATO's Military Committee, Brussels, January

Thus, the objective which France set herself decades ago appears finally to be coming to fruition. As 1993 merged into 1994, the prospects for a sensible division of labour between an enhanced WEU and a restructured NATO looked promising. There is still a very long way to go, and the problem of military intervention, particularly as exemplified by the Bosnian situation, remains as intractable as ever. But, to parody Churchill, while it is not the beginning of the end, it may well prove to be the end of the beginning of a new transatlantic structure.

1994. However, notwithstanding these developments on the security front, it seems clear that France still intends to promote a purely *European* diplomatic initiative, with Edouard Balladur's proposal on the European Security Conference leading to a Security Pact (an updated version of President Mitterrand's ill-fated *Confédération* idea of 1990–1991), a proposal which received the blessing of the European Council on 10 December. France is also very serious about Europe acquiring an independent intelligence-gathering capacity through her own space programme. Officials have always argued that this was the most important lesson learned from the Gulf War.

# MILITARY INTERVENTION FOR EUROPEAN SECURITY: THE GERMAN DEBATE

HARALD MÜLLER*

## Introduction

WHEN the Cold War ended and Germany was united, the strategic vision for keeping peace in Europe, as prevailing in Bonn, was through a multi-lateral network of institutions; CSCE should be the place where conflicts would be recognised early on, prevented and, if prevention failed, settled by peaceful means. NATO was to provide the stabilising backbone, and the European Community the economic embrace for new market economies/democracies. It was a vision basically based on the rule of law rather than of any thought about the use of force. It was, in other words, a typical expression of the German aversion to thinking seriously about war, which had become a cornerstone of the self-image and the world view of West Germany after the Second World War, and is largely dominating in the united country as well. First traces of an emerging debate went back to 1988, but it took the watershed years of 1990/91 to put this issue into the centre of the discussion on foreign and security policy.

This view was shaken by the Gulf War and shattered by the bloodshed that followed the dissolution of Yugoslavia. While Germany had watched the rising assertive Serbian nationalism with greater concern and the responding striving of Slovenia and Croatia for autonomy with greater sympathy than some of her partners, it was the beginning of shooting in the former Yugoslavia that turned German preferences from keeping a united, though decentralised, Yugoslavia to recognition of the former provinces as independent states.[1] In the second half of 1991, the German government was under growing domestic pressure to move towards recognition. Only part of this pressure emerged from those on the con-servatives side, such as the editors of the *Frankfurter Allgemeine Zeitung*, who drew on historical analogies to justify pro-Slovenian and pro-Croatian sympathies. For the larger part of the German public, including the outspoken Social Democrat (SPD) critics of the government's too timid position, what counted was a desire to stop the bloodshed, and, to an increasing degree, the stream of refugees from Yugoslavia into Germany

---

* Dr Harald Müller is Director of International Programmes, Peace Research Institute, Frankfurt.

[1] It was after the outbreak of hostilities that Chancellor Kohl publicly stated that Slovenia and Croatia should be recognised, *Neue Zürcher Zeitung* (NZZ), 3 July 1991, p. 2.

(until February 1993, more than 250,000 would seek shelter in Germany). Also, the fact that Germany had just exerted its right to self-determination made Germans more sympathetic to the respective claims from Slovenia and Croatia.[2]

Germany's strategy of recognition was the last gasp of a policy of negating the possibility that force might be used in war in Europe again. By turning what started as the internal affair of a member state of both the CSCE and the United Nations into an interstate war, Bonn believed that the conflict could be brought under control. The instruments available in the Paris Charter and the Charter of the UN could be applied, and the fighting would end quickly.[3] This vain hope, rather than sinister imaginings about German influence in the Balkans or a replay of the game that led to World War I, motivated Germany's insistence on early recognition of Slovenia and Croatia. The consequences of recognition, in particular for the fate of Bosnia, were hardly thought through. By default of other political instruments, recognition became virtually a placebo for public opinion, a pretence that the political leadership was doing something about the conflict, without, in fact, doing much.[4]

The policy of recognition, stubbornly pushed through to December 1991, was conducted—and probably meant—as a demonstration of a new, self-confident, assertive Germany. However, this attitude quickly gave way to an even more reticent, self-contained demeanour when it became clear that the policy was not only patently unsuccessful in Bosnia, but that, given its own restrictions, the best Germany could do was to ask its unwilling partners to deal with the policy's consequences militarily. Rather than being a harbinger of new power and assertiveness, December 1991 turned into a new lesson to the Germans that successful foreign policy was only possible in a thoroughly multilateral framework.[5]

It became clear, however, that the issue of the legitimate use of force in international relations was back on the German agenda. Initially, this was unwelcome to everyone, including the conservative-liberal government. Given the broad popular aversion against war, or even military matters in general, to stir up such a debate was a political loser. No party wanted to take it up. On the other hand, given strong external pressure on Germany to come to grips with this problem, the government could not avoid it; and after it started to address the issue, the opposition also had to take a stance.

---

[2] cf. Heinz-Jürgen Axt, 'Hat Genscher Jugoslawien entzweit? Mythen und Fakten zur Außenpolitik des Vereinten Deutschlands', *Europa-Archiv*, Vol. 48, No. 12, 1993, pp. 351–60, part. pp. 353–54; Bruno Schoch, 'Anerkennen als Ersatzhandlung. Ein kritischer Rückblick auf die Bonner Jugoslawienpolitik', in Peter Schlotter *et al.*, *Der Krieg in Bosnien und das hilflose Europa. Plädoyer für eine militärische UN-Intervention*, Frankfurt, HSFK-Report 5/6, 1993, pp. 37–53.

[3] cf. letter of Foreign Minister Genscher to UN Secretary General Perez de Cuellar, *Frankfurter Allgemeine Zeitung* (FAZ), 16 December 1992, p. 1.

[4] Wolfgang Wagner, 'Auch Lehren aus dem Fall Jugoslawien', *Europa-Archiv*, Vol. 47, No. 2, 1992, pp. 31–41, part. p. 37.

[5] Axt, *op. cit.*, pp. 354, 359.

126

In the German debate, the issue of military intervention is rarely combined with what is seen as one of the most pressing security issues for the country: the stabilisation of Eastern Europe and the former Soviet Union. Increasing turmoil in this part of Europe concerns Germany in two distinct ways: through the threat of an ever-increasing influx of refugees and asylum-seekers, maybe the only possibility to destabilise the otherwise quite robust fabric of German democracy; and through the horizontal escalation of uncontrolled violence that could, one day, reach the German border. However, the problem is dealt with conceptually in the institutionalist framework mentioned earlier: by integrating the Visegard states (Poland, Hungary, the Czech Republic and Slovakia) into the European Union at an early date, by drawing them closer to NATO and, perhaps, admitting them as full members. (The bilateral military cooperation with these countries, most notably Poland, should also be mentioned in this context). Another element of this approach is to expand the mediation and peace-keeping activities of the CSCE in the hot spots in the former Soviet Union such as Moldova, Georgia, and the Transcaucasian region.

In Germany, the question of intervention in European conflicts is embedded, as indicated, in the broader issue of the legitimate use of force for peace-making and peace-keeping out of the North Atlantic Treaty area. In the European context, only the issue of intervention in Yugoslavia has been discussed, and it was one of the very few points of all-party agreement that in this area German soldiers could not be involved because of the crimes committed by Hitler's Germany in that region during the Second World War. For this reason, this paper describes this broader debate and points to its implications for the European theatre wherever it is relevant. It starts with a description of the German reaction to the Gulf War—when the debate started—and then analyses the various dimensions of the controversy: legal, political, institutional, and organisational.

## Prelude: The Gulf War

The special character of the German situation was first fully exposed during the Gulf War. Germany found itself the target of much criticism for having supported the allied war effort only in a most lacklustre way. Whatever the merits of this accusation, it remains true that the German government, until the very day when the fighting started, put far more emphasis on a peaceful solution to a conflict that—to realistic observers—had been poised for some time to end in war. In addition, anti-war demonstrations were larger and more visible in Germany than elsewhere—in the largest, on 26 January 1991, about 200,000 participated, even though average public opinion was not strikingly different from that in other European countries (about 60 per cent said that it was right to take military action against Saddam Hussein).

During the war, both the government and the opposition agreed that the Constitution (the Basic Law) did not permit German participation in the fighting; only defensive troop deployment to a NATO ally, Turkey, was legally possible, and these troops would only fight if and when Turkish territory was attacked by Iraqi forces. Interestingly enough, support for the allied support included some of the most high-profile German leftists, such as singer Wolf Biermann and writer Hans Magnus Enzensberger, as well as leading Social Democrats, such as caucus leader Klose, and Minister of the Environment in North Rhine Westphalia, Matthiesen.

After the fighting had ended, however, this apparent agreement dissipated quickly. While there was a shared feeling that a united Germany must reconsider (not necessarily completely change) its foreign policy in the light of a new world, and, of course, a new shape of the country, it was by no means clear that military power was to play a role in this policy, and if so, what role this should be.

## The Legal Dimension

The first controversy centred on the question of whether or not the German Constitution, as it stood, permitted out-of-area deployments of the Bundeswehr. What is clear is that the Basic Law permits the maintenance and use of armed forces for self-defence only. Exceptions to this rule must be explicitly stated in the Basic Law (Art. 87,1,2). One such exception, embedded in many substantial and procedural precautions, authorises the employment of the Bundeswehr, under exceptional circumstances, in national emergencies. What is contested, however, is the second possible exception. Art. 24,2 of the Basic Law empowers the Federal Republic to participate in systems of collective security.

A majority of constitutional lawyers, supported by the CDU/CSU, read this as authorising German membership of NATO, and as a blank cheque for participation in activities taken in accordance with the United Nations Charter, be it peace-keeping or enforcement actions under Chapter VII. The German government expressed no reservation on this matter when Germany acceded to the U.N.: nor did Parliament on the occasion of the ratification of this accession. The same applies, incidentally, to the former East Germany. The united Germany, as successor to both states, cannot claim any exception. Since the United Nations, under Chapter VII, acts as a system of collective security, it fits the conditions of Art. 24, and participation is fully permitted.[6] A change in the constitution is thus unnecessary.

The counter-argument embraced by both the governing Free Democrats (FDP) and the leading opposition party, the SPD (as well as all other parties in opposition), argue that NATO participation is not a case of

---

[6]  cf. *Zeitschrift für Rechtspolitik*, June 1993, pp. 201–5.

128

collective security but rather of collective defence, and that it therefore does not invoke Art. 24 at all. Furthermore, it views Art. 24 as a general authorisation that does not supersede the priority of and the need for a case of defence. Thus, the argument goes, any new mission of the Bundeswehr that goes beyond its NATO commitment necessitates a substantial change in the constitution.

Initially, there was agreement that for legal and political reasons the Constitution had to be changed. But the more it proved difficult to agree on the substance of such change, the more the conservative parties became inclined to assume the position that the Basic Law permitted all they wanted. For some time in 1992, an intermediate position was held that what was needed was no real 'change' but a 'clarification', not the least because a changed interpretation of the same law would disavow forty years of political practice, and most particularly this government's stance during the Gulf War. However, as time dragged on and no solution was in sight, the conservatives led the government into a piecemeal strategy of more and more extensive participation in U.N. military actions without a prior change in the basic law.

This started with the deployment of minesweepers to the Persian Gulf in the aftermath of the war, followed by air support for the UNSCOM and IAEA missions in Iraq following U.N. Security Council Resolution 687. A medical unit in Cambodia (Spring 1992) was the first unit ever to assist in a U.N. peace-keeping action. This mission—as a 'purely humanitarian mission'—attracted the opposition's consent. The consensus broke, though, when German destroyers were to help supervise the embargo against Serbia. This time, the opposition went to the Constitutional Court. It argued that decisions taken by NATO and WEU surpassed the boundaries of the objectives enshrined in the respective alliance Treaties, and that, in particular, the WEU Petersberg declaration implied a change of the Treaty that should be subject to parliamentarian ratification.[7] The next 'escalatory step' was the continued participation of German air force personnel in NATO AWACS planes watching the airspace over the former Yugoslavia (with responsibility for directing fire in the case of the use of aircraft in Bosnia) after the U.N. Security Council decided to enforce the ban on military air movements over Bosnia. That such 'salami tactics' were effective was all the more surprising as the coalition partner, the FDP, had left no doubt that it saw a change of the Constitution as a legal requirement.[8] This intra-government controversy led to a more absurd consequence: when the decision on AWACS was taken in cabinet, the FDP ministers voted against, and the FDP, led by its new chairman, foreign minister Klaus Kinkel, sued the government of which it was part for a transgression of constitutional authority.[9] The SPD, of course, did not miss the opportunity to join the case before the Constitutional Court.

[7] Report to the Constitutional Court, 7 August 1992, courtesy Prof. M. Bothe.
[8] *SPIEGEL*, 1/1993, pp. 27–8.
[9] *SPIEGEL*, 13/1993, pp. 13–24; 14/1993, pp. 18–21.

The plaintiffs wanted an 'urgent ruling'. This is different from a Court decision in the 'main case', in that it is only decided when the action in question must be prevented because of overwhelming reasons. The Court technique of consideration was as follows: the negative consequences of German participation, if this proved to be unconstitutional in a later 'main case' decision, were weighed against the negative consequences of non-participation. In the event that non-participation could be more harmful, the Court ruled participation to be principally in accordance with the Constitution. On the basis of evidence presented by the government—that non-participation would compromise Germany's reliability as a partner in the Atlantic Alliance and generally weaken its reputation—the Court deemed the consequences of non-participation less acceptable. In this decision, the prospect of a relatively risk-free mission played a major role. The Court stated that, if there was a high risk of death for the participating German soldiers, the weighing of negative consequences might have been different.[10] This, in turn, leads to the somewhat absurd consequence that the government has to prove that German soldiers are leading a riskless life whenever they are deployed for UN-missions. Why, if this is so, soldiers are needed for the job in the first place, is a natural question that is not easy to answer. Encouraged by this court ruling, and contrary to FDP preferences, the hardliners in the governmental parties (particularly the CSU) denied the need for further discussions about the involvement of Parliament in this kind of decision: the executive, they maintained, was empowered to send German soldiers on U.N. missions.[11]

The issue came before the Court again when the executive decided to send troops to Somalia, and the Bundestag—with the governing majority—applauded this decision in a resolution. This time, the SPD went to Court alone, on the grounds that the 'unconstitutional' decision hurt the inalienable constitutional rights of the Parliament.[12] The Court accepted part of the complaint. It ruled that while the SPD could not request revoking the mission before the Court ruled in the main case, the Bundestag had to share fully in the decision-making, especially as this deployment meant more risks for the participating soldiers. This involved, as the Court stated, an orderly preparation of the decision in the respective parliamentary committees, and a substantial debate in parliament.[13] This ruling was promptly obeyed, and, after a one-day preparation by the foreign and defence committees and a day of debate in the plenary, the same majority endorsed the Somalia mission again.[14]

This is where the legal issue stands presently. Both in the AWACS and in the Somalia issue, the 'main case' is still pending. It may well be in

[10] *Süddeutsche Zeitung* (SZ), 11/12 April 1992, p. 5.
[11] *Ibid.*, 11/12 April 1992, p. 5.
[12] *Das Parlament*, 23, 18 June 1992, p. 1.
[13] *Neue Juristische Wochenschrift* (NJW), 32, 1993, pp. 2038–9.
[14] *Das Parlament*, 28, 9 July 1993, p. 1.

1994, the Constitutional Court will rule that both deployments were constitutional and that the government was fully authorised by its executive prerogative to take the respective decisions. However, it cannot be excluded that the Court will find a substantial change in the Constitution necessary to permit such deployment of German troops.

## The position of the government and the ruling parties

The issue has caused the biggest rift on a foreign policy issue since Ostpolitik was adopted by the conservatives as a mainstay of German foreign policy. Not even the INF deployment in Germany, though causing far more public action, split the political elite as much as the present dispute. Here are the main positions of the parties.

Both governing parties agree that Germany must participate in all actions mandated by the United Nations, peace-keeping as well as peace enforcement, for the united country to play its appropriate role in international relations. This position is based on four considerations:

— that Germany's role as a reliable partner of a common foreign and security policy in the European Union, and as a NATO ally, excludes a pacifist 'Sonderweg'. Germany must be ready to stand by its allies in whatever contingency
— that Germany has duties as a 'world citizen', that is, as an ordinary member of the United Nations. This includes the possibility of full participation in all UN-mandated actions, even if this possibility is not realised in each and every single instance
— that Germany loses 'capability for action', and thus its capacity to influence international events, if it excludes itself from actions the world community deems necessary
— that Germany will stand no chance of obtaining a permanent UN Security Council seat if it denies itself a military role within the organisation's purview (though it took almost forty years for the first Russian peace-keepers to appear, and we are still waiting for the first Chinese blue helmet).[15]

Initially, the government sought some rapprochment with the SPD. Defence Minister Volker Rühe proposed an amendment to the Constitution that would permit fighting missions for the Bundeswehr under U.N. auspices, but with assurance from the executive at the same time that for a certain period, German troops would only serve as peace-keepers proper. This proposal was not acceptable to the SPD, as there was no legal barrier for a government to break this assurance.[16]

---

[15] cf. Chancellor Kohl, *Das Parlament*, 38/39, 17/24 September 1993, p. 9; Foreign Minister Kinkel, according to *FAZ*, 11 September 1992, p. 4. See also *Das Parlament*, 29/30, 17 July 1992, p. 9; a more extensive argument is Kinkel, 'Keine UN-Mitgliedschaft à la carte', *Der Überblick*, 4/1992, pp. 56–8.
[16] Randolph Nikutta, 'Bundeswehr out of area. Stationen einer Fehlentwicklung', *Blätter für deutsche und internationale Politik*, No. 8, August 1992, pp. 934–45.

A compromise draft for a constitutional amendment, introduced by the governing coalition in January 1993, authorises the government to decide upon the participation of Bundeswehr soldiers in a multinational context and as permitted by the U.N. Charter. While this sounds innocent at first glance, it contains the seeds of some major controversy within the coalition: the FDP, with Foreign Minister Kinkel at the top, has acted quickly to distance itself from the draft's language.

The draft would authorise the deployment of troops not only for peace-keeping and under Chapter VII UN enforcement action (both missions subject to a simple majority in the Bundestag), but also under Art. 51, that is, in the context of collective defence. This means that Germany—within its proper alliance organisations, to satisfy the prescription for a multilateral context—would be free to conclude ad-hoc alliances with threatened or supposedly threatened countries, even without an explicit U.N. mandate. A two-thirds Bundestag majority would be required to confirm such a decision.[17] This latter condition was the result of FDP resistance, while a simple majority would have been the preference of the CDU/CSU.[18] Still, the compromise ran into some criticism from within the FDP, where many deputies believed that there should be no action outside a UN or CSCE framework (assuming that the CSCE evolves into a true collective security system). It was also clear that there was no chance for a compromise with the Social Democrats on this issue. Thus, Kinkel proposed a changed draft whereby only UN-mandated deployments would be permissible, and whereby all non-peace-keeping missions would be required a two-thirds, rather than simple, majority in Parliament. Kinkel's position is based on an explicit endorsement of a 'political culture of reluctance', that stresses non-military means of foreign policy and rejects any further 'militarisation' of German policy.[19] This position was explicitly endorsed by other party leaders.[20]

The CDU/CSU was far from happy with Kinkel's initiative. The CSU, the more conservative Bavarian sister party, already had difficulties with the requirement for multilateralism in the original draft. The Bavarians thought that Germany should be as free in its foreign and security policy as its European partners, Britain and France, and that a constitutional amendment should attach no strings, other than those found in ordinary international law, to the employment of German troops abroad. But in the CDU, too, there were great misgivings about the proposed changes. Waiving Art. 51 employments would prevent all missions that were not

[17] Deutscher Bundestag, 12. Wahlperiode, Drucksache 12/4107, 13 January 1993, and Drucksache 12/4135, 15 January 1993.
[18] cf. Ole Diehl, 'UN-Einsätze der Buneswehr. Außenpolitische Handlungszwänge und innenpolitischer Konsensbedarf', *Europa-Archiv*, Vol. 48, No. 8, 1993, pp. 219–27, part. pp. 221–2.
[19] *SPIEGEL* 40/1992, p. 33; *SZ*, 11/12 September 1993, p. 2; for this intragovernmental controversy, cf. also *SPIEGEL* 31/1992, p. 29/30; *SPIEGEL* 16/1993, pp. 18–22.
[20] *Freie Demokratische Korrespondenz*, No. 96, 22 June 1993.

endorsed by all of the five permanent Security Council members, and the situation in Bosnia proved that this could be disastrous for peace-enforcing activities. This was an argument against the whole multilateral rule, as neither NATO nor WEU nor EPC could agree on a joint military position towards the Bosnian situation, though this point was elaborated. Making all such deployments contingent on a two-thirds majority in the Bundestag, i.e. on SPD consent, would, in many CDU members' view, paralyse the system and petrify the very status quo which an amendment was meant to overcome in the first place. The Art. 51 authorisation is seen by the right wing of the CDU/CSU as putting Germany on an equal footing with France and Britain 'with equal rights and equal duties'.[21] This more far-reaching ambition found expression in a guideline adopted by the Ministry of Defence in 1993, which defined, among Germany's vital security interests which would inform defence requirements, 'the mainten-ance of free trade and the global access to markets and raw materials', a formula that attracted much criticism and suspicion from the German left.[22]

It must be emphasised that in the CDU rank and file, there is strong criticism against what is perceived as an appeasement policy towards Serbian aggression, and even of the government's policy that is seen as being too lenient towards the interests of the hesitant partners, and too inactive in responding to the suffering in Bosnia. Former Post Minister Schwarz-Schilling left the government in protest over the issue (ad-mittedly just before Kohl would have asked for his resignation anyway), and junior MP Schwarz made his name through emotional pleas to help the threatened Muslims.[23]

On a more general plan, the Christian Democrats strive for the 'normalisation' of the role of the German state. A closed session of the caucus, devoted to foreign policy, concluded that Germany must learn to deal with its international power and its newly won freedom of action—though prudently, and with due regard to its interdependent position, which binds it inevitably together with its neighbours and allies. This role requires going with the allies wherever they go. A special restraint, separating Germany from its allies, would be tantamount to a new 'Sonderweg' and replace the 'hypertropical' power policy of the past with an equally objectionable 'hypermorality'. They see a distinct danger that this policy may prevent the development of a common European foreign and security policy, from the Eurocorps to the WEU. They emphasised that the government's draft amendment would permit out-of-area deploy-ments only in a multilateral framework and that the opposition's suspicion

---

[21] cf. Deputy Glos, leader of the regional CSU party group, *Das Parlament*, 29/30, 16/23 July 1993, p. 7.
[22] Der Bundesminister für Verteidigung, *Verteidigungspolitische Richtlinien für den Geschäftsbereich des Bundesministers für Verteidigung*, Bonn 1992.
[23] *SPIEGEL* 2/1993, pp. 76–7.

of an imminent 'German intervention policy' was thus void.[24] Since many conservatives are convinced that the Constitution is largely permissive to out-of-area missions, they would agree to a change only if what they perceive as presently available options would not be constrained. This runs directly against the central desire of the SPD.[25]

It was also emphasised by the Chancellor and the Foreign Minister that out-of-area activities should be conducted, as far as possible, as a multilateral endeavour, with WEU and the Eurocorps in a prominent role.[26]

## The Opposition Parties

If the government is split, the same must be said, with even more emphasis, about the opposition parties—the SPD and the Greens.

The debate within the SPD is truly pathetic. In 1991, then party leader Engholm succeeded, by employing all his personal prestige to persuade a reluctant convention majority to agree to German participation in peacekeeping activities: blue helmets and nothing more.[27] Even then, there were dissenting voices on both sides. The pure pacifists wanted Germany to focus completely on nonviolent means of foreign policy and to renounce all use of force out-of-area (however, they did not question self-defence within NATO). On the other side, pragmatists in the SPD Bundestag Caucus, such as Caucus leader Klose, foreign policy speakers Gansel and Voigt, and the SPD's nestor of foreign policy, Egon Bahr, saw participation in U.N. enforcement actions as justified and inevitable. They would agree with the rest of their party, however, that Art. 51 actions should not be authorised through a constitutional amendment.

In summer 1993, with a new party convention approaching and a new party leader—Mr. Scharping—at the helm of the SPD, the debate intensified. There has been hardly one day since May without a statement, counterstatement, or clarification by a leading SPD member, or a regional or functional subgroup concerning the 'out of area' issue.

The SPD Foreign Policy Commission—a body in which both party wings are represented—voted down a proposal by Klose (quietly supported by Scharping) that asked for a principal constitutional authorisation for all deployments under U.N. command (but not for Gulf-type

[24] *SZ*, 27 August 1992, p. 4; see also several statements by Foreign Policy Speaker Lamers, e.g. *CDU-Pressedienst* 5249, 11 January 1992; Karl Lamers, 'Zum Einsatzzweck deutscher Streitkräfte', Bonn, January 1992; and Caucus Whip Jürgen Rüttgers, 'Elemente einer neuen Friedenspolitik', Bonn, without date.

[25] cf. K. H.-Hornhues (deputy CDU/CSU caucus chair), Erklärung 'Zum Einsatz deutscher Streitkrafte im Rahmen kollektiver Sicherheitssysteme', Bonn, 1992.

[26] *Bulletin der Bundesregierung*, 32, 23 April 1993, pp. 277–80; 58, 2 July 1993, pp. 609–11.

[27] Oliver Thränert, 'Germans Battle Over Blue Helmets', *Bulletin of the Atomic Scientists*, October 1992, p. 33–5; in summer 1993, this position was expressed in a proposal for a constitutional amendment, cf. Deutscher Bundestag, 12. Wahlperiode, Drucksache 12/2895, 23 June 1992.

blank cheque mandates) in each single case and subject to a two-thirds quorum in the Bundestag.[28] Instead, the Commission proposed an extension of the past Convention line but only by a little: a constitutional amendment would permit the Bundeswehr to participate in blue beret missions, including 'mission defence', but in a 'defensive, de-escalatory way', aiming at the 'consent of all conflict parties'. This additional restraint was included by the left wing of the Commission to terminate far-reaching interpretations of 'mission defence' that had been discussed in the Caucus.[29] Another new element was the consideration of proposals to enable Bundeswehr action in the enforcement of UN-embargos, if necessary by military force. However, the German presence in the Adriatic is still rejected, because, in the words of the left-wing leader Wiecorek-Zeul, this was not a UN mission, but one 'usurped' by NATO and WEU.[30] She was supported by SPD prime ministers of Saarland and Lower Saxonia, Lafontaine and Schröder, as well as the party's leader in Bavaria, Renate Schmidt.[31] This line was criticised as unrealistic, rendering the party incapable of taking over the government, by caucus leader Klose, caucus whip Struck, and defence experts Voigt and Niggemeyer.

Party leader Scharping himself pleaded also for a less restrictive mandate. To constrain Germany only to certain UN actions and to deny sharing in others was tantamount to a 'partial withdrawal' from the United Nations. A SPD government, Scharping believed, would not be in a position to withdraw from international responsibilities in that way. Scharping would also prefer to work out a compromise with the government before the Constitutional Court issued its 'main case' ruling, but he recognised considerable resistance in the rank and file to such a step.[32] To echo his concerns, the Commission's draft decision guidance was endorsed in the Presidium of the party (the highest inter-convention body).[33] A few days later, a regional party convention in Schleswig Holstein opposed even 'blue helmets' and asked instead for an 'international peace policy with non-military means under the umbrella of the United Nations', against the declared intentions of the regional party leadership.[34] Consequently, the party leadership took refuge in avoiding the critical question—what to do against aggression and genocide—and pointed to its opposition against a 'German role in warfare' and the priority of nonmilitary means for peace-keeping and conflict prevention.[35]

[28]  *SZ*, 24 August 1992, p. 1.
[29]  *SZ*, 18 August 1993, p. 2.
[30]  *SZ*, 30 August 1993, p. 2.
[31]  *SZ*, 21/22 August 1993, p. 1; 28/29 August 1993, p. 2; *Sozialdemokratischer Pressedienst*, Vol. 48, No. 166, 1 September 1993.
[32]  *FAZ*, 18 August 1993, p. 3; *SZ*, 1 September 1993, p. 2; *SPIEGEL* 27/1993, p. 22.
[33]  *FR*, 25 August 1992, p. 1.
[34]  *SZ*, 13 September 1993, p. 2.
[35]  e.g. Scharping during the Bundestags debate on the budget, *Das Parlament* 38/39, 17/24 September 1993, p. 6.

Sometimes, it counterattacked by accusing the government of striving for an 'intervention army'.[36] This is to keep the rank and file, particularly the intellectual cadres of the party, close to the leadership. It does little to solve the issue at stake. The leadership draft won a compromise that included 'defensive, de-escalating mission defence' in blue helmet missions which the party would endorse.[37]

Even among the Greens a controversy rages, caused by the events in Bosnia. The party convention of April 1991, in the aftermath of the Gulf war, took a clearcut stance against any deployment of German soldiers abroad.[38] But in response to the bloodshed in Bosnia, several leading politicians demanded a U.N. intervention to stop what they viewed as genocide.[39] The feminist wing of the party, not renowned for its pro-military stance, was particularly shaken by the raping of Bosnian women by the Tetschnik soldateska; it turned out to be the loudest supporters of military action.[40] The party's Regional Council (composed of politicians from all Länder) voted for a U.N. military intervention in Bosnia, and beyond that, for a German participation in the U.N. system of collective security that should act in cases of outright aggression and genocide.

This position, which has the support of a couple of 'realist' green politicians, met the decisive opposition of other forces within the party. The Green Federal Board and its Foreign Policy Working Group both recalled the principled antimilitaristic position of the Green Party, renewed the call for the dissolution of the Bundeswehr, and dismissed the Regional Council's initiative as a slap in the face of the party. In a biting critique, Jügen Trittin, a minister in the Länder government of Lower Saxonia and one of the prominent party members, accused the 'bellicose' wing of jumping in the arms of an interventionist government.[41] For the Greens, the issue is delicate; the party's success in the eighties was partly contingent on its uncompromising opposition to the double-track decision, and its rank and file is composed of many principled pacifists. In the German antimilitaristic movement all forms of Bundeswehr activity are anathema. The U.N. is seen as captive of the United States and NATO, still the 'bêtes noires' of the pacifists.[42]

Among the parties represented in the Bundestag, only the PDS, the successor to the former ruling party in the GDR, takes a unanimous

---

[36] Party secretary Verheugen, *FR*, 25 August 1993, p. 1; cf. the strong denial by Chancellor Kohl, *Das Parlament*, 38/39, 17/24 September 1992, p. 9.

[37] Perspektiven einer neuen Außen- und Sicherheitspolitik. Leitantrag des SPD-Parteivorstandes zum Ordentlichen Parteitag in Wiesbaden im November 1993, Bonn, 15 October 1993.

[38] Resolution A3, 13. Ordentliche Bundesversammlung der Grünen, Neumünster, 26–28 April 1991.

[39] *SPIEGEL 35/1992, p. 68; Die Tageszeitung* (taz), 2 February 1993.

[40] cf. *SPIEGEL* 5/1993, pp. 76–83; *SPIEGEL* 8/1993, pp. 50–4.

[41] *FR*, 1 September 1993, p. 12; cf. also deputy Ullmann, *Das Parlament*, 29/30, 16/23 July 1993, p. 9.

[42] *FR*, 1 September 1993, p. 7.

136

position: rejection of any expansion of the role of the Bundeswehr. The party takes visible pleasure in opposing a time-honoured enemy; 'Germany imperialism'.[43]

At the end of 1993, the parties appeared firmly entrenched in their chosen positions.[44] But, remarkably enough, when the first German solider was killed in United Nations service in Kampuchea in October 1993, this caused no political controversy. The protagonists of the political debate joined in mourning the young man's death. The reason may have been that the deployment of a medical unit in Kampuchea was never contested.[45]

## Military Planning for Intervention

While the debate was going on, the Ministry of Defence was not idle. In the hotly-contested Defence Guidance of November 1992, German participation in global missions played a central role.[46]

Planning is actively under way for future out-of-area employments. Two battalions of 1400–1700 soldiers each will be specially trained and earmarked for U.N. missions. Planning changes for the navy and airforce (mainly close air defence and air transport) have been made accordingly.[47]

The Bundeswehrplan 94 discusses procurement with a perspective of out-of-area utilisation. This includes a new assessment of the specification for weapon systems that have long been on the wish list, but in the context of alliance defence only. Among the systems are an antitank helicopter, light armoured personnel carriers, a tactical transport aircraft, a tactical enhanced air-defence system with limited ATBM capabilities, a new air-surface missile for the Tornado, a new frigate, blue water corvettes, and a logistic ship for task force groups.[48]

But planning will be to no avail until a point of consensus has been found among the diverging positions. This puts the German military into a sort of quagmire. Officers and troops are integrated into military units— the Eurocorps and the Multinational Rapid Reaction Corps—whose avowed mission is to be flexible and mobile and to react quickly to crises. The site of the crisis as with the reaction thereto is not necessarily limited

[43] Deputy Gysi, *Das Parlament*, 29/30, 16/23 July 1993, p. 8.
[44] As demonstrated in the most recent parlamentary debates, cf. *Das Parlament*, No. 40, 1 October 1993 and No. 49/50, 3/10 December 1993.
[45] *Badische Zeitung*, 16 October 1993, p. 5.
[46] Bundesministerium der Verteidigung, Verteidigungspolitische Richtlinien, Bonn, 26 November 1992.
[47] Dieter Mahnke, 'Wandel im Wandel: Bundeswehr und europäische Sicherheit', *Aus Politik und Zeitgeschichte* 15/16, 1993, pp. 40–6; *EUROPE*, 6048, 23/24 August 1993, p. 3.
[48] Katrin Fuchs, 'Mit deutschen Soldaten eine Neue Weltordnung schaffen? Die Planungen zum Aufbau von "Krisenreaktionskräften"', *Sicherheit + Frieden (S+F)*, Vol. 11, No. 1, 1993, pp. 36–43, part. pp. 39–40.

to the areas of the Brussels and the Washington treaties, at least in the minds of the allies. Yet given the present constitutional and political situation, it is plain that German forces would not be permitted to participate. This is a clear consequence of putting the cart before the horse: that is, deciding on the creation of new military formations before the political rationale—and the domestic conditions—have become clear. Nowhere is this as striking as in the case of the Eurocorps. This unit emerged not from any consistent military planning in the Defence Ministry, but an interest at the top of government to intensify military cooperation with France in the context of allaying French fears over unification; the evident corollaries of the 'double hat' were thought through only afterwards.[49] It can be surmised that German officers in the units in question pray daily lest no contingency arise where they would suffer the humiliation of explaining to their fellow officers that they had to stay home.

## Evaluation of the debate

In looking at the contents of the positions taken by the various sides in the intra-German discussion, two features stand out: first, the connection of the issue to German security and the complex institutional strategies proposed for order in Europe is not in the least clear. The rationale given by governmental forces for a change in the Constitution relates to Germany's reputation as a reliable partner and a 'good citizen' of the United Nations.[50] This case was rarely made for CSCE, even though it was a German initiative that led this body to declare itself a 'regional organisation' under Chapter VIII of the UN Charter. That a collective security system in Europe would need an enforcement structure is largely left out of the debate—with the exception of the specific case of Yugoslavia. But here, there is almost unanimous agreement that, for historical reasons, German soldiers could not share in an enforcement mission.

Another interesting characteristic is the persistent reluctance of a great part of the German public—and the political elite—to look at military forces as instruments of legitimate national policy. Contrary to many fears expressed abroad when the unification train ran full steam, the powerful antimilitary, pacifist undercurrent that has characterised the Federal Republic, and became highly visible—and largely unwanted in the West—during the INF deployment controversy, is also a political factor of considerable weight in the new Germany. The strange combination of militaristic heroism and antimilitaristic rhetoric in the former GDR has resulted in a public opinion where these traits are even stronger than in the

[49] Otfried Ischebeck, '30 Jahre nach dem Elysee-Vertrag. Die deutsch-französischen Pläne für eine europäisches Korps', *S+F*, Vol. 11, No. 1, 1993, pp. 44–7.
[50] cf. Caucus leader Schäuble, *Das Parlament*, 38–9, 17/24 September 1993, p. 7; Chancellor Kohl, *ibid.*, p. 9.

138

Western part of the country. This undercurrent reaches to the far right of the centre. While all Western democracies are having serious and sombre debates as elected officials are considering sending the sons and daughters of their voters into danger, none shares this political undercurrent with Germany where it is the heritage of two terrible, bloody and lost wars.

In the old Federal Republic, this ideology was well entrenched: either in a principled aversion to matters military in general, or in what one could call pacifism by nuclear over-emphasis. This stance, more frequently found on the political right, insisted on a seamless escalatory ladder that would lead from the first shot to an intercontinental nuclear exchange between the US and the Soviet Union. Because this was unbearable even for hard-nosed communists in the Kremlin, all fighting would be impossible. What this stance shared with the pacifist wing was the serious aversion to the mere possibility of conventional fighting. The strength of this conservative version of German pacifism became visible during the SNF debate in the late eighties, when staunch NATO supporters like Alfred Dregger or Volker Rühe, surprisingly for some of their friends abroad, suddenly took a stand among the opponents of SNF modernisation.

The very difference between the German majority view on military action and that of its European allies was for long blurred because of the shared interest in an ironclad nuclear guarantee from the U.S. The difference was, however, that for the allies it was no great political problem to fight small wars elsewhere, in the Falklands or in Chad, or to devote soldiers to U.N. actions. In Germany all military action was seen with awe, suspicion, and instinctive moral resentment. For Germans to agree to military enforcement of an international rule of law (not to speak of national interest) is not, as for others, a matter of instinctive reaction that then might be countered by cool consideration of national interest. To the contrary, it starts with an instinctive rejection of the military instrument that might then be contained by protracted rational considerations of right and wrong.[51]

This interpretation is consistent with public opinion polls. In late summer 1992, 39 per cent thought that the Bundeswehr mission remain unchanged: national and NATO defence. Forty-four per cent for unarmed peace-keeping missions and only 14 per cent supported fighting engagements for U.N. peace enforcement. The split within the country was remarkable: the figures for the Eastern part were 63, 24, and 11 respectively.[52] In spring 1993, a small majority (53:42, 5 undecided) opted for German participation in the violent enforcement of Bosnian airspace control, with SPD voters responding 54:41 in favour.[53] In April 1993, 80:17 of those polled agreed that German soldiers in Somalia

[51] cf. Karl-Otto Hondrich, 'Wenn die Angst nachläßt', *SPIEGEL, 30/1992, pp. 30–1.*
[52] *SPIEGEL* 27/1992, p. 44; 44/1992, p. 61.
[53] *SPIEGEL* 13/1993, p. 19.

should be entitled to use force in order to secure the transport of food; but 58:17 opposed their employment for fighting against armed gangs.[54] In mid-1993, the share of support for participation in United Nations military actions in general (58:37) and fighting in Somalia in particular (55:43) had reached a majority in the West, but not in the East (41:49 and 30:68 respectively).[55]

More than 70 per cent of the Germans think it would be appropriate to take a seat in the Security Council on condition that Germany would participate in the future in U.N. mandated military actions. Even among the sceptical Green voters, this option obtained a small majority (57:41).[56] Generally, there is a visible trend of growing support for blue helmet as well as enforcement activities from 1991 on; but strong minorities are still opposed, and, even more important, majorities in the new Länder. In order not to strain a fragile national unity, this issue can obviously not be pushed too far.[57]

Finally, a two-third majority of Germans wants the Bundestag to take the final decision on UN deployments of the Bundeswehr. Even among CDU/CSU voters, distrust of the executive hold a clear majority (52:40).[58] Reluctant support for participation, with sizeable opposition still existing, and a strong quest for parliamentary control, characterises the attitude of the German public towards the issue of military enforcement of peace.

Taken as it is, and in the light of the German past, this is not the worst possible case, to say the least. The political culture of military reluctance should certainly be more welcome to Germany's neighbours than the quest for 'normalcy' (with some Wilhelminian overtones) that is heard at the fringes of the German right. However, this would only be so if the 'reluctance' would not collide with the other main pillar granting Germany's role as an accountable, reliable and peaceful player in Europe: its organised solidarity with its neighbours and its institutionalised ties with its allies. An isolationist pacifism that distinguishes Germany fundamentally and irretrievably from its allies would amount to a new 'Sonderweg' whose final destination no one could know. It is for this reason, more than for any specific action in which German soldiers may be useful to achieve mission objectives, that a reasonable compromise must be found in the German debate. Germany's friends should accept that the issue of legitimacy—a U.N. mandate—and selectivity with regard to the historical meaning of places German soldiers might be sent to—act as constraints that might still create a difference between Germany and themselves, but one that is more of nuances, and not as fundamental as the one that would result from pacifist isolationism. This may be the optimum

---

[54] *SPIEGEL* 17/1993, p. 21.
[55] *Stichworte zur Sicherheitspolitik* 6/1993.
[56] *SPIEGEL* 28/1993, p. 77.
[57] *Stichworte zur Sicherheitspolitik* 4/93 and 6/93.
[58] *SPIEGEL* 25/1993, p. 29.

to extract from Germany in the foreseeable future without the risk of polarising public opinion in a most dangerous way.[59] In this case, a creative solution to the German debate might contribute quite useful aspects to the international discussion about collective security in Europe: considerations about legitimacy, embedding military missions in a broad spectrum of non-military means to prevent, manage, and terminate conflict, and the definition of precise criteria on which military action might be considered will predictably be part of any package deal resulting from the present German debate.

[59] For an imaginative scenario cf. Ole Diehl, *op. cit.*, pp. 224–7; also the lecture of Chancellor Kohl to the Wehrkunde Conference, *Bulletin der Bundesregierung* 13, 10 February 1993, pp. 101–5.

# THE NETHERLANDS AND MILITARY INTERVENTION

## JAN WILLEM HONIG*

'THE Netherlands and Military Intervention' may sound like an oxymoron. Few other countries have a more established reputation for being peaceful and peaceloving. The Dutch last intervened militarily in another European country in 1830 when they tried—and failed in a mere ten days—to keep Belgium as a part of the Kingdom of The Netherlands. Although colonial interventions have occurred until more recently, the 'police actions' in the Dutch East Indies in 1948 and 1949 encountered such domestic unease—despite their military success—that they hastened rather than prevented Indonesian independence.[1] The perception of The Netherlands, both at home and abroad, is that of a thoroughly unmartial, strongly anti-militaristic society. In the eyes of many, this national quality is forever exemplified by the long-haired, unionised conscripts of the 1970s and the massive anti-nuclear protests of the 1980s. As a result, it is difficult to imagine a Dutch foreign policy in which the military instrument plays a role of any significance.

In the past few years, however, the unimaginable has been happening: Dutch foreign policy is increasingly emphasising the use of military means. In September 1991, the Dutch took the initiative in proposing a massive European Community peace-keeping intervention in Yugoslavia (a move that was vetoed by Britain). This was not an empty gesture. By September 1993, they were deploying slightly over 3,000 troops in peace-keeping operations around the globe—both in absolute and relative terms one of the largest deployments among the NATO allies. In November of that year, they announced the sending of an additional 1,100 soldiers to Bosnia in the beginning of 1994. Do these examples present an instance of a country radically redefining its foreign policy after the end of the Cold War? Before exploring the reasons behind this interventionist attitude and considering its implications, we will first have to bring into focus the extent of the recent military contributions to peace-keeping operations.

* Dr Honig lectures in the Department of War Studies, King's College, London. He is author of *Defense Policy in the North Atlantic Alliance: The Case of The Netherlands*, Praeger, 1993.

[1] During the Second Police Action in December 1948, Dutch forces managed to capture the government of the Republik Indonesia, including Sukarno. A second important factor was the widespread international condemnation, especially by the United States, which led to a speedy vote of censure from the UN Security Council.

## Dutch Forces In Action Abroad

During the period of the Cold War very few Dutch troops could be found outside the NATO treaty area. After the loss of Indonesia in 1949, a Dutch army battalion saw action in Korea under the aegis of the United Nations.[2] Subsequently, no other Dutch forces participated in active combat operations. The only instance when they came close was between 1960 and 1962, when it was feared that The Netherlands would be involved in a war with Indonesia over New Guinea (which was the only territory in the Far East that had remained under Dutch control after Indonesian independence). But again, domestic opposition to unilateral military action and a desire to 'internationalise' the dispute by involving the UN, ultimately led to the territory being handed to Indonesia peacefully.[3]

After this colonial misadventure, the Dutch limited themselves to contributing small numbers of troops to peace-keeping operations. The largest single force sent overseas was an infantry battalion which went to the Lebanon from 1979 to 1983 as part of UN Interim Force in Lebanon (UNIFIL). For the rest, The Netherlands has had some 15 observers with the UN Truce Supervision Organisation (UNTSO) in the Middle East since 1956, and a communications and military police unit with the Multinational Force and Observers (MFO) in Sinai since 1982. It also participated with two minehunters in a joint Dutch-Belgian force that operated under WEU auspices in the Persian Gulf in 1987.

But since the Iraqi invasion of Kuwait in 1990, there has been a dramatic increase in Dutch military contributions to UN and other international operations. Two frigates and a supply ship were dispatched to the Gulf to help enforce the UN-sanctioned embargo against Iraq. At the start of hostilities, these ships were put under U.S. command, although they were not authorised to undertake offensive operations. Their proudest moment came when one of the frigates acted as the first line of defence of the carrier U.S.S. Midway. Three minehunters were also sent as part of a WEU anti-mine task force and other naval forces beefed up NATO defences in the Mediterranean. The Netherlands also offered a squadron of F-16 fighters, but this was turned down because of the over-crowding already occurring in airbases in Saudi Arabia and the United Arab Emirates.[4] When NATO decided to strengthen Turkey's defences

---

[2] Interestingly, in line with the conviction that the Dutch abhor violence, it is widely believed that the UN battalion was made up of marginal elements from society, such as veterans from the former Netherlands-Indies Army and the German SS.

[3] And again, the U.S. failed to support Dutch initiatives to retain control of the island: P. B. R. de Geus, *De Nieuw-Guinea Kwestie: Aspecten van buitenlands beleid en militaire macht* (The New Guinea Question: Aspects of Foreign Policy and Military Power), Martinus Nijhoff, Leiden, 1984.

[4] 'Squaring the Dutch Circle', *Defence*, June 1992, p. 15.

with the ACE Mobile Force, The Netherlands contributed an air defence capability in the form of two Patriot and one HAWK surface-to-air missile batteries, and when Scuds began to hit Israel it quickly followed the United States by offering a Patriot battery.[5] Operation 'Provide Comfort' could again count on immediate Dutch support: a company of marines with some army personnel was stationed in Northern Iraq to assist the Kurds between April and July 1991. Thus The Netherlands, along with the U.S., Britain, France, Canada and Italy was among the select group of NATO countries technically involved in open hostilities with Iraq.

Although the UN effort to supervise the elections in Angola in 1991–1993 was helped by only 15 Dutch observers, the UN Transitional Authority in Cambodia (UNTAC) in 1992–1993 was supported by the deployment of a marines battalion, an engineer unit, three transport aircraft and three helicopters—a total of around 890 personnel.

The largest deployment to date, however, came with the conflict in Yugoslavia. The Dutch contribution to the various peace-keeping forces in and around the former Yugoslavia amounted to some 2,000 personnel by September 1993. One signals battalion and a mixed Dutch-Belgian transport battalion were on the ground in Croatia and Bosnia. Eighteen F-16s were controlling the airspace above Bosnia enforcing the UN no-fly zone, and six F-16s were on stand-by to provide close air support to the UN troops in Bosnia in case of need. In the Adriatic, three frigates and two Orion maritime patrol aircraft were keeping a watchful eye over the former Yugoslav coast. These forces were set to be reinforced by another 1,100 ground troops in the beginning of 1994, including the first combat unit: the newly created volunteer battalion from the airmobile brigade.[6]

These have been significant efforts which compare well with those of other countries. In the Gulf, The Netherlands was the only smaller NATO ally to put forces in harm's way (albeit not in offensive operations). In Cambodia, the Dutch and the French were the only NATO allies to send infantry battalions. In Bosnia and Croatia, the Dutch made up fifteen per cent of the total troops on the ground (about the same as in Cambodia). In comparison with the total worldwide French and British peace-keeping contributions of about 8,700 and 4,100 men respectively, by the middle of 1993, the Dutch contribution of about 3,000 is

[5] Both initiatives were marred by embarrassing moments. Initially, the Dutch government publicly announced they were sending a F-16 squadron to Turkey before having notified the Turks, who then turned it down. The first public offer of Patriots for Israel by the Prime Minister surprised his cabinet colleagues—including the Defence Minister—who said it was out of the question. A looming row was nipped in the bud by a speedy Israeli rejection. A second, better prepared, attempt was accepted by Israel (and the Defence Minister). *De Telegraaf*, 26 September 1990; *NRC/Handelsblad*, 23 January 1991.

[6] 'Niederlande entsenden Soldaten', *Frankfurter Allgemeine Zeitung*, 15 November 1993. By that time the marine battalion will have been withdrawn from Cambodia, so the total peace-keeping effort will only increase by a few hundred.

proportionally larger.[7] In absolute terms, the Dutch figures are larger than those for any of the smaller NATO allies, surpass those of Canada, and are beginning to rival those of Italy.

Are we seeing then, since the Gulf War, as one American journalist put it, a 'turnaround' in Dutch foreign policy 'strikingly at odds with The Netherlands' reputation for abhorring military force'?[8] The answer to this question is no. On the contrary, Dutch foreign policy has been remarkably consistent, even to the extent that virtually all of the basic premises developed since the end of the Second World War have remained in place. What has changed as a result of the end of the Cold War is the opportunities and scope for Dutch foreign policy and the peace-keeping forces are merely its most concrete manifestation. So what are the premises that underpin this foreign policy?

## The Premises of Dutch Foreign Policy

The experiences of the Second World War impressed upon the Dutch that their traditional foreign policy was no longer suited to the modern world.[9] Although officially described as a policy of neutrality, it had always possessed a bias. Because of the Dutch dependence on trade and open access to the world seas, it relied on an implicit British security guarantee following from the conviction that the British could not allow the Low Countries to be occupied by a continental power and threaten their sea lanes. The experience of war showed that such a guarantee was, if not wholly reliable, certainly impractical. The pace of war was such that the country was long occupied before effective help could be given. The lesson was clear: the security of The Netherlands could only be assured through a military alliance which would prepare a defence in peacetime.

---

[7] Figures for the French and the British per 1 June 1993 taken from *The Military Balance, 1993–1994*, Brassey's for the International Institute for Strategic Studies, London, 1993. French figures exclude two frigates in *Sharp Guard* and three C-130 transport planes in *Provide Promise*. British figures also exclude the carrier, frigates, support ships and Nimrod aircraft in *Sharp Guard*. For the Dutch, *The Military Balance* gives a total of almost 1,900 which excludes the 30 F-16s in *Disciplined Guard* and *Deny Flight*. The Dutch Statement on the Defence Estimates for 1994 gives a total of 'ca. 3,025' per 1 September 1993 (which includes the F-16 and *Sharp Guard* contributions): 'Rijksbegroting 1994', *Handelingen Tweede Kamer der Staten-Generaal 1993–1994* (Parliamentary Proceedings, henceforth *HTK*), 23400 X, p. 17. The main difference with the *Military Balance* lies in the increased contribution to UNPROFOR. As a percentage of their active armed forces, the French, British and Dutch, respectively, contribute 2.1, 1.5, and 4 per cent. In these terms, only Luxembourg and Norway (who have very small armies) are on a par with 4.4 and 4.5 per cent.

[8] Joseph Fitchett, 'Dutch Show New Toughness on Defense', *International Herald Tribune*, 29 February 1991.

[9] On Dutch foreign policy in general, see J. H. Leurdijk, ed., *The Foreign Policy of The Netherlands*, Sijthoff & Noordhoff, Alphen aan den Rijn, 1978; J. J. C. Voorhoeve, *Peace, Profits and Principles: A Study of Dutch Foreign Policy*, Martinus Nijhoff, The Hague, 1979.

Although the great hopes entertained in this respect for the United Nations were quickly disappointed due to the onset of the Cold War, the more limited and practical Brussels Treaty of 1948 and the North Atlantic Pact of 1949 were warmly embraced as cornerstones of Dutch security.

Once in the North Atlantic Alliance, the Dutch had two options: either to exploit the protection offered *de facto* by the large allies, especially the United States, and minimise their defence and foreign policy efforts; or to seek to maximise their role and influence in the Alliance. Contrary to what many (especially American political scientists) have posited regarding small ally behaviour, the Dutch rejected the first, 'free-rider', option and chose the second. The reasons for this choice were a combination of idealism and pragmatism. Free-riding contradicted a strong Dutch sense of the importance of international agreements and the necessity to accept the obligations that came with them. This sense was fed by the country's prevailing protestant ethic with its moral emphasis on justice, duty and obligation, and which was embodied in a strong tradition of international law, stretching back to Hugo Grotius. On the pragmatic side, because of their dependence on free trade the Dutch increasingly had to rely on the cooperation of other nations. International law provided a useful tool in codifying the principles of cooperation as well as the sanctions to be applied in case of non-cooperation. It provided an independent authority which, to some extent, could make up for the lack of military power of The Netherlands.

Having chosen to become a loyal ally, however, the paths of the various actors involved in foreign and defence policy have not always followed the same line. The purest exponent of loyalty could be found in public opinion. Support for Dutch NATO membership, for example, has hovered between 60–80 per cent of the population since the 1950s. Even in the darkest days of the anti-nuclear protests, a majority—which included many of the protesters—continued to support NATO member-ship.[10] What many people abroad did not realise was that opposition to nuclear weapons did not necessarily mean opposition to NATO. Nuclear weapons were widely perceived to be an amoral means of defence for an essentially moral and lawful alliance, established according to principles recognised by the UN. Public opinion remained true to its principles after the end of the Cold War. If anything, hopes went up. Instead of acquiescing in the limited contribution NATO as a regional organisation could make to international justice, an opportunity now appeared to achieve the grander aim of the United Nations, finally to establish a just world order. International operations designed to help build working democracies, such as in Cambodia and Angola, could count on overwhelming support. After an initial moment of doubt (largely due to distrust of the speed with

[10]  E.g., Jan G. Siccama, 'The Netherlands Depillarized: Security Policy in a New Domestic Context', in Gregory Flynn, ed., *NATO's Northern Allies: The National Security Policies of Belgium, Denmark, The Netherlands, and Norway*, Rowman & Allanheld, Croom Helm, London, 1985, pp. 130–1.

which the U.S. seemed to intervene to protect its oil supplies), the public also rallied behind the anti-Iraq coalition and strongly favoured a hard line.[11] The act of unprovoked aggression by an undisputed tyrant was so manifestly unlawful and morally reprehensible that only strong action could right the wrong. With the seemingly interminable conflict in the former Yugoslavia, public sympathy also came to favour some form of peace-making. In a poll taken in early 1993, two-thirds of respondents supported peace-enforcement in Bosnia and would accept Dutch casualties.[12] It is entirely consistent that one of the pre-eminent leaders of the anti-nuclear protest movement has called for a NATO peace-keeping intervention in Bosnia.[13]

The broad principles informing these beliefs have been shared by the Ministry of Foreign Affairs. However, its enthusiasm for NATO has not been based solely on the convictions that the Alliance was the best organisation to provide for the security of The Netherlands and, after the Cold War, that it offered the best instrument for peace-making. Institutional self-interest and pragmatism led the Ministry to see two additional attractions in the organisation. NATO is the only international body in which The Netherlands can have direct and immediate contact with the world's foremost superpower, the United States. No other organisation has offered a comparable opportunity for exercising influence on the world stage. As a result, Dutch foreign ministers have always emphasised the importance of consultation and consistently sought to broaden it beyond addressing simple issues of security to include 'matters of common concern'.[14] A second attraction of NATO is that it prevents either domination by France, Britain, and Germany, or deadlock as a result of irreconcilable differences between these powers. In NATO, all European powers occupy a second rank after the U.S. Bargaining focuses on two actors, the U.S. and the Europeans, rather than on a multitude as in the European Community. A major foreign policy objective therefore has

---

[11] Jan van der Meulen, 'Het verlangen naar de ideale oorlog' (The Longing for the Ideal War), *Maatschappij &Krijgsmacht*, August 1993, pp. 4–7.

[12] *Ibid.*, p. 3. A Eurobarometer poll taken in the twelve EC countries in the summer indicated support for intervention to restore peace in the former Yugoslavia to be among the highest in the Netherlands.

[13] Interview with Mient-Jan Faber in *NRC/Handelsblad*, 17 September 1993. Foreign Minister P. H. Kooijmans (a professor of international law) noted in an interview that he had asked his Swedish counterpart 'whether there also existed in Sweden such a sense of restiveness to intervene in Yugoslavia if need be with military means. No, she said, that is not at all the case with us.' 'Op je dooie eentje kun je als Nederland niet zo vreselijk veel' (The Netherlands Can't Do Too Much All By Itself), *NRC/Handelsblad*, 24 April 1993.

[14] E.g., 'Memorie van Toelichting bij de begroting van Buitenlandse Zaken' (Statement on the Budget of the Ministry of Foreign Affairs), *HTK 1993–1994*, 23400 V, p. 6. On the importance of this political function of NATO, see Jan Willem Honig, *NATO: An Institution under Threat?*, Institute for East-West Security Studies, New York, 1991, pp. 27–37. For some examples of the Dutch experience with consultation, see Cees Wiebes and Bert Zeeman, '"I Don't Need Your Handkerchiefs": Holland's Experience Of Crisis Consultation In NATO', *International Affairs*, Vol. 66, 1990, pp. 91–113.

long been to keep the EC focused on improving economic cooperation in Europe, while keeping foreign and security policy—the ultimate guarantors of national independence—within the domain of NATO. Moreover, it should be pointed out that the Foreign Ministry monopolises the political consultation process in NATO, whereas in the EC they must cooperate and coordinate with all the other national ministries.

These attractions of NATO have not been diminished by the end of the Cold War. If anything, fear of Franco-German domination has increased. The Dutch foreign minister at the time, Hans van den Broek, immediately rejected an October 1991 proposal to create a five-country European 'security council' to hammer out the EC's approach to defence policy—even though his country was included among the five.[15] The initiatives of France and Germany to establish a common European foreign and defence policy have met with a consistently cool response.[16] Unsurprisingly, The Netherlands has refused to join the Eurocorps.[17] It is within this framework that peace-keeping is seen by the Ministry as a golden (and domestically popular) opportunity to maintain the importance of NATO and retain, if not strengthen, its ties with the United States.

## Peace-Keeping Initiatives

In early August 1991, while it held the presidency of the Community, the Dutch government proposed to send what was called an 'interposition force' to the former Yugoslavia. In other words, instead of pure peace-keeping which requires the consent and cooperation of all parties involved in the conflict, this force would have a broader remit—although still falling short of a unilateral intervention. The proposal found support from Germany, while France and Luxembourg had already backed an intervention coordinated by the WEU.[18] Nevertheless, this plan quickly slipped from the headlines. Four days later, Foreign Minister Van den Broek lamely stated that the EC would oppose the changes of borders that were occurring in the former Yugoslavia 'by all peaceful means'.[19] But in

[15] 'EC "Security Council" Mooted: Smaller Nations Fear Defence Policy Takeover by Europe's Big Four', *The Independent*, 30 October 1991.

[16] E.g., the interviews with Van den Broek: 'A Hawk From The Netherlands Takes Flight Against EC's Plan to Set Defense Policies', *Wall Street Journal*, 26 April 1991; '"Les Douze ne peuvent pas monopoliser la politique de sécurité en Europe"', *Le Monde*, 8 February 1991. One of Van den Broek's most illustrious predecessors, Dirk Stikker, opposed the European Defence Community in the early 1950s on the same grounds. Only after the U.S. and the Dutch Parliament expressed support did he reluctantly join the negotiations: Jan van der Harst, 'The Pleven Plan', in Richard T. Griffiths, ed., *The Netherlands and the Integration of Europe, 1945–1957*, NEHA, Amsterdam, 1990, pp. 137–64.

[17] See, for example, 'L'Europe "ne doit pas être soumise au consensus franco-allemand" déclare M. Van den Broek', *Le Monde*, 18 October 1991; 'Viel Fragen an die Deutschen', *Frankfurter Allgemeine Zeitung*, 18 October 1991.

[18] 'EC Troops Set for Role in Yugoslavia', *The Independent*, 3 August 1991.

[19] 'Stay Out of Yugoslavia, Moscow Warns West', *The Independent*, 7 August 1991.

September, the government tried again at a WEU meeting of foreign and defence ministers in The Hague. Again Germany, France and now Italy backed the proposal. The German Foreign Minister, Hans-Dietrich Genscher, even talked about 'peace-making' as the necessary objective. However, the British government vetoed the move. Reproaching their EC counterparts for failing to provide the necessary detailed logistical and operational planning, it presented a study of its own which showed that intervention would be too demanding for the Community. Publicly, Foreign Minister Douglas Hurd cited the Northern Ireland example, where the British had been 'fighting from village to village and street to street ... for 22 years', implying that the dangers of being drawn into another interminable quagmire were too great.[20]

The fact that these initiatives were undertaken in an EC and WEU framework may, at first glance, appear to contradict the primacy of NATO in Dutch foreign policy. However, since the U.S. made it clear repeatedly that Yugoslavia was a European problem to be dealt with by the Europeans, the initiatives can be seen as attempts to curry favour with the U.S. by showing that some European countries were taking the problem seriously. The Dutch were not alone in concluding that a willingness to engage in peace-keeping efforts had now become a principal means of acquiring influence with the U.S. and in the world. The same point was made in Britain and Germany, though with less effect.[21] The absence of a Northern Ireland experience and the strength of feeling regarding international law and human rights made the Dutch more hawkish regarding the need for active peace-keeping. Also, the Dutch Foreign Ministry knew full well that at some point NATO would have to be involved in any major operation because of its superior organisational and logistical resources (as indeed happened).[22]

However, by increasing peace-keeping commitments, the Foreign Ministry has run into the problem that the available military means do not fit the mission. The existing heavy-armoured forces manned with conscripts are not well suited to peace-keeping. Because of constitutional limitations, conscripts can only participate in peace-keeping operations

[20] 'Europe Split on Military Force', *The Independent*, 18 September 1991; 'Mitterrand Calls for Talks to Settle Border Dispute', *The Independent*, 19 September 1991; 'EC Pulls Back from Sending Troops to Yugoslavia', *The Independent*, 20 September 1991.

[21] E.g., 'As far as Britain is concerned, there must be an understanding that the power of influence comes with the hefty price tag of larger and better-equipped military forces than are envisaged in *Options for Change*'. 'A World Role for NATO', *The Independent*, 30 January 1993. See also 'MPs Urge Government To Offer More UN Troops', *Financial Times*, 1 July 1993. For Germany: 'German Influence In NATO In "Rapid Decline"', *Financial Times*, 8 March 1993.

[22] Foreign Minister Van den Broek repeatedly emphasised the need for the U.S. to be involved in enforcing a political settlement in the former Yugoslavia and the concomitant need for the EC to support U.S. initiatives. See, for example, 'Un entretien avec M. Hans van den Broek', *Le Monde*, 28 November 1992, and the interview with him in his new capacity as European Commissioner responsible for external policies: 'A Brief to Build Bridges', *Financial Times*, 8 March 1993.

outside the NATO treaty area on a voluntary basis. As a result, to date the only available combat forces have been the marines (an almost entirely professional force, part of which went to Cambodia). For the rest, the Dutch army has only been able to commit support units, mainly logistics and communications personnel. The less hazardous tasks required from these units make them more suitable for conscripts. Even so, the army is reaching the limit. In one case, a UN request for a medical unit could not be met because of insufficient volunteer conscripts.[23] Thus, the Ministry of Defence has concluded that in order to be able to immediately deploy units for crisis management operations conscription should be abolished by 1998 and an all-volunteer force established.[24]

Peace-keeping has given the armed forces a new rationale which they have embraced with enthusiasm. The January 1993 Defence White Paper states that 'The Netherlands will have to be prepared and possess the ability to contribute, in an international framework, to a broad range of peace-keeping and peace-enforcing activities. It is mistaken to exclude in advance Dutch participation in certain assignments'.[25] In practical terms, the armed forces are preparing to participate simultaneously in four peace-keeping operations with a battalion, two frigates, or an F-16 squadron for a maximum period of three years each. In addition, they are establishing 'an adequate contribution to peace-enforcing operations' at the level of a brigade, naval task force, the marine corps, three squadrons, or a combination thereof.[26] These new assignments have meant that the Navy and Air Force (which both largely consist of volunteers already) have escaped major cuts. The Navy is even increasing its strength from fourteen to sixteen frigates and will also get an amphibious transport ship (a project already desired during the Cold War). This force will be more modern than ever before: in 1996 the average age of the frigates will be less than eight years. The Air Force will lose 70 of its 192 F-16s (leaving six, instead of formerly nine, operational squadrons), but gain an air-refuelling capability (also a long-standing wish), a much increased and

---

[23] See the interview with Defence Minister Ter Beek: 'Het warme bad en de koude douche van Relus ter Beek' (The Hot Bath and Cold Shower of Relus ter Beek), *Vrij Nederland*, 12 December 1992. In contrast to the marines in Cambodia, there have also been a number of cases of psychological problems with the conscripts in Yugoslavia: 'Psychotrauma's bij VN-soldaten' (Psychological Traumas with UN Soldiers), *Elsevier*, 16 January 1993.

[24] Even though a government commission had advised in September 1992 to retain conscription because of the great risk of not finding enough volunteers, the problems involved in changing the constitution, and the increased costs of recruiting and paying volunteers.

[25] 'Prioriteitennota: Een andere wereld, een andere Defensie' (Statement of Priorities: Another World, Another Defence), 12 January 1993, *HTK 1992–1993*, 22975, p. 12. This paper updates the earlier March 1991 White Paper which still took a possible Soviet resurgence into account: 'Defensienota 1991: Herstructurering en verkleining, De Nederlandse krijgsmacht in een veranderende wereld' (1991 Defence White Paper: Restructuring and Reduction, The Dutch Armed Forces in a Changing World), 7 March 1991, *HTK 1990–1991*, 21991.

[26] 'Prioriteitennota', *op. cit.*, pp. 14–15.

150

modernised transport capacity, and a fleet of 70 combat and transport helicopters.

The Army is the big loser. It had escaped the previous round of cuts in early 1991 fairly well, because at that time it was still accepted that a resurgence of the Soviet threat was conceivable. That possibility being more remote than ever, coupled with the reliance on conscription for 60 per cent of its military manpower, together with difficulties in mobilising units quickly for peace-keeping operations, have made deep cuts unavoidable. Five of its ten brigades will be disbanded. The core peace-keeping unit will be the new airmobile brigade. A newly formed light brigade, as well as an old-style mechanised brigade are earmarked for higher intensity peace-enforcing operations. More airmobile units are considered unrealistic because of the cost involved. Already the brigade will eat up much of the savings achieved by cutting the rest of the army.

If all goes according to plan, The Netherlands will possess an impressive array of forces dedicated to peace-keeping and even peace-enforcing. However, this will take time. For example, the airmobile brigade will have its infantry complement ready by 1995 (its first battalion went to the former Yugoslavia in early 1994), but its helicopter complement will only be in place by 2001.[27] A great uncertainty hovering over army plans is whether enough volunteers can be found. The service possesses none of the special attractions of the Navy and Air Force and is likely to suffer from the Dutch seeing themselves as an unmartial nation.[28] The Navy and Air Force are in a much better position. They are relatively small, less labour-intensive, and have had no great problems to date in finding volunteers.[29] Moreover, the amphibious ship will be ready in 1996 and the air-refuelling and transport aircraft in 1995. Nevertheless, all three services share serious financial uncertainties regarding the feasibility of their plans. It remains to be seen whether they can be achieved within budgetary limits and within the allotted timeframe.

In the short term, therefore, the Dutch armed forces are not able to do much more peace-keeping than they are already doing at present. Once the new forces become available a new question will arise: in line with foreign and defence policy statements that peace-keeping and crisis management are the new objectives of national security policy, will the

---

[27] *Ibid.*, pp. 37, 48. The first seventeen helicopters were ordered in October 1993.

[28] The Army leadership had wanted to keep conscription because it fears severe difficulties in this regard. The top MoD leadership shared the concern to some extent and wanted a total of only four brigades. Insistence from the Foreign Ministry that the Dutch reputation in NATO would suffer in case of a 60 per cent reduction in the number of brigades forced them to settle on five brigades. It remains to be seen whether that is feasible. See Leonard Ornstein, 'In drie weken raakte Nederland zijn leger kwijt' (The Netherlands Lost Its Army in Three Weeks), *Vrij Nederland*, 28 November 1992; Jan Hoedeman and Arend Joustra, 'Veldslagen om nieuwe defensieplannen' (Battles over New Defence Plans), *Elsevier*, 2 January 1993.

[29] The Army needs to recruit 6,000 people annually; the Navy, Air Force, and Royal Military Police, 1,550, 1,450, and 300 respectively: 'Prioriteitennota', *op. cit.*, p. 28.

Dutch actually be able to commit themselves to peace-enforcing? Even with recent operations, differences of opinion have emerged between the Foreign Minister and the Ministry of Defence. Van den Broek (and Development Cooperation Minister Pronk) have repeatedly wanted more extensive commitments and broader remits than Defence Minister Ter Beek.[30] An offer to send Patriot missiles to defend Israel against Iraqi Scud attacks during the Gulf War was labelled 'out of the question' by Ter Beek.[31] The defence minister was less hesitant about committing naval forces to the Gulf—but only in defensive operations. This hesitation is not simply related to the conscript problem, but is a common phenomenon among defence ministers and their military advisers. They prefer to avoid operations in which their contribution is only a relatively minor one and whose process and outcome is mainly influenced by political, rather than military, factors and considerations.[32] This difference of opinion is bound to recur each time troops are sent to dangerous places, and it will complicate the preferred Foreign Ministry policy.

If the government faces tensions, public opinion presents another problem. There is broad support for upholding international law and human rights, but this does not necessarily mean that there is broad support for active combat operations by Dutch troops. The extent of the congruence between ideals and reality has not been put to the test, but the signs are that they do not wholly coincide. Defence Minister Ter Beek certainly had an eye on the electorate when he hesitated before supporting the afore-mentioned military commitments. Breaches of international law must be as blatant as in the Gulf War, and solutions must be clearly known and within grasp before public support can be assured for any large-scale peace-enforcing operation. Moreover, the Foreign Ministry might wish for peace-keeping and peace-enforcing operations to take place in a NATO framework under U.S. leadership, but many in the electorate have never overcome their suspicions regarding U.S. foreign policy intentions aroused during the Vietnam War. It took some time, for example, before it was accepted that more was at stake in the Gulf War than simply oil. Public opinion also does not share the Foreign Ministry's objections to EC and WEU peace-keeping operations. The catalogue of failures of the past two years may have pushed these two organisations out of the limelight, but they are still trying hard to achieve a greater role in security matters. Their competition, in addition to the electorate's unreliability and the Defence Ministry's hesitations, could easily put a stop to the more ambitious peace-keeping designs of any foreign minister.

The Netherlands is developing a high profile in international peace-keeping. It is certain that the country will be among the most significant

---

[30] See the interview with Ter Beek cited in n. 23.

[31] Ter Beek revised his view after cabinet consultations and after the Israelis—who initially declined the offer—accepted it: *NRC/Handelsblad*, 23 January 1991.

[32] Richard K. Betts, *Soldiers, Statesmen, and Cold War Crises*, Columbia University Press, New York, 1991.

contributors to peace-keeping operations in the foreseeable future.[33] The long-standing, peculiarly Dutch concern, not with questions of national interest and sovereignty, but with the moral nature of the international system, assures this. On the other hand, it is uncertain whether the country will get involved in peace-enforcing operations. Despite the official statements supporting such initiatives and a massive reorganisation of the armed forces with this objective in mind, a consensus on the actual application of violence is not assured. Public opinion, unfamiliar with Dutch involvement in war, may easily turn against peace-enforcement. Although two-thirds said it would accept Dutch casualties in case of a peace-enforcement operation in Bosnia, poll results are contradictory regarding the question of how firm that support will remain in the actual event, especially if there are civilian casualties or significant Dutch losses.[34] Parliament and government can be forgiven for hesitating to put their voters' idealism and moralism to the ultimate test of battle in far-off regions. The military are also hesitant about getting involved in what are likely to be politically confused conflicts which necessitate long-term commitments and have no predictably positive outcome. Their forces, in spite of the reorganisation, are also not all well-suited for such operations. The best and most popular services, the Air Force and the Navy, have as their mainstay fighter aircraft and frigates—weapons systems that are not good instruments for keeping or enforcing peace between people fighting on land. Army volunteer manpower may well fall short of targets and affect the availability of those units most appropriate for peace-enforcing.

Finally, will the strong commitment to peace-keeping and the uncertain commitment to peace-enforcing be sufficient to allow the Foreign Ministry to establish The Netherlands in a position of some influence with the United States and in the world? The prospects are quite good. Given the strength of public feeling, the Foreign Ministry can be expected to continue to take a hawkish line on peace-keeping and peace-making. Nonetheless, the blows to the Dutch reputation in NATO in the not too distant past should serve perhaps as reminders that the world is a thankless place. The Netherlands has never been a free-rider in the international community and, most likely, never will be, yet its long-haired soldiers and anti-nuclear protesters effectively undermined the perception abroad that the country was in fact a very loyal ally. In other words, it does not take much to bring down a hard-won international reputation. Political substance counts for remarkably little. One easily imaginable instance of hesitation to join a peace-making operation could again send the reputation plummeting.

[33] They have already reacted positively to the UN Secretary-General's idea to establish an international pool of rapid deployment forces: 'Prioriteitennota', *op. cit.*, p. 19.
[34] Van der Meulen, *op. cit.*, p. 8.

# RUSSIAN VIEWS ON MILITARY INTERVENTION: BENEVOLENT PEACE-KEEPING, MONROE DOCTRINE, OR NEO-IMPERIALISM?

ELAINE M. HOLOBOFF*

'I am fighting not for money but for an idea'.
*Sergei Leonenko, Lieutenant-Colonel in reserve, ex-officer of the Russian Army, fighting on the side of the break-away region of Abkazia in the Georgian civil war.*[1]

IN the case of the Russian state, what is the *idea* behind military intervention, or indeed, is there one? Certainly one of the driving forces is the need to maintain the belief that Russia is still a great power, despite the failure of ideology, the loss of empire, humiliating economic conditions, and frequently absurd domestic politics. To be a great power requires that a state acts in certain ways and accepts certain responsibilities. But how will this be accomplished when it comes to dealing with the many conflicts on Russia's borders and beyond? Will Russia set new standards for humanitarian peace-keeping? At the other extreme, will hardline nationalists or even fascists attempt to reconstitute the old Soviet Union or a new imperial Russia through military adventurism and intervention? Or is the most likely scenario the implementation of a Russian Monroe Doctrine[2] which seeks to define a sphere of influence in regions of the former Soviet Union (FSU) and perhaps Central and Eastern Europe (CEE)?

In this paper it is argued that the last scenario is the most likely, though in the longer term an even more aggressive Russian policy can be expected if fascist politicians such as Vladimir Zhirinovsky continue to increase their power and influence. A Russian Monroe Doctrine has already been

---

* Dr Holoboff is Director of The Programme on Post-Communist Security Studies and Lecturer in the Department of War Studies at King's College. She is a specialist on Soviet/ CIS military and security policies.

[1] 'Dogs of War', *Moscow News*, 16 July 1993, p. 2.
[2] The Monroe Doctrine was enunciated in 1823 by the fifth US President James Monroe. It stated that European colonising powers were no longer welcome to intervene on the American continents. It effectively defined the parameters of America's sphere of influence for over one hundred years.

put in place and Russia maintains that it now has a right to intervene militarily in regions of conflict in the FSU, especially when its national interests are threatened. Correspondingly, countries to the south such as Iran and Turkey are unwelcome on the territories of the FSU, as is any type of NATO involvement which would seek to draw the newly independent states into Western Europe's sphere of influence. In this context Russian 'peace-keeping' activities are largely a method of seeking international legitimacy for the use of military force in support of Russian national interests on the territory of the FSU. This position strengthened progressively as 1993 proceeded.

To begin with it is necessary to look at why the Russian debate on military intervention is qualitatively different from Western policy debates on these same questions. Next, Russian rationales for military intervention will be examined, as well as the way in which the debate on this issue has proceeded. Then actual and future applications of force are looked at, including a critical view of the Russian approach to 'peace-keeping'. Finally, policy implications for the West are considered, with particular consideration given to the election success of Vladimir Zhirinovsky in December 1993.

Most of the debate on military intervention in Russia has concerned events in the FSU. Intervention in the former Yugoslavia has been a matter for some debate, but it has by no means been the central issue under discussion, so I devote only a small portion of the paper to this problem. The second emphasis is on Russian 'peace-keeping' activities, because it is under this name that most interventions have taken place.

## The Context of the Debate on Military Intervention

Several characteristics about the Russian case distinguish it from Western debates on military intervention. To begin with, there is no Russian debate *per se* on this issue which is comparable, for example, to the American debate. Instead it has been inextricably tangled up in a larger debate about the general orientation of Russian foreign policy, the requirements of military doctrine, and definitions of national interest. In Russia it is not a matter of debating and changing existing policies, but more often than not coming up with policies from scratch.

The chaotic post-communist environment has also meant that much of what takes place is *ad hoc*, and therefore often inconsistent and unpredictable. It is difficult if not impossible to set and maintain clear policies in the environment that characterises Moscow and the rest of the country. Western policy makers in established democracies are blessed with stable economies and political systems of the type that most Russian policy makers can only dream of. In post-communist societies 'policies' come and go like so many poker chips in a high stake card game.

It is also difficult to define issues of national interest when Russia must be ultra-sensitised to Western concerns if it is to receive financial assistance. Western nations are anxious that Russia's great power sensibilities are not offended when the issue of aid is considered, but if the Emperor has no clothes, then the Emperor has no clothes. No amount of public posturing will make the situation any different. Yet how does Russia distinguish what are truly national interests from the interests of Western countries who are offering substantial sums of economic aid?

Even if identifiable policies can be discerned and maintained, there is no guarantee that they can or will be implemented. Large and unanswerable questions loom about the ability of the political and military leaderships to control military units stationed within and beyond Russia. Control is even more difficult when it comes to seemingly autonomous military forces such as the Cossacks and illegal paramilitary forces that frequently operate across borders with impunity. There is also the issue of regular Russian army units operating alongside Russian 'peace-keeping' forces in zone of conflict. Who are the 'peace-keepers', who are the 'occupying forces', and who are government military forces?

Finally, how are allegedly democratic aspirations to be reconciled with political expediency? If 'democratic Russia' ends up supporting communist governments through military interventions in the FSU, is this a cause for concern? If so, for whom? There are few clear-cut answers to any of these questions, however identifying them serves to highlight the fact that in Russia decisions about issues such as military intervention are subject to the tumultuous ebb and flow of domestic politics which has been left in the wake of communism's dissolution.

### The Fragile Consensus on National Interests and Rationales for Military Intervention

Many of the unique characteristics of the Russian situation would seem to mitigate against a coherent point of view on national interests and military intervention. Yet it is possible to identify five rationales about which there is a rough consensus. There seems to exist a general agreement that military intervention can be justified as long as it fulfils one or more of the conditions below:

  i. contributes to the maintenance of Russia' great power status;
 ii. protects Russians residing in the 'near abroad' (*blizhnyeye zarubye-zhye*), including military personnel and their families;[3]
iii. prevents the spread of instability, especially to regions of Russia itself;

---

[3] The 'near abroad' is the frequently-used Russian term for all the countries in the FSU. Throughout the world military intervention has frequently been justified to protect nationals threatened in other countries. In the Russian case the intention to protect Russians in the 'near abroad' is no different. This is no surprise when there are 25 million Russians living outside Russia, with the highest percentages in Kazakhstan, the Baltics and Kyrgyzstan.

iv. looks after Russia's geopolitical interests, for example, protecting Russia's southern borders and preventing the spread of Islamic fundamentalism;

v. coincides with nationalist public opinion.

How did this rough consensus arise? For over a year the Russian Federation functioned without a clear foreign policy. Foreign Minister Andre Kozyrev in particular was under constant criticism from the Russian parliament and others for being little more than a lapdog of the West. As a holdover from the Gorbachev period, Kozyrev and many of his protegés had adopted the idealistic notion of a foreign policy based on 'all-human values' and cooperation, as opposed to a policy based on national interests.[4] Failure to develop a coherent foreign policy also meant constant bickering between 'westernisers' and 'slavophiles' about how to deal with countries in Western Europe and Asia. The Yeltsin government and the Ministry of Foreign Affairs (MFA) were criticised for lacking a strategy to deal with the newly independent republics, and placing too much emphasis on relations with the West in order to obtain large amounts of foreign aid.

On 23 April 1993, however, after much discussion and debate, a final document detailing Russia's foreign policy concept was accepted as government policy by President Yeltsin. Remarkably, this represented something of a consensus between various competing factions such as the Security Council, the MFA, the Ministry of Foreign Economic Relations, the Ministry of Defence (MOD), the intelligence services, Civic Union, the non-governmental Council for Foreign and Defence Policy, and others, all of whom contributed in one way or another to the development of the concept.[5]

The document clearly identified what were understood as Russia's vital national interests and reiterated the fact that Russia is a great power. National interests were understood to include the protection of Russia's statehood and territorial integrity, stability and continued reform, the protection of human rights in the FSU (i.e. protection of Russians outside Russia), stopping armed conflicts and preventing their spread to Russia, integration of the Commonwealth of Independent States (CIS) and strengthening of its external borders. The most serious threats to national security were likely to arise from instability along Russia's perimeters,

---

[4] This was perhaps the Russian equivalent of the Bush administration's idea of a 'new world order', which itself also met a tarnished end.

[5] The document titled 'Fundamental Positions of the Concept of Foreign Policy of the Russian Federation' was published in *Nezavisimaya Gazeta*, 29 April 1993. The way in which the policy was formulated is discussed in Vladimir Orlov, 'Head of Security Council forced to resign', *Moscow News*, 30 April 1993, p. 9. Other influential groups such as the Council on Foreign and Defence Policy followed with publications of their own. See for example, the Council's 'Strategy for Russia' in *Nezavisimaya Gazeta*, 19 August 1992. For a general survey of the development of this consensus see Suzanne Crow, 'Russia Asserts Its Strategic Agenda', *RFE/RL Research Report*, 17 December 1993.

Islamic fundamentalism, the integration of Europe without Russia (i.e. entry of CEE and FSU countries into NATO), and additional nuclear powers on the territory of the FSU (i.e. Ukraine). The presence of foreign military bases and forces on the territory of the FSU was explicitly rejected. Emphasis was placed on collective security and the maintenance of an integrated military infrastructure which would ensure the military security of Russia and others in the FSU.

Evgenii Ambartsumov, the influential chairman of the Russian parliament's Committee on International Affairs and Foreign Economic Relations (and formerly liberal advisor to President Gorbachev), had earlier published an article defining Russia's national interest which emphasised many of the same issues.[6] By June he said that previously tense relations between his Committee and the MFA had improved considerably, even on contentious issues such as former Yugoslavia and relations with the West. Andrei Kozyrev would no longer have to resign because Russian foreign policy had been appropriately 'reoriented' towards the most significant area of Russian interest, the 'near abroad'.

However, not only were 'westernisers' like Kozyrev forced to moderate their views, so too were conservatives like Yuri Skokov, head of the Security Council.[7] In a document titled 'Programme for National Security of Russia' developed in April 1992 Skokov had argued for a Russian Monroe Doctrine which would have challenged the US for predominance in *all* regions of the globe, not simply in the 'near abroad'.[8] Following Yeltsin's acceptance of the new foreign policy concept, which itself came out of the Security Council process, Skokov was asked to resign despite his seemingly powerful position within Yeltsin's administration.

The military leadership had also begun to clarify their own ideas about national interests in mid-1992. A draft military doctrine was published in a special edition of *Voennaya Myls* in May (with a final draft appearing a year later). Though a rather contradictory document, this highlighted the fact that Russians in the 'near abroad' constituted a major part of Russia's vital interests. It was suggested that the Armed Forces should have a special mission to protect Russians outside the country. In addition, any placement of foreign troops near Russia's borders would be considered a direct military threat. Many in the military have found it difficult to move away from the view that NATO is no longer a threat, and view the prospect of NATO enlargement with some trepidation.

By November 1993 the military had consolidated their power considerably, following their support for Yeltsin in the armed struggle against his opponents in the Russian parliament. A final version of the military doctrine was accepted with little controversy, this very likely being one

[6] *Krasnaya Zvezda*, 11 February 1993.

[7] On Skokov's influence see Vladimir Orlov, 'Chief of Russia's Diplomacy', *Moscow News*, 11 February 1993, p. 9.

[8] Orlov, 'Head of Security Council', *op. cit*.

condition of the MOD's support for Yeltsin in the October uprising.[9] On the one hand the doctrine states that Russia regards no state as its enemy, while at the same time emphasising that very real external and internal threats continue to exist. The gravest threats will arise from local wars and conflicts, and internal armed conflicts.[10] In line with the view of many conservatives in the military, the doctrine states that a direct threat to Russia could include a build-up or movement of troops on Russia's borders (for example, NATO troops in CEE or the Baltic states). The doctrine also confirms that the armed forces can be stationed outside Russia, take part in peace-keeping operations, and assist Internal Ministry troops in quelling domestic instability. Some prominence is also given to the idea that the use of armed force against another state is justified, not only by an attack on Russia itself, but also by attacks on its citizens (presumably a reference to Russians in the 'near abroad').

With these clarifications of policy has come a slow but steady expansion of the boundaries of Russia, and an ever increasing willingness to assert Russian interests in the 'near abroad' and even beyond. In February 1993 the MFA stated that the United Nations (UN) and Western European Union (WEU) would have to obtain Russian approval if they wished to send warships into the Black Sea and Danube basin to enforce sanctions against rump Yugoslavia, this despite the fact that Russian territory is 800 km. away.[11] Regions outside Russia, where Russian military units are still based, have been explicitly identified as Russian territory as personnel become angered and alarmed by the threats to safety of themselves and their families.[12] With 600 incidents recorded against military personnel in the 'near abroad' in 1992 (including 73 deaths and 160 injuries) the military has decided that it has no choice but to defend itself.[13] Even the distant borders of Tajikistan were identified as belonging to the Russian Federation when in July 1993 24 Russian border guards were killed during a clash with armed opposition members on the Afghan border. As early as February Russian Defence Minister Pavel Grachev had identified Tajikistan as being of strategic importance to Russia.[14] In particular, fears

---

[9] This point is argued in Stephen Foye, 'Updating Russian Civil-Military Relations', *RFE/RL Research Report*, 19 November 1993, p. 47. Grachev's announcement of the doctrine and its contents are published in *Krasnaya Zvezda*, 4 November 1993.

[10] Concerning internal conflicts, this includes an opaque reference to the fact that other states may exploit such situations by using internal instability as an excuse for intervening in the domestic affairs of Russia. This is a frequent argument of ultra-conservatives and nationalists who fear that the West will use any excuse to intervene, with the ultimate aim of dissolving Russia.

[11] *RFE/RL News Brief*, 22–26 February 1993.

[12] For example, after an incident in which a helicopter was shot down in Abkhazia in December 1992, military officials stated that 'Russian helicopters land on the territory of Russian military units, which is the territory of the Russian Federation', cited in *RFE/RL News Briefs*, 10–23 December 1992, p. 10.

[13] *Krasnaya Zvezda*, 30 December 1992.

[14] *RFE/RL News Brief*, 1–5 February 1993.

exist about the rise of Islamic fundamentalism in the south. With 20 million Muslims residing within Russia itself, the military leadership believes the country cannot afford to be complacent on this subject.[15]

The Northern Caucasus in particular has consistently been identified as a region of concern. In February 1993 Grachev spoke about the strategic importance of the south. Forces returning from Germany, including 9,000 officers, are being relocated to this region in order to create a 'combat district'; three airborne and two motorised brigades will form the core of the regional mobile forces; and the first regional formation for the MVD Internal Troops will also be located in the North Caucasus. Russia has also sought a revision of the Conventional Forces in Europe (CFE) Treaty so that it can devote more forces to the area.[16]

The process of extending Russia's border was made more explicit during a Yeltsin speech to military officers in June 1993. He suggested that Russia should adopt basing practices similar to those of the US, formalised by bilateral agreements to establish a Russian military presence in places like Moldova, Armenia, Georgia and Central Asia.[17] Russia has been proceeding with this policy and has concluded bilateral military agreements with a number of states which formalise the presence of Russian bases, and financial support for them.[18]

Another significant development has been the end of the idea of a CIS joint command for the Armed Forces in June 1993 due to a lack of enthusiasm on Russia's part. In its place a 'joint staff for coordinating military cooperation between states of the Commonwealth' was agreed upon.[19] In practice, this involves an endorsement of *Russia's* efforts to develop bilateral military cooperation between itself and other CIS states, for there is little that any of the other newly independent states can offer each other in terms of significant cooperation. Many new states like Tajikistan and Turkmenistan have no armies of their own as yet, thus 'cooperation' means Russian assistance in building such structures. Ultimately the price for this 'cooperation' may be monetary (e.g. payment for services rendered by the Russian Armed Forces), or it may be the ceding of autonomy to Russia.

[15] *Nezavisimaya Gazeta*, 7 May 1993, p. 1.

[16] 25 February 1993, Russian TV, 'Vesti'; *Rossiiskie vesti*, 6 March 1993; *RFE/RL News Brief*, 11–15 January 1993; and on CFE see for example the *Washington Times*, 31 March 1993 and 11 June 1993, and Jane Sharp, 'CFE Treaty Under Threat as Russia Requests Revisions', *Bulletin of Arms Control*, No. 12, November 1992.

[17] *RFE/RL News Brief*, 7–11 June 1993, p. 5. The idea was automatically rejected by countries like Moldova who have been trying to reduce the Russian military presence in Dniester Republic.

[18] For example, agreements have been concluded with Georgia and Turkmenistan which include financing of Russian troops by the host country. See Alexander Zhilin, 'Russian military presence in Georgia, Central Asia reaffirmed', *Moscow News*, 10 September 1993, p. 3.

[19] *RFE/RL News Brief*, 14–18 June, p. 8 and 23–27 August 1993, p. 8; Alexander Zhilin, 'The CIS Army starts from scratch', *Moscow News*, 3 September 1993, p. 3.

On 15 May 1992 a Collective Security Agreement was signed by Russia, Armenia, Kazakhstan, Kyrgyzstan, Tajikistan, and Uzbekistan. Initially this appeared to mean little without the involvement of the other newly independent states, and apparent inaction on cases such as Armenia made this a rather weak agreement. However, by the spring of 1993 the six signatories, clearly under Russia's leadership, were acting in a more concerted manner. In March they discussed a need to create a joint security zone as a counterbalance to Western Europe, Iran, China, and Japan.[20] In August they signed an agreement on eleven areas of military cooperation including a common air-defence system.[21] This too has served to consolidate Russia's leadership in the security sphere within the CIS.

In the near term it seems doubtful that Russia intends to extend its sphere of influence beyond the boundaries of the FSU in any substantial way, though there are certain to be cases where it will be forced to defend its own particular interests. Failure to condemn Serbian aggression in Bosnia is one example; warnings about former Warsaw Pact countries joining NATO is another.[22] The situation could of course change dramatically, for example if Zhirinovsky wins the next Presidential election.

What is clear from this progression of events is that since early 1993 Russia has worked with deliberation to reassert its leadership politically and militarily in the regions of the FSU. The issue of defending Russia's interests in the 'near abroad' is something which few have been willing to take a stand on. Indeed, it is one of the few areas of clear consensus between liberals and ultra-conservatives. This in turn has guided the issue of Russian military intervention incalculably.

## Military Intervention As 'Peace-keeping'

Prior to the end of the Cold War it was easy to identify and define military intervention: guns went off, bombs were dropped and people were killed. Intervention had little to do with keeping the peace unless it was one's own peace. In the post-Cold War era, however, the distinction between peace-keeping and military intervention has become blurred, as supposedly

[20] *RFE/RL News Brief*, 15–19 March 1993, p. 5.
[21] *RFE/RL News Brief*, 23–27 August 1993, p. 8.
[22] In August 1993 Andrei Kozyrev suggested that the entry into NATO of the Czech Republic, Slovakia, Poland would threaten democracy in Russia. He also defined the Baltics as an area of strategic interest for Russia. However, policy was confused on this issue for some time. The day after Kozyrev's comments Yeltsin said that he had no objections to Poland's NATO membership, but then backed away from this position. See *RFE/RL News Brief*, 23–27 August 1992, pp. 12 and 16. Since the election success of Zhirinovsky, however, Yeltsin has come out clearly against the expansion of NATO eastward. For a view which says that Russia's influence does not extend as far as CEE see Crow, 'Russia Asserts Its Strategic Agenda', *op. cit.*

161

neutral forces are drawn deeper and deeper into combat. Nowhere has this been more true than in the conflicts of the FSU.

In mid-1992 Russian concepts of peace-keeping were poorly defined and policy was *ad hoc*.[23] Yet military forces were already being introduced (or maintained) in regions of conflict without detailed forethought about their role, rules of engagement, or methods of disengagement. By April 1993 at least 18,000 Russian forces were carrying out 'peace-keeping' functions in regions of the FSU, this despite the fact that no legal framework existed for their deployment.[24] Whether it was the urgency of the situation on Russia's borders, or calculated differences of opinion on the role of peace-keepers, the Russian view of such forces has from the beginning manifest several major differences with the conventional understanding of peace-keeping. Russian/CIS 'peace-keeping' forces:

i. can enter a zone of conflict before hostilities have ceased;
ii. involve mediation by self-interested parties (e.g. Russia) rather than neutral parties;
iii. allow troops from each hostile side to be incorporated into the 'peace-keeping' force;
iv. have the clear right to defend themselves if attacked, and are usually heavily armed;
v. have the right to use a high level of force, regardless of whether attacked or not;[25]
vi. have the right to use force *before* being attacked in some cases (e.g. confrontation with unidentifiable armed groups).

All of this has served to make Russian 'peace-keeping' forces look more like actual combat forces, or at least 'peace-enforcement' forces.

### The Application of Force: Russia's Existing 'Peace-keeping' Operations and Their Problems

During 1993 Russian 'peace-keeping' forces were deployed in three regions of the FSU (South Ossetia in northern Georgia, the Dniester Republic of eastern Moldova, and Tajikistan), as well as one region outside the FSU (Croatia in the former Yugoslavia). In addition, the Russian army has been involved in, or accused of being involved in, conflicts in Nagorno-Karabakh and also the break-away republic of Abkhazia in western Georgia.

[23] This was certainly the author's impression from interviews about Russia's approach to peace-keeping in the Russian Ministry of Foreign Affairs in May 1992.

[24] *Nezavisimaya Gazeta*, 22 April 1993, p. 2.

[25] For example, in South Ossetia peace-keeping forces are allowed to open fire 20 minutes after the beginning of hostilities. See James M. Greene, 'The Peace-keeping Doctrines of the CIS', *Jane's Intelligence Review*, April 1993, p. 157. This creates a volatile situation when troops from both sides of the conflict are incorporated into the 'peace-keeping' force.

The Russian 'peace-keeping' force in South Ossetia was the first to be deployed. Since 1989 South Ossetia has been seeking independence in order to rejoin North Ossetia which is located in the Russian Federation. After a bitter conflict with the Georgian government a peace-keeping force, consisting of roughly one battalion (500 men) each of Russian, Georgian, and North and South Ossetian troops, was to be deployed on 14 July 1992. The final numbers were different, however, with Russia contributing 700 troops consisting of paratroopers brought in from Russia, instead of regular troops which were already deployed in the region, as had been expected. The Ossetians contributed 469 men (some of whom were accused of being criminals) and Georgia only 320 men. Hardly a traditional 'peace-keeping' force, the Russians were attacked upon their arrival and continued to suffer fatalities as the mission went on.[26]

The second 'peace-keeping' force to be deployed in Dniester Republic has been one of the most controversial. In this conflict the Russian 14th Army, located in the eastern part of Moldova, openly sided with opponents of the Moldovan government and indeed, promoted succession. The result was a short but bloody civil war. In one of the great ironies of Russian 'peace-keeping' it was actually suggested that perhaps the 14th Army could itself act as a 'peace-keeping' force. This route rejected however, a 'multilateral peace-keeping' force was deployed on 29 July 1992. The Russian military presence in Dniester was increased considerably with the addition of 3,800 Russian 'peace-keeping' troops from outside the country. Moldova contributed 1,200 troops and the Dniester national guard in the conflict region contributed 1,200 to a total of 6,200 men. Originally other countries (Romania, Bulgaria, Belarus and Ukraine) had expressed an interest in becoming involved, but later backed out of involvement. Moldova appealed repeatedly for UN or CSCE troops, but when this failed had little recourse but to accept 'peace-keeping' forces on Russia's terms.[27]

Despite a rather large contingent of Russian 'peace-keeping' forces in Dniester one hears little about their activities. The 14th Army, led by the outspoken and hardline General Aleksandr Lebed, has dominated the news from this region. Lebed fully expects a revival of the FSU and communism. He and others have deliberately developed contacts among like-minded individuals in Ukraine and Abkhazia. This has included a friendship and cooperation treaty with Abkhazian insurgents which pledges military assistance if one side is attacked.[28] It is also apparent that the military and political leaderships in Moscow tolerate the controversial activities of Lebed. Following the cessation of the conflict Lebed was

[26] Details of this deployment can be found in Suzanne Crow, 'The Theory and Practice of Peace-keeping in the Former USSR', *RFE/RL Research Report*, 18 September 1992, pp. 33–4.

[27] Crow, *op. cit.*, p. 35.

[28] *Izvestia*, 26 January 1993; Interfax, 27 January 1993 reported in *Foreign Broadcasting Information Service-Central EurAsia* (hereafter FBIS-CEA), 28 January 1993, p. 41.

promoted in rank, and Yeltsin has refused to discuss a timetable for the withdrawal of the 14th Army. Lebed is now pursuing his own political career in Dniester and hopes to be elected to the Supreme Soviet. There can be no better example of the politicisation of the military than General Lebed.

The civil war in Tajikistan is the third region in which Russian 'peace-keeping' troops have been deployed, though in this case it is hard to distinguish these from actual combat forces. There has been a substantial involvement of the 201st Russian Army, paramilitary formations, and Ministry of Interior and KGB troops. This conflict began in May 1992 when opposition forces (Islamic and democratic groups) attempted to oust communist President Rakhmon Nabiev. As the conflict spread outward from the capital Dushanbe inter-clan conflict exacerbated the situation. Casualties have been heavy with 20,000 dead (not counting persons who have disappeared), and at least 200,000 refugees.[29]

Agreement to deploy CIS 'peace-keeping' forces was reached in August 1992: however, actual deployments did not take place until February 1993, with troops from Uzbekistan and Kazakhstan being the first to arrive. In April the Russian Supreme Soviet approved the deployment of a 500-strong peace-keeping force for the region; and 500 troops from Kyrgyzstan arrived in July. Though the CIS Collective Security Agreement has proven insignificant in other conflicts, in this case it was used as a justification for military intervention by the Russian government.

Prior to the arrival of peace-keeping forces, the Russian's 201st Army played a significant role in protecting infrastructure from attack and guarding the porous borders in the south of the country. In effect the 201st Army was the only option for defending strategic points in the country. Tajikistan, like many other newly independent states, has a number of paramilitary groups operating throughout the country, but no regular army of its own. As the conflict has progressed, however, the 201st Army has been drawn further and further into the conflict. After the death of Russian troops in the Tajik-Afghan border in July, Grachev requested the rapid deployment of more combat troops, aircraft and heavy weapons in order to bring the 201st Army up to full strength.[30]

Though the neutrality of the 201st army has often been praised by Russian observers (in contrast to the 14th Army in Dniester), there can be no doubt that, without the involvement of this military force, the communist government would have had great difficulties staying in power. It is also true that Russia would far rather see the present government in power than face the unknown threat of the first Islamic government in the FSU.

Several common features can be found concerning the Russian involvement in these regions. First, in all cases Russian forces have provided the

[29] These are official government figures, *RFE/RL News Brief*, 1–5 February 1993, p. 9; real fatality figures could be much higher.

[30] *RFE/RL News Brief*, 12–16 July 1993, p. 6.

lion's share of any 'peace-keeping' contingent. In some cases contributions by other countries have only been symbolic and this has had unsavory results. Countries such as Moldova and Georgia, which had expected that Russian troop levels in their countries would steadily decline, had found instead that these have increased via the introduction of 'peace-keeping' forces. Despite protestations Russia has stalled on a timetable for the withdrawal of its regular forces.[31]

Another common feature is that Russian interventions have frequently resulted in direct support for hardline communist governments in regions of conflict, despite Russia's own ostensibly democratic aspirations. This has been true for the Dniester Republic, Tajikistan, and as will be seen below, Abkhazia. Russia's softness on the Serbs in former Yugoslavia is also consistent with this pattern. Consequently Russia has on more than one occasion supported secessionist movements in other countries, despite its own concerns about the fragmentation of Russia itself.[32]

What is behind these seeming contradictions? One explanation is that a certain portion of Russians stranded beyond Russia maintained a belief in communism and the eventual resurrection of the FSU. These groups also tend to be the most outspoken on the rights of Russians or Slavs in the 'near abroad'. If Russia has a policy of defending Russians in the 'near abroad', it can hardly have a policy based on 'good' and 'bad' nationals, therefore there is little choice but to support Russians whatever their political persuasion. The question of support for secessionist movements is not so easily justified. Governments in Moldova, Georgia and Azerbaijan are angered by what they see as Russian support for individuals or groups who seek to tear their countries apart. Support for individuals of a disagreeable political orientation is one thing, support for secessionist movements quite another.

Finally, and not unrelated to the above, is the fact that Russia stands to gain certain strategic advantages by these 'peace-keeping' interventions. In the case of South Ossetia, intervention allows the military to justify its continued presence in an area which it considers to be the front line against instability and resurgent Islamic fundamentalism. The same applies to Tajikistan, where there are concerns that instability will spread domino-style across Central Asia and into Russia itself. There is also concern about the 200,000 Russians in the region. Moldova offers the military another strategic outpost to the West, though why Russia would want the trouble of another 'Balkan Kaliningrad' is not immediately clear.

---

[31] In Moldova there has been no agreement on a timetable for withdrawal, and in Georgia the end of 1995 has provisionally been agreed upon, though without details of how this will proceed.

[32] The exception to this rule is Russian support of non-communist Armenia in the conflict over Nagorno-Karabakh, though this can partially be explained by the fact that Moscow has been loth to come down on the side of Muslims in Azerbaijan, especially given concern about the threat of Islamic fundamentalism. Ironically, though, accusations of Russian military support in Nagorno-Karabakh, if true, are another example of support for a secessionist movement.

### 'Out of Area' Interventions and the Case of Former Yugoslavia

Russian peace-keeping forces numbering 900 (an airborne battalion) have also been deployed in Croatia in the former Yugoslavia under UN mandate.[33] The deployment of these troops, and Russia's participation in attempts to find a solution to the war, have been the subject of some debate within Russia.[34] For Yeltsin, Kozyrev and the MFA there has been an obvious interest in maintaining an active role in the region in order to reaffirm Russia's status as a great power, despite the country's dire economic problems and chaotic political environment. And though few would admit it, early on there was also probably an element of 'kowtowing' to the West for reasons of economic gain. The contribution of troops has also guaranteed that the Russian government will have a continued say about developments in the region.

On the diplomatic front Russia differed little from Western Europe in its policies throughout 1991 and the first half of 1992.[35] This included condemnation of Serbian aggression in Croatia, and support for economic sanctions against Serbia. By the latter half of 1992, however, the government had to take into account voices critical of Russia's policy. Positions less overtly in line with Western policies started to be adopted. Even so, substantively Russian policy maintained remarkably similar to some Western positions: for example, British and French opposition to military intervention. The Yeltsin government supported the Vance-Owen agreement until its demise, and *might* have considered a contribution to a multi-national force if a cease-fire had been achieved in Bosnia under this plan. In addition, several detailed plans for a resolution of the conflict were put forward by Russia, one in February and another in May 1993.

In contrast to the government's position, at the core of the Russian parliament's overtly pro-Serbian position were the following: (i) a rejection of all foreign military intervention in the region, including, obviously, Russian intervention; (ii) the *equal* application of sanctions and delivery of humanitarian aid to all sides (or equal withdrawal of these); and (iii) continuance of the arms embargo.[36] By spring 1993 the parliament was arguing against continued sanctions against the Serbs. Some of the more conservative parliamentary members believed that Yugoslavia was

---

[33] The activities of this force have not been without criticism. The troops and their commander have been accused of openly fraternising with the Serbs and engaging in private profiteering.

[34] For two Western analyses see J. Lough, 'Constraints on Russian Responses in the Yugoslav Crisis', *Occasional Brief 22*, Conflict Studies Research Center, June 1993; and Suzanne Crow, 'Russia Adopts a More Active Policy', *RFE/RL Research Report*, 19 March 1993, pp. 1–6.

[35] For a useful description of the evolution of Russian policy on the Balkans see Allen Lynch and Reneo Lukic, 'Russian Foreign Policy and the Wars in the Former Yugoslavia', *RFL/RL Research Report*, 15 October 1993.

[36] *RFE/RL News Brief*, 10–23 December 1992, pp. 6–7.

simply a practice run for eventual UN/Western involvement in the FSU, and therefore the idea of military intervention on the ground was especially worrying. Ironically it was Kozyrev who came up with one of the most salient reasons for *not* supporting the Serbs, an argument that had some resonance even with hardline conservatives and nationalists. He argued that open support for the Serbs could potentially alienate Russia's own Muslim populations in Tatarstan and Bashkortostan, with the ultimate result of fracturing Russia itself.[37] In the end, although the parliament's anti-western orientation put constant pressure on the government not to associate itself too closely with Western positions, Russia was able to offer as constructive an approach as any of the other powers involved in the region.

The MOD has also consistently been reluctant to participate in any direct military intervention for fear that it will become involved in another Afghanistan, and possibly a conflict that spreads beyond the Balkans. Grachev openly rejected the enforcement of the no-fly zone over Bosnia and the idea of air strikes, in contrast to Kozyrev's statements on the issue.[38] The concern with conflicts within the FSU also means that the MOD has neither the interest nor the manpower to go very far beyond the borders of the 'near abroad'. While a commitment of further troops was ruled out, there was some willingness to provide air-delivered humanitarian assistance under UN mandate.

Until April 1993 pressure from conservatives in the Russian parliament and the military meant that Russia's position on the Serbs had to be dealt with cautiously, and that a further commitment of Russian troops for Bosnia was almost impossible. However, after the Russian referendum on 25 April Yeltsin's position was strengthened considerably, and by May Kozyrev played an active diplomatic role in the attempt to find a solution to the war. He suggested a plan involving safe areas for the Muslim population in Bosnia which was accepted by the US, Britain and others. He also hinted that Russia might contribute as many as 2,000 additional troops to enforce the Vance-Owen plan, and that a smaller contingent could act as monitors along the Serbian-Bosnian border, something which was rejected outright by Grachev and the parliament.[39] Given the political environment in Russia at the end of 1993 further military intervention (i.e. troops) can probably be ruled out at this time, though diplomatic activities will continue.

## Future Cases of Military Intervention?

There are no shortages of places for Russian 'peace-keeping' forces to be deployed in the future if the country wants to continue to extend its army

[37] *Nezavisimaya Gazeta*, 16 February 1993, p. 1.
[38] *RFE/RL News Brief*, 29 March–2 April 1993, p. 7.
[39] *International Herald Tribune* (hereafter *IHT*), 20 May 1993.

in this fashion. Russian forces may well be deployed in Georgia again, this time in Abkhazia. Hardline communists in this region have been attempting to break away from Georgia in an increasingly bloody battle with the central government. (Indeed, the Abkhazians would like to join Russia as a protectorate.) Russia has been involved in trilateral negotiations with Georgia and Abkhazia and it seems possible that, following the Ossetian and Moldovan models, Russia will send 'peace-keeping' troops into the region. The UN has agreed to play a role in achieving a peace settlement, but it seems very doubtful that this would include an actual commitment of troops. Russia, along with Ukraine, has also been fulfilling a humanitarian role in the region by delivering humanitarian aid and evacuating refugees (both Abkhazians and Russians).[40]

The conflict over Nagorno-Karabakh is one region where there has been some reluctance on the part of the Russians to become involved militarily. This five-year war has resulted in at least 15,000 casualties and one million refugees. In addition to Armenia's numerous requests for UN and CSCE involvement, it has also requested military intervention under the CIS Collective Security Agreement. However, Russia and others have shown little interest in being drawn into the hostilities. In lieu of military intervention Russia became involved in trilateral peace negotiations with Turkey and the US in April 1993, though these have achieved little success thus far. In September Kozyrev did suggest that Russia was prepared to send troops to Nagorno-Karabakh once a peace settlement was worked out; however it is unclear whether the MOD would be willing to participate in this activity.[41]

In both Abkhazia and Nagorno-Karabakh there have been constant accusations of Russian military involvement, including combat support and the supply of heavy arms and equipment. Individual incidents are almost impossible to verify; however, overall it seems undeniable that some Russian regular forces are contributing to hostilities. Relations between Russian military units and Abkhazians have been described as 'friendly'.[42] On the other hand the MOD accuses Georgia of drawing the Russian military into the conflict in Abkhazia, and in the conflict over Nagorno-Karabakh accuses Azerbaijan of obtaining arms and supplies from other countries in the FSU (though the MOD declined to specify where).[43]

The dismal conditions and morale within the military make it inevitable that command structures have progressively loosened. In many regions

[40]  *RFE/RL News Brief*, 14–18 June 1993, p. 6.

[41]  Kozyrev made his comments on CNN, 14 September 1993. He also stated that Russian and Ukrainian mercenaries are active in the region and are paid $5,000.00 per month to assist the military forces in Nagorno-Karabakh.

[42]  *Moscow News*, 18 July 1993. This report is from a Russian officer who worked as a mercenary for the Abkhazians. He also said that Afghan veterans and Cossacks were assisting the rebels as well.

[43]  *RFE/RL News Bulletin*, 14–21 May 1993, p. 4.

servicemen have gone for long periods without pay, units are severely undermanned due to the failure of conscription, and there is no social network for military personnel.[44] In these conditions it becomes more and more difficult to control the activities of individuals who, for profit or principle, seek to become involved in conflict situations.

There are other regions where open hostilities have not broken out yet, but which may provide fodder for Russian military interventions in the future. The Crimea has been a constant source of tension between Ukraine and Russia.[45] The Russian parliament exacerbated matters by claiming that Crimea is part of Russia. With a large Russian population in this region there will be any number of excuses for Russia to intervene militarily in the future if it wishes to risk a major confrontation with Ukraine. It is conceivable that if relations deteriorated seriously, or if a change of government occurs in Moscow, Russia could easily pursue a military presence in Ukraine under the pretext of protecting the Russian population in Crimea.

In the Baltics, too, the threat of Russian military intervention has intermittently loomed. Russia has been especially concerned about what it sees as discriminatory citizenship laws in Estonia and Latvia. As of August 1993 there were 7,000 troops left in Estonia and the Russian military has suspended troops withdrawals in the Baltics several times to show its disapproval of the treatment of Russians in this region. More provocatively, in April 1993 the Northwestern Group of Forces, without notification, carried out exercises involving a strategic takeover of the Baltics.[46] Military intervention in the Baltics would obviously be a high-risk venture and have serious repercussions for Russian relations with Europe and North America. It is doubtful that Yeltsin would contemplate or allow any military intervention in this region; however, once again it is impossible to predict the actions of future presidents.

Finally there is the Russian Federation itself which may provide plenty of opportunity for military intervention as numerous regions call for increased autonomy and/or outright independence. Tatarstan, Bashkortostan, Sakha (Yakutia), and Karelia have been particularly insistent on increased independence from Moscow, threatening to launch their own currencies and collect their own taxes. The republic of Chechnya has already declared complete independence, though for the time being

---

[44] For example, sailors in Severomorsk did not receive pay for three months, and 60 per cent of servicemen's salaries remained unpaid in July 1993. See Moscow Russian Television Network, 9 August 1993 in *FBIS-CEA*, 10 August 1993, pp. 25–6, and Moscow Russian Television Network, 31 August 1993, *FBIS-CEA*, 1 September 1993, p. 22.

[45] During the Yeltsin-Kravchuk summit in Massandra on 3 September 1993 the contentious issues of the Black Sea Fleet and Ukrainian nuclear weapons appeared to have been resolved. Ukraine agreed to sell its part of the fleet and return all nuclear weapons as payment for its debts to Russia. However the agreement still has to be passed by parliament,and the outlook is not good; the Prime Minister Leonid Kuchma was forced to resign over the issue.

[46] *RFE/RL News Brief*, 19–23 April 1993, p. 20.

Russia has chosen not to intervene militarily. However, Russia has already deployed military forces to deal with a conflict on its southern border between the North Ossetians and the Ingush. Some additional 5,000 troops from the Interior Ministry are to be stationed in this region after the Russian head of a newly appointed local provisional government and a high ranking military official were assassinated in July 1993.[47]

## Russia's Self-Assigned Role As Regional 'Peace-keeper'

In February 1993, in a statement to the Civic Union, Yeltsin said that 'the time has come for distinguished international organisations, including the United Nations, to grant Russia special powers as a guarantor of peace and stability in regions of the former USSR'.[48] Russia's neighbours viewed this approach with some alarm. Ukraine accused Russia of neo-imperialism, Moldova expressed 'astonishment and concern', and others such as Latvia and Azerbaijan added their protests. Nonetheless Russia proceeded with a formal submission on the subject to the UN on 3 March. The UN Committee on Charter Review looked at Russia's 'peace-keeping' proposal and failed to raise any issues of principle, though overall the response of the UN was lukewarm.[49]

What is behind Russia's self-promotion? First, there can be no doubt that Russia has adopted a more interventionist policy in the FSU for the variety of reasons pointed out earlier. If the international community endorses Russia's Monroe Doctrine, so much the better. Promoting Russia as the leader in 'peace-keeping' is also necessary for domestic reasons. It allows Yeltsin to portray himself as a strong leader and demonstrate that his sympathies are with the 'near abroad', rather than the West. The MOD and conservatives are also loth to see Western involvement in the FSU, and Russia's monopoly on 'peace-keeping' is one way of ensuring that no Western troops, UN or otherwise, will shadow Russia's sphere of influence. Cooperative east-west peace-keeping activities in the FSU would severely curtail the strategic advantage that the MOD is currently free to obtain from its activities in non-Russian regions. There has been an agreement between Grachev and the former US Defence Minister Les

---

[47] The multiple conflicts of this region provide a good example of the type of domino effect that Russia is justifiably afraid of. The conflict between North Ossetia and Ingush began after the Chechnya republic (previously Chechen-Ingushetia) declared complete independence from Russia. The Ingush then looked westward to their previous homelands in North Ossetia, with some 16,000 wanting to relocate. This conflict was overlaid on the already ongoing conflict between South Ossetia (which wants to join with North Ossetia) and Georgia.

[48] Cited in *RFE/RL News Brief*, 1–5 March 1993, p. 5. Russia's desire to be the 'gendarme' of the FSU and the idea of a Russian Monroe Doctrine goes back to mid-1992. For a background see Suzanne Crow, 'Russian Peacekeeping: Defense, Diplomacy, or Imperialism?', *RFE/RL Research Report*, 18 September 1992, pp. 38–9.

[49] *RFE/RL News Brief, 8–12 March 1993, p. 3.*

Aspin on joint training for peace-keeping forces which will involve two heavy combat divisions.[50] Whether this is a symbolic exercise or something more serious remains to be seen.

Finally one cannot exclude a financial aspect. Given that Russia will be drawn inevitably into conflicts on its periphery, it will attempt to seek significant financial compensation for its role from the international community, rather than bearing the full brunt of expenses itself. In July 1993 Yeltsin asked the UN to grant Russian/CIS troops in Tajikistan the status of a UN peace-keeping force, *and* to finance the operation out of the UN budget.[51] With expenses for peace-keeping operations running upwards of 2.2 billion roubles for 1992,[52] it is no wonder the Russian government would like an international mandate and budget for its activities.

Curiously, one hears few voices in Russia who oppose a more interventionist role in the 'near abroad', whether under the rubric of 'peace-keeping' or not. One might have expected that the country's experience in Afghanistan would have made some Russians cautious about further adventurism in unfamiliar territory. In fact the opposite seems to have occurred. Intervention is motivated not only by strategic concerns, but on occasion it is also justified for humanitarian reasons. Among many there is a belief that only Russia can stop a bloodbath on the rim of the FSU, thus it cannot shirk this historical responsibility.[53]

## The Zhirinovsky Factor

Zhirinovsky's parliamentary victory in the 12 December 1993 elections was viewed with surprise and alarm by many. His authoritarian, expansionist and racist views make it certain that Yeltsin will face even greater difficulties with the new parliament than he did with the previous body. Zhirinovsky has advocated recreating Russia with its former Soviet borders. Simple but effective election slogans such as 'I will bring Russia off its knees' found sympathy with many.[54] He has also advocated provoking wars between different tribes and clans in order to 'annihilate' ethnic groups such as Azerbaijanis, Armenians, Tajiks, Uzbeks Turks, and others. If wars do not work, starvation might serve to rid the region of those who live off Russia.[55] Zhirinovsky is also known for his anti-Semitic

[50] *IHT*, 10 September 1993.

[51] 'Decree By Russian Federation President On Measures To Settle The Conflict On The Tajik-Afghan Border And Bring About A General Normalisation On The Borders Of The Russian Federation', 27 July 1993, RIA-Novosti, London.

[52] *Nezavisimaya Gazeta*, 22 April 1993, p. 2.

[53] See for example the comments of Grachev on Russia's Radio, 23 February 1993 in *Summary of World Broadcasts*, 25 February 1993, SU/1622 C1/6.

[54] Reported in Steven Erlanger, 'For Zhirinovsky, Rise Is Linked To Russia's Fall', *IHT*, 14 December 1993, p. 7.

[55] Comments reported in *RFE/RL Daily Report*, No. 241, 17 December 1993.

views, and has gone so far as to blame Jews for anti-Semitic provocations, this despite the fact that his father may well have been Jewish.[56] He has for some time been an advocate of the 'purity of the nation', in this case the Russian nation.[57]

Zhirinovsky is also intent on advocating grossly belligerent policies towards Russia's neighbours, professing intransigence towards the Japanese and the Kuril Island dispute, disdain towards Poland, impatience with Germany, and aspirations of reincorporating Finland and Alaska back into Russia. In one of his more alarming statements, Zhirinovsky suggested he would not be against the use of nuclear weapons on Germany and Japan if they aggravated Russia.[58]

Of gravest concern is the prospect that Zhirinovsky will win a presidential election in 1996. With strong presidential powers, complements of Yeltsin's newly approved constitution, this would be a nightmare scenario for the former Soviet republics. Zhirinovsky's power and influence have increased consistently over the past few years. In the 1990 presidential elections he came in third with 7.8 per cent of the vote. By December 1993 he received 22.79 per cent of votes cast (compared to 12.35 per cent for the Russian Communist Party; and 15.38 percent for Russia's Choice).[59] During his election campaign Zhirinovsky packed halls to standing-room only, while other candidates often could not even attract a few dozen people.[60] There is little to indicate that his popularity will decline. Indeed, Zhirinovsky is now in a position to sit back and play the 'loyal' parliamentary opposition. With an economy unlikely to improve over the next two years, the Liberal Democrats only stand to gain.

If Zhirinovsky gains power, he believes that at least 15 years of authoritarian rule will be necessary before democracy can be introduced to Russia. The security forces would assist in this process, and it would also be necessary to purge the communists.[61] All of this makes Zhirinovsky's brand of authoritarianism sound more like fascism. And he has left little doubt about the kinds of policies that he would pursue towards the former republics of the Soviet Union. What until now has been military intervention for geopolitical advantage could well turn into outright war if Zhirinovsky is as good as his word, and there are few reasons to doubt that he will be.

[56] Lee Hockstader, 'Ultranationalist Assails Jews For "Provocations" /, *IHT*, 15 December 1993, pp. 1–2. Of interest is the fact that Zhirinovsky visited far right-wing individuals in Germany and Austria less than two weeks after his election victory, leading to speculation that some of his funds and support may have come from these sources.

[57] *FBIS-CEA*, 30 April 1993, p. 32.

[58] Hockstader, 'Ultranationalist Assails'. Zhirinovsky's comments were recorded in an interview with a German radio station before the election.

[59] *The Economist*, 8–14 January 1994, p. 38. Due to the pecularities of the Russian voting system, Zhirinovsky's Liberal Democrats did *not* win a majority of seats in the new parliament. They came away with only 64 seats, compared to 70 for Russia's Choice.

[60] See for example, the report in Andrew Higgins, 'Nationalism: The Trump Card', *Independent On Sunday*, 19 December 1993, p. 11.

[61] *RFE/RL Daily Report*, No. 244, 22 December 1993.

## General Implications for Western Policy

In virtually all of the conflicts on the territory of the FSU there have been calls for the involvement of international organisations and outside states. Requests for assistance have been made to the CSCE, the UN, the Council of Europe, NATO, and specific countries such as the US, Turkey, and Ukraine.[62] In the majority of cases the motive is the same. There is grave dissatisfaction and suspicion about Russian involvement in regional conflicts, and international observers are desired as a counterweight to Russian military involvement (overt or otherwise).

What should the Western response to such requests be? Should Russia be allowed a free hand when it comes to intervening in regions of the FSU? Is there anything the West can do to contain the 'Zhirinovsky factor'? Should international organisations play a greater role in order to reduce Russia's potentially hegemonic aspirations? Is there a rationale for Western diplomatic or military intervention in the FSU? Should there be involvement to maintain some consistency in international diplomacy, by not excluding the FSU from humanitarian assistance? Should the West try to prevent a 'Yugoslavia writ large' in the FSU? What is desirable and, perhaps more important, what is practical? There is no simple answer to these questions, nor is this the place for a detailed discussion of Western policy. However, it should be said that despite several self-interested requests for UN observers, Russia's general response to any intended Western military intervention in the FSU is likely to be negative. This is all the more so since Zhirinovsky's election success.

This was demonstrated as early as August 1993 when the Clinton administration indicated that it would be adopting a seemingly new approach to conflicts in the FSU. 'Directive 13' argued that US policy should involve more active diplomatic initiatives and would not rule out the participation of US troops in UN peace-keeping missions in conflict regions of the FSU. (The Bush administration's policy had been to hold the FSU at arm's length on the issue of diplomatic and humanitarian intervention.) The response from Moscow was immediately hostile, especially from conservatives, the parliament and the military. By the end of the

---

[62] As examples, Armenia and Azerbaijan for some time requested international involvement in the conflict over Nagorno-Karabakh, and the CSCE is currently engaged. In Georgia, Shevardnadze made repeated calls for the involvement of the UN, the CSCE, the Council of Europe, and NATO in the conflict over Abkhazia. Moldova has also asked on numerous occasions for intervention by the CSCE, UN, NATO, and the US to assist in the withdrawal of the 14th Army. In the Baltics there have been various requests for international observers to monitor the negotiations on the status of Russian troops and their actual withdrawal, as well as involvement in negotiations over a border dispute between Estonia and Russia. Russia too has requested observers in Estonia to monitor human rights violations against Russians, and on one occasion at least has requested UN peace-keepers in Abkhazia. The UN and/or CSCE have indicated a willingness to commit (or have already committed) observer missions to Moldova, Tajikistan, the Baltics, and Abkhazia.

month the US backed away from its original policy directive, emphasising in particular that the US would not intervene unless the UN or CSCE were involved, and that aid *would not* be made conditional upon Russian policy or behaviour towards any other states in the FSU.[63] In large part this exchange was a tacit acknowledgement of Russia's Monroe Doctrine and its right to an emerging sphere of influence.

However, if Zhirinovsky continues to expand his powerbase, these nuances of diplomacy will seem trivial compared to the threat which may emerge from this quarter. If this unfortunate scenario materialises Russia's Monroe Doctrine will very likely fall by the wayside, replaced by an overtly aggressive policy of intervention in the FSU and possibly further afield. Thus it may not be too soon for the West to reevaluate its acquiescence to Russia's military intervention in the 'near abroad', and suggest more international solutions to the instability and bloodshed which plague the regions of the FSU.

## Conclusion

A benign interpretation of Russia's Monroe Doctrine is that Russia is simply doing what great regional powers do, that is, taking advantage of weak states in its direct vicinity in order to use these states to the utmost advantage of Russia itself, militarily, politically, and economically. Carving out a sphere of influence in this manner also defines the parameters of military intervention. Intervention will take place when and where it serves Russia's national interests (as defined earlier in the paper).

But is there a more alarming interpretation of the Russian Monroe Doctrine? Will the country seek ever greater advantage by securing influence in the regions of the FSU, with the ultimate aim of reconstituting the boundaries of the USSR. Certainly some such as former Vice President Aleksandr Rutskoi and the former parliamentary speaker Ruslan Khasbulatov believed so. And Zhironovsky has given every indication that he intends to promote as belligerent a policy as possible towards the new states of the FSU. Given the unpredictability of Russian politics, one cannot exclude the possibility that today's strategic advantage is tomorrow's neo-imperialism, or even neo-fascism.

---

[63]  *IHT*, 6 August and 30 August 1993.

174

# SECURITY CHALLENGES IN POST-COMMUNIST EUROPE

## PAUL HIRST*

THE security situation in Europe has obviously changed out of all recognition since the collapse of Communism that began in 1989. The principal change is that economic issues have taken precedence over military ones. Up until 1989 the key issue remained the division of the continent into East and West. As the Second Cold War thawed, policy shifted from the need to contain the Soviet Union to the aim of reducing the military confrontation between the two armed blocs of NATO and the Warsaw Pact. Now the most advanced post-Communist states—the Czech Republic, Hungary, Poland and Slovenia—are predominantly concerned with economic reconstruction and with seeking support from eventual membership of the European Union. Neutral states like Austria, Finland and Sweden face a fundamental re-appraisal with the demise of the blocs, the development of major domestic economic problems, and the objective of European Union membership in the near future. Thus the future of European security can best be considered by concentrating on the policy of the European Union as it defines its relations with the rest of Europe. These relations are predominantly economic, and it is the pace of the Union's own political and economic integration that will define the security situation in the next two decades.

The European Union will not become a super-state and it is unlikely to possess its own supra-national military forces for the foreseeable future. It has, however, become the primary focus for member nations in approaching their relations with the rest of the continent and the wider world. In this respect and because of the primacy of economic issues in external policy, the European Union is far more important than any of the possible frameworks for the regularisation of the military aspects of security, such as NATO or the WEU. The European Union's member nations have overwhelmingly military and economic superiority over their immediate neighbours. The major external powers, who once structured the affairs of the continent, are now either gravely weakened and removed from direct presence in Central Europe, as is the case with Russia, or are in process of military disengagement and in potential economic conflict with the Union, as is the case with the USA. Western Europe enjoys a degree of security without parallel in this century, it is threatened neither by external enemies

* Paul Hirst is Professor of Social Theory at Birkbeck College, University of London. Author of *After Thatcher* (1989), *Representative Democracy and its Limits* (1990) and editor of *The Pluralist Theory of the State: Selected Writings of G. D. H. Cole, J. N. Figgis and H. J. Laski* (1989). Member of the editorial board of *The Political Quarterly*.

nor by the possibility of internal inter-state armed conflicts. However, it faces a complex variety of economic, social and low-level security threats that are serious and, if not addressed, could present significant problems for the European Union. The danger is that they will not be effectively addressed because they do not have the compelling necessity of an overriding external threat. Western European nations may exploit their immunity from military threat to evade their responsibilities and the absence of a unifying external threat may slow the pace of European integration, leading to an intensification of conflicts between national policies and to an inability for coherent action in relation to the economic and social problems of the countries on the periphery of the Union.

The collapse of Communism is clearly an immense benefit to the whole of Europe. The ex-Soviet world offers the western European nations investment opportunities and potential markets that could, if decisively exploited, launch it and its neighbours into a period of sustained boom similar to 1945–1973. The collapse also poses a very real challenge, because it has removed the vital impetus to unity and integration provided by the Soviet threat. The Union has lost an enemy that provided it with much of its political identity and rationale, and it is now faced with the problem of finding an effective source for identification with and legitimation of the European project. Severe recession has compounded this problem. It is forcing the member nations of the Union to compete economically and is revealing divergent interests. It has shown the fallacy of the technocratic conception of European unity, in which economic development and integration would inevitably create the conditions for political integration. Now it is clear that the strengthening of central political institutions and the building of legitimacy for them is a condition for effective economic policies that restore prosperity, and that the Union's economic progress is closely tied up with the success of its neighbours in Eastern and Central Europe in reconstructing their economies.

## Europe: The Cold War and After

It would be foolish to ignore the extent to which the European Union was a product of the Cold War and that the ending of that conflict poses problems for it as well as advantages. The European Community was never coterminous with NATO, it included neutrals like Ireland and military independents like France, but it has been inescapably structured by the division of the continent that began at Yalta. It is worth beginning our discussion by characterising the fundamental features of the period 1945–1989 and then trying to assess those of the subsequent state of affairs.

It is an obvious fact that after 1945 the position of Western Europe was defined above all by the Cold War. It is now easy to forget how rigidly and radically the continent was divided. The Western powers, hitherto enemies, became allies—united by a common and overwhelming threat. The societies of Central and Eastern Europe became members of an enemy bloc, and virtually passed out of normal political and economic contact for decades. These societies hardly had an independent existence, and were primarily appendages of Soviet policy. Western Europe's security was defined by a single major threat, the possibility of a war with the Soviet Union along a common land frontier. Europeans recognised that their fate in this respect would be determined externally, as a function of a crisis between the Soviet Union and the USA. Europe's armed forces were organised to fight a war in Germany. It was a war that most politicians knew to be a remote contingency, but one that threatened to devastate the continent should it occur. The very scale of the threat and its consequences ensured that it was more apparent than real. The risk of mutual extinction, understood in a primitive way on both sides, paralysed both of the Superpowers from too active and too direct a confrontation. Europe was lucky that the leaders of its external hegemonic powers were possessed of at least minimal rationality, that the various Superpower crises resolved themselves, and that the need for dialogue and *rapprochement* constantly reasserted itself.

Thus the Western European countries gained in many ways from the Cold War despite the threat of disaster should it turn hot. Above all they enjoyed a unity imposed on them by an enemy who was too serious to be ignored but who it was unlikely they would ever actually have to fight. The threat of the Soviet Union and of domestic Communist takeovers in the immediate post-1945 period led to large-scale US economic aid to Western Europe as part of a strategy of political containment. Marshall Aid may not have been decisive in European recovery, but it certainly contributed to it. Throughout the Cold War the USA provided a significant portion of the forces and much of the military infrastructure for Europe's defence. This allowed most European states to spend a relatively low percentage of GDP on the military, and undoubtedly contributed to domestic economic growth in consequence. The massive threat just across the border hastened and deepened the Franco-German reconciliation that was the core of the European Community. The Soviet threat and American leadership of the Atlantic Alliance made it easier for European states to see what they had in common and facilitated the process of the surrender of their national sovereignties in the course of the integration of the Community and the growth of its powers. Union was possible without 'blood and iron', something very rare in the construction of larger political entities. From having been for centuries a hotbed of conflict, Western Europe became one of the most stable and peaceful regions in the world. In this Cold War regime, most European states became accustomed to peace and accepted US military hegemony. They either ceased to have experience of fighting or were constitutionally prevented from acting except in self-defence, as was the case with West Germany. During the

Cold War there could be no question of military intervention elsewhere in Europe, short of starting World War Three. Western Europeans may in retrospect see this period nostalgically as one in which politics were simplified and the concord of their national states assured by a common external threat.

From the signing of the Treaty of Rome until the collapse of Communism the Community enjoyed two other fundamental characteristics that ensured its political stability and coherence. The first was prosperity. Most member states of the European Union have enjoyed relatively rapid growth in national wealth since the 1950s, with brief recessions, and have been able to return to growth despite severe external shocks such as the oil price hikes of 1973 and 1979. Some, like Italy and Spain, have gone from relative industrial backwardness to advanced nation status as a result of Community membership. The second, closely connected with the first, is political homogeneity. Politics has been dominated by centrist parties since the 1950s, with the extremes of left and right being politically contained and excluded from government. This homogeneity of the main political actors, most being either Christian Democrats or Social Democrats committed to pragmatism, a market economy, and social welfare, facilitated the inter-governmental accommodations that were central in creating and developing the Community. Politicians enjoyed high autonomy from their national publics in Community policy-making because prosperity allowed social conflicts to be contained or bought off, even if at immense cost (as with the CAP). Western Europe's homogeneity was historical and contingent, it depended on the utter discrediting and defeat of Fascism and on the identification of Communism with an external threat. It was, however, real, unlike the false uniformity imposed in the Soviet satellite states by political repression and ideological indoctrination.

Each of these fundamental features has changed since 1989. The continent is no longer divided militarily and there is no hegemonic power in the East. Russia is penned-up, immured in the east behind Belarus and the Ukraine. Neither of the latter states, nor Poland, nor any lesser power could credibly threaten Eastern Europe. The military strength of the Union's states is unassailable in Europe. There is no no need for US forces to be stationed in Western Europe for the purpose of its defence. However, if the military division of Europe has vanished, the Continent remains as divided as ever. A GDP *per capita* curtain has replaced the old frontier. The gulf in wealth and living standards between the core states of the Union and the ex-Soviet world is vast. For example, Poland's GDP *per capita* is less than a sixth of that of Germany's. The economic conditions in most ex-Soviet states are intolerable, not least because they have highly educated populations accustomed to living in industrialised and urbanised societies. These populations have been sustained by the hope that the destruction of the command economy would lead to a rapid increase in prosperity. With the possible exceptions of the Czech Republic and

178

© The Political Quarterly Publishing Co. Ltd. 1994.

Slovenia, they are likely to be substantially disappointed. The ex-satellite and post-Communist states of Eastern and Central Europe have few options but to struggle on trying to convert to market economies. This seems to be the case even when ex-Communist-based parties return to power, as in Poland. The immediate neighbours of the Union—the Czech Republic, Hungary, Poland and Slovenia—are all desperate to develop trade with it and ultimately to join it. In these countries, the consequences of slow economic adaptations are likely to be domestic political and social conflict, rather than inter-state violence requiring Western military intervention.

The other post-Communist and ex-Soviet states pose no direct threat to the European Union and are unlikely to lead it to large-scale military intervention in local inter-state conflicts and internal crisis.

## Why Western States will Avoid Military Intervention

Some advocates of military intervention by the Western powers in the former Yugoslavia have argued that inaction is short-sighted and contrary to the longer-term interests of those powers. The claim is that the existing Balkan conflicts carelessly neglected may lead on to wider wars. This is to see current events in the light of the situation leading up to 1914. But the analogy is far from apt. Then both Austria-Hungary and Russia had what they perceived to be vital and conflicting interests in the region. Now the states of Western Europe have no fundamental interests in the region. Despite the horrors of the war in Croatia and Bosnia, and deplorable as the West's failure to protect human rights may be, the fact remains that the dismemberment of Bosnia and the rise of a Greater Serbia poses no serious threat to any of the Western European states. The Balkans have no vital economic significance to the Union and are, after the end of the Cold War, of no great strategic consequence. The same is true of Russia's interests in the Balkans, Slavophile posturing by elements of the Opposition aside. There is little likelihood that the major powers in Eastern and Western Europe will take sides and clash over the Balkans.

Greece is the one member of the European Union with a direct interest in the region. Even then, its concerns are more symbolic than economic and strategic. Greece has experienced the rise of the ugliest and most intransigent ultra-nationalism over the Macedonian question, and this position is common across the political spectrum. Greek interests in this matter are divergent from those of the rest of the Union. The most dangerous possible outcome would be a serious conflict between Greece and Turkey over the Balkan crisis, inflamed by long-standing differences over the Aegean and Cyprus. Both are members of NATO, Greece is a member and Turkey a potential member of the European Union. Undoubtedly the EU and the USA would put intense pressure on both states to prevent an open clash, both having a great deal to lose

179

economically if they were to refuse mediation. Greece, moreover, would almost certainly be defeated if it came to war. But, in the extremely unlikely event that war were to happen, the major powers would not actively intervene. Britain did nothing during the Turkish invasion of Cyprus, and that is likely to be the model for the response of the Western powers to further Balkan wars.

In the case of conflicts on the periphery of Russia, Western interests were even less salient than in the Balkans. The EU and the USA have little option but to concede Russia's primacy of interest in its 'Near Abroad'. The Western powers might as well accept Russia's version of the Monroe Doctrine in this area. Neither the EU nor the USA will challenge Russia over conflicts in Central Asia, especially when ethnic Russians are under threat. The loss of Russian goodwill would be too great a price. Russia, although in economic crisis, remains a formidable military power. It can also obstruct Western policy elsewhere in the world were it to use its Security Council veto. In the case of a serious clash between Russia and the Ukraine, the West would presumably offer mediation and press the threat of such economic sanctions as it could apply. Should it go beyond sparring to armed conflict, the Western powers would remain horrified spectators. Giving military guarantees to Belarus, the Ukraine, the Baltics, Georgia, or any other state on Russia's periphery would be an act of utter folly, as would building a greater Europe in the East by letting the Czechs, Hungarians, and Poles join NATO. This would threaten the Russians and make them insecure, pushing them towards hostility through fear of encirclement. Better to assist and appease Russia, cajoling it into being a better neighbour rather than deterring it from being an enemy. At best, therefore, Western troops may be required for peace-keeping missions in the former Soviet world and only with Russian agreement.

Thus, the odds against the European Union's states intervening militarily and on a large scale in any local conflict in the ex-Communist countries are very great indeed. Had Bosnia's integrity been of vital interest to enough of the Union's states then the odds are that the Serbs would have been intimidated by a massive show of force early on. The conflict in the former Yugoslavia has exposed the very real divisions between the member states of the Union on foreign policy issues. The collapse of Communism has exacerbated those divisions by lessening the risks of independent national policies; and yet the illusion of common action has made no state truly responsible for the outcome of the Union's initiatives. Germany played a decisive role in pushing the recognition of Slovenia, Croatia and Bosnia and yet is constitutionally incapable of guaranteeing their sovereignty. A truly common foreign and security policy is a long way off. Even then, the likelihood of a majority of member states actively intervening in a purely local conflict is small; such conflicts will seldom directly impinge on more than one member.

The Bosnian Muslims have suffered, as do most of the conflict zones in the Third World, from the fact the advanced countries are more and more absorbed in their own affairs. They no longer have to fear Communist advances and to contain hostile revolutionary forces in conflicts by proxy. Western, and particularly US, intervention has in the past helped to create many of the worst of those conflicts, from supporting UNITA in Angola to funding Pol Pot after his expulsion by the Vietnamese. They are now mostly messy conflicts without sponsors and have degenerated into being just bad news on the TV for most Western citizens. The interests of the advanced world's states are overridingly economic and the bulk of world trade is conducted between these states themselves, overwhelmingly within the triad of the European Union, Japan and North America. Oil is the only exception to this self-absorption. The massive Western intervention in the Gulf was not unconnected with the need to secure the oilfields of Kuwait and Saudi Arabia against Saddam Hussain. Slobodan Milosevic poses no comparable threat, and a greater Serbia is a power in a region of minimal economic interest to the Western powers. I am not making this point as opposition to the Gulf War, or because I am indifferent to the fate of the Bosnian population who do not want to be part of a greater Serbia. The point is that one is obliged to consider how the advanced states do and will behave, not how in conscience one would wish them to act.

It is naive to imagine that Western states will commit vast resources and face the death of many of their soldiers when neither their territorial integrity nor their vital external economic interests are at stake. Western states are above all concerned with economic issues, since material prosperity is the dominant concern of the bulk of their populations. Moreover, as they are democracies their leaders have to justify large-scale military intervention to the voters. The threat of large numbers of sons and daughters dying in foreign countries the existence of which most citizens are hardly aware does not appeal to elected politicians.

To many Western citizens with an altruistic and justified concern for human rights, basing foreign policy upon economic interests appears nothing less than sordid. But such interests are a necessary core of external policy in states whose citizens' primary concerns are economic. They can be perfectly legitimate, provided they involve no unjustified seizure of the resources of others. Economic interests have one great advantage, they limit the causes of wars and large-scale military interventions to circumstances where such interests or assets are actually threatened and thus impose a degree of rationality on the use of force. It is by no means inherently immoral or unreasonable for states to go to war in defence of legitimate economic interests. States have the right, for example, to defend the world free trading order against authoritarian regional powers annexing wealth by force. In doing so they will use the traditional grounds of international law, the defence of the sovereignty and integrity of states and the preservation of international agreements. But they will do so only in cases of violations of those principles central to their own interests. War for oil sounded obscene to the opponents of the Gulf War in the West. Yet the defence of economic interests is a legitimate *casus belli*, particularly when compared with the main causes of war in the modern world—the aim of ethnic homogeneity, religious fanaticism or dictatorial ambition. Economically motivated war is limited in its aims and governed by a calculus of the proportionality of costs to benefits. For this reason, such interests must be vital before liberal states with democratically account-able governments will commit themselves to war on economic grounds.

On the other hand, going to war to defend human rights—while apparently easier to justify in moral terms—is by no means unproblematic. Western publics as a whole are not yet ready to impose the new inter-national law of human rights, and they will only give sanction to the old international law of the sovereignty and territorial integrity of states when some other major national interest compels them to do so. Of course, it would be better if the international community could act to prevent horrors like Pol Pot's seizure of power in Cambodia or the rape of East Timor. One doubts, however, that a Western crusade to secure and defend human rights in the rest of the world would not founder on the inevitable ambiguities of military intervention. The unsettling experience of Somalia is all-too-likely to be the norm in such a new world order.

To say this is not to abandon all hope of the protection of human rights. To begin with Western States can best do it by *not* intervening to arm factions and give political forces the capacity to prolong civil wars. The disasters of Angola and Afghanistan are all-too-evident arguments for doing nothing, not actively intervening in local conflicts and civil wars in the future. Western states can achieve more by judicious economic aid and economic sanctions than they can by armed force in most cases. Western direct economic aid is well below the levels deemed the barest minimum by the UN.

### Prosperity and Security—East and West

The second fundamental feature of the period from 1945 to 1989—economic prosperity—may also be changing. Europe's growth and prosperity are by no means assured. This is not just for conjunctural reasons connected with the current depression. Europe's long-term growth rates and capacities for technical innovation are slowing. The political settlements that have underpinned the national production systems of key areas like Western Germany and Northern and Central Italy are failing and are threatening to undermine those systems them-selves. The Community's policy makers staked a great deal on the boost to growth provided by the creation of the Single European Market and the processes of economic and political union that were its essential accom-paniments. It looks like calculations of the benefits of the Single Market were profoundly wrong and that a more activist economic policy than monetary union is required to create both a coherent economic zone and

182

acceptable rates of growth and employment. The difficulties in ratifying the Maastricht Treaty, the improbability of its provisions for monetary union in the current economic crisis, and the virtual collapse of the ERM show that integration in economic policy is if anything going backwards. National states are edging toward competitive macro-economic policies, such as competitive devaluations and the poaching of inward direct investment.

Most ex-Communist states would be glad to enjoy the Union's problems. It remains a fact that none of those states (with the possible exception of the Czechs) will be able to join the Union for the foreseeable future, their GDP *per capita* simply will not let them conform to common Union standards. Greece, Portugal and Spain entered when the European Community was a much less integrated entity, they enjoyed substantial regional development funds, and they benefited from a period of Western European economic growth. The ex-Communist states are standing at the door at a time of severe recession. Further, if the 'neutrals' (Austria, Finland and Sweden) are to join in the near future they will dilute the political mechanisms of the EU at the very moment when they are faltering. Those political forces most opposed to European integration, a sizeable chunk of the Conservative Party being chief among them, wish to admit the Central and East European states as fast as possible, in effect diluting the Union into a free-trade area. This is by no means in the long-term interests of the ex-Communist states, unless they wish to remain low-wage appendages of the richer states.

The third fundamental feature of the period up to 1989, political homogeneity, is also under severe threat. This threat is principally from the Far Right and it is the more serious because these political forces are aided by two objective features of the current situation. The collapse of Communism and demographic pressure in Africa threaten the advanced states with the steady pressure of migrants driven by political turbulence and economic hardship. The ageing and economically stagnating societies of the EU are increasingly unwilling to admit large numbers of migrants. Migration is particularly explosive given the very large numbers of unemployed in the EU and the fear that migrants will accept jobs at wages Western Europeans are unwilling to consider. That migrants might be a source of economic growth is generally discounted. The Far Right is willing to exploit the issue of migration and put pressure on immigrant communities within the Union. It is unlikely to take political power, but its main effect is to drive the parties of the Centre-Right that do have power to compete with it in cracking down on migrants. The Right is also able to define economic policy in nationalist terms, promoting competition with other member states and favouring protection against non-EC competitors. Faced with large quantities of cheap food from Eastern Europe and highly competitive manufactured goods from the Pacific Rim, the farmers and industrial workers of Western Europe may see protection as a salvation. That this is a retreat from effective competition into subsidies and tariffs will seem a less than convincing argument if Europe is failing to compete and to grow. In this sense the Right has real issues that it can exploit and which the centrist political forces have found few means of addressing in terms other than those the Right proposes.

The only way to tackle these issues of migration and protectionism that the Right can exploit so well is to find policies that restore full employment and promote competitive performance. The EU is missing a golden opportunity to restore prosperity. Whereas none of the member states is a large enough economic entity to follow an expansionary policy, the EU has the resources and the scale to pursue a quasi-Keynesian strategy of internal reflation linked to external aid. This would only work if it did not simply boost domestic consumer demand and public spending, which would rapidly lead to budgetary and trade deficits of the kind spawned by Reaganomics. A large-scale programme of aid and specifically long-term trade credits and capital grants for the renewal of capital goods and infrastructure targeted at Central and Eastern Europe would have the combined effect of boosting effective demand in the post-Communist countries and exports and employment in the Union. Falling unemployment in the Union would reduce social costs and budgetary deficits, promoting domestic consumption.

Both halves of the continent would benefit from such a 'Euro-Keynesian' policy. Eastern Europe is a reservoir of frustrated demand, which (if it could be converted into effective demand) would offer vast markets to European producers. Western Europe has significant levels of over-capacity in a wide range of industries, particularly in heavy capital goods and motor vehicles. A means of linking Eastern frustrated demand to Western excess supply could well inaugurate a period of prosperity. Eastern Europe generally has a serious capital shortage that prevents the formation of new enterprises, or the restructuring of old ones. It is unlikely that private capital will invest on the scale required to turn such societies around, the risks and uncertainties are too great. Eastern Europe generally has a chronic foreign exchange shortage that prevents the acquisition of foreign machinery and other capital goods. Targeted trade credits would ensure that such boosting of effective demand was sourced in Western Europe.

By boosting employment and output in the West, trade credits would also facilitate exports from the East. In a period of stagnant demand and high unemployment, there is great resistance to imports from the East in the EU. Promoting effective demand in this way would do a great deal to reduce social conflicts in Eastern Europe and to facilitate the more rapid integration of these countries into the EU. A new trading system of this Euro-Keynesian kind would undercut pressures for protection, since it would promote domestic output and it would mitigate pressures for migration, providing the peoples of Eastern Europe with hope that they can prosper and find work in their own states. One cannot be sure that such a large-scale programme would work in the absence of appropriate

184

structural transformation in the domestic economies of Eastern European countries. In all likelihood it would make a material difference in the Czech Republic, Hungary and Poland. In Russia the question of whether aid can facilitate transformation is open, but to do nothing will make the situation worse. Moreover the immediate benefits of such aid to the West would be real. Even if much of the aid to Russia were 'wasted' it would have the same effect as Keynes' only half ironic advocacy of buying money and have the unemployed dig it up.

Jacques Delors wanted to launch a modest version of such a programme. He was refused the expansion of the EU's central budget that was necessary to facilitate it. Only if the EU makes rapid progress in political integration could it devise a coherent economic policy of this kind and have the legitimacy to implement it. That it would benefit EU citizens is irrelevant, the member states could not agree upon and coordinate such an ambitious programme in the absence of stronger central structures in the EU and a far greater common budget under central control. The EU is unlikely to make such political progress in the near future. It is faced, if anything, with greater fragmentation and competition between the national states. The problem, moreover, of the wider political sources of support for such a programme seems almost insuperable. In many states, Italy being the most glaring example, the electorate has lost confidence in the traditional political parties and what they can accomplish. Nationalist, local and single issue organisations are growing in political strength throughout the Union. The Northern League, for example, is unlikely to support an ambitious programme of aid for Eastern Europe if it is unwilling to subsidise Southern Italy.

Eastern Europe is not the only peripheral region of the EU that raises security issues. The southern Mediterranean littoral, Syria, Egypt and Algeria, are all threatened by rapid population growth, a failure of economic development to keep pace with this growth, and large-scale unemployment. Coupled with this the rise of political Islam in Egypt and Algeria in particular is feeding off popular discontent and the perception that integration into Western markets has led to nothing but poverty and gross inequality. The consequences of rapidly growing populations, where the majority are under twenty, are combined pressures to migration and to religious fanaticism. In no case can the regimes be regarded as strong enough to contain the political pressures or competent enough to address the economic problems. The threat to secular regimes and open societies in this region is too serious to ignore. It cannot be coped with by military means and is potentially far more serious than any of the problems posed by the post-Communist world for Europe. Add to it large numbers of migrants and residents from North Africa in Western Europe, and particularly France, and one has the makings of an explosive situation. This will be particularly so if conservative governments are restricting migration and discriminating against current residents. Europe will pay dearly if it neglects this issue, if it follows an illiberal course with migrant

185

communities, and if it fails to make every effort to sustain secular regimes and open societies by greater economic aid.

The European Union is faced with an historic opportunity by the collapse of Communism. It has two basic courses of action open to it. To carry on as at present, that is, to do very little to address the problems of its own political unity, to neglect Eastern Europe, and to ignore the Southern littoral. The odds are that political and economic union will stall until at least the end of the century. There is likely to be no more than a moderate recovery from the slump, growth rates will remain low and levels of spending high. The EU will remain profoundly cautious in its external policy. The alternative is to follow the combined policy of deepening political and economic integration and large-scale economic aid both to Eastern Europe and to the southern Mediterranean littoral. The result of promoting full employment through a 'Euro-Keynesian' policy would be to reduce social and inter-country strains within the EU and to promote economic development and prosperity in its neighbours, thus reducing their own internal conflicts and any tendency toward external conflict with the Union. The promotion of prosperity remains the best security policy, Such a policy would enable the EU to weld the greater part of Europe into one coordinated trade bloc, larger than NAFTA. This would strengthen its hand in dealing with the other two major blocs.

## Security and the Future of the European Union

Such a radical policy departure is no more than a remote possibility.[1] Lack of credible political forces to sponsor it dooms it to irrelevance. It has value, however, in showing that Europe is not inevitably trapped into its present impasse. Doing nothing about the economic and social conditions of its neighbours is simply not an option. A European Union that is surrounded by failing economies that can do nothing to counter its own tendency toward stagnation, that has an ageing population and low birth rates but refuses to accept migrants from surrounding countries, that will find it difficult to maintain its current international competitiveness in a world free trade system, and that has no hope to offer its neighbours, cannot be secure in the long-run. The EU will be encircled by poverty and political failure, whilst offering no lead and little material help. Western Europe would remain able to bomb its opponents into the stone age, but it will not be threatened by invading armies. Security has many other dimensions than military force or war. Multiple economic, political and low-level security problems will breed a self-defeating 'fortress Europe' mentality.

[1]  For a developed outline of such a policy see P. Hirst and G. Thompson, '"The Problem of Globalisation": international economic relations, national economic management and the formation of trading blocs', *Economy and Society*, Vol. 21, No. 4, November 1992, pp. 357–96.

186

The one great exception to this analysis is the future of Russia. It is evident to all that the present situation is unsustainable. The Russian economy has not effected a transition to a viable market economy, output and living standards are still falling. The introduction of market relations has not favoured new investment or resulted in a more efficient allocation of resources, at best it has benefited merchants not manufacturers and at worst it enriches gangsters. The Russian birthrate has fallen below replacement levels, and Russians are now paranoid about competition from minority peoples within the Russian Republic as well as the fast-growing populations of Muslim Central Asia. The political system lacks the capacity to administer in this crisis or to ensure legitimacy for the new order. A weak 'civil society', that is, social fragmentation and the absence of strong independent secondary associations, leads to weak, unstable and numerous political parties and, therefore, to no stable link between social forces and the regime. Russia, once the classic example of strongly authoritarian government, both Tsarist and Communist, now has a 'weak state' more typical of Latin American democracies. The state has neither a high degree of autonomy *vis-à-vis* society, as did the Communist autocracy, nor is it a stable regime based upon powerful social forces. The state is faced, moreover, with serious peripheral conflicts and the difficult task of protecting minority Russian populations in the ex-Soviet republics.

No sensible person would predict what is going to happen. However, it is worth cautiously entertaining the worst scenario, short of complete anarchy and the falling of the Russian nuclear arsenal into the hands of the highest bidders, and assessing the consequences for European security. One possible outcome of the current crisis might be the fall of the democratic, market-oriented government and its replacement by a Great Russian nationalist regime.[2] Nationalism and economic conservatism might stem current discontents, directing anger outwards, and buy-off the numerous losers in the new economic order with guaranteed prices and subsidies. This regime could best be called a 'Red-White' coalition based upon conservatives in the Army and the Church, upon ultra-nationalists and the remnants of the Communist Party. This neo-Slavophile regime would be the most unlikely to enter into direct confrontation with the West: it would be bankrupt, it would share no common land frontier, and it would have conflicts near enough at hand. It would squeeze the Baltics economically, although it would be unlikely to provoke a full-scale crisis with the West re-annexing them. It would be a bad neighbour to its western neighbours Belarus and the Ukraine, constantly squabbling with them over economic issues and the rights of ethnic Russians. It might very well be further embroiled in shooting wars in Central Asia than is the present government. It would not be like the old Soviet Union, but concerned above all with Eurasian rather than world affairs. In short, it would be

---

[2]  This was written before the Russian elections of December 1993 and the success of Mr Zhirinovsky's Liberal Democrats.

containable, well short of large-scale re-armament in Europe and a return to the Cold War.

We should not assume that the Yeltsin regime will not be driven into some of these actions by necessity or to stave-off conservative political success. For example, it is possible that Russia might be forced to intervene should the Ukraine collapse into civil strife, the predominantly Russian populations of its eastern industrial zones revolting against economic failure. The West should do no more in these circumstances than act as a honest broker, seeking to prevent war and acting to support the populations of the western part of the Ukraine in retaining their independence.

Europe's security is best sought, not through military intervention, but through economic partnership with its neighbours to aid their social reconstruction. Europe would benefit from measures to restore its growth rate, employment levels, and, therefore, economic power, measures directly connected to aiding its neighbours. It would benefit greatly, given a reduction in unemployment and a restoration of growth, from allowing a steady flow of migrants into Europe and ensuring their security once there.

Military and security issues would remain, even if socio-economic policies aimed at reducing threats were successful. Even allowing for a substantial measure of migration the EU would still require strict frontier controls and the policing of immigration quotas. The supply of economic migrants fleeing wretched conditions throughout the world is inexhaustible. Italy and Spain are serious weak points for illegal entry. Even a liberal policy toward migrants would require Europe to put far greater resources into border security. The Union's states also need to create more mobile and professional military forces capable of external intervention if need be, and to switch away from conscript armies. Many of the conscript forces are little better than militias and are unfitted for demanding roles like supporting the UN relief effort in Bosnia. Had the EU wanted to intervene effectively to keep the peace in Bosnia, rather than to engage in the gesture politics of bombing the Serbs, it would have been faced with a serious shortage of fully-trained soldiers. Lastly, the European Union continues to depend for a great deal of its extra-European security upon the USA. It could not, for example, have defeated Iraq or led the coalition against Saddam Hussein. European nations played at best a secondary role. The EU, like Japan, relies on the USA for the defence of the world free trade order against regional powers that threaten vital Western economic interests. It continues to rely on the US for its nuclear deterrence. Europe's nuclear arsenals are either ultimately dependent on the USA, like Britain's, or still too weak credibly to confront a power like Russia, as with France's. Lastly, although Europe as a whole would benefit from a trade war with Japan (Japan having a vast positive trade balance), the same is not true of its relation to the USA and so the EU needs to be cautious in following protectionist policies. The European Union may be without rival in Europe, but in world terms it needs to remain on good relations with the USA and cultivate the Atlantic Alliance, even though the Soviet threat that brought the alliance into being has disappeared.

The European Union is quite unlike the states of the old pre-1945 Europe. The ensuing half-century of peace and prosperity has changed the outlook of Western Europe's politicians and citizens alike. They have no interest in war or territorial expansion, and are reluctant to intervene militarily even for active peace-keeping. This is a positive change for which we should be grateful. Western Europe has no desire aggressively to exploit the situation created by the collapse of Communism, pushing its military frontier eastwards at the expense of Russia. The problem is now the reverse of bellicosity, the passivity and economic self-absorption of the states of the European Union. This has led to a failure actively to engage with the economic and social problems of Eastern Europe on the scale that they require. If Western Europe is to enjoy military security and social stability in the longer term it has to provide a measure of economic security and hope for its eastern neighbours now. This lesson needs to be learnt rapidly, that mutual prosperity is the key to security, and that economic action now will obviate the possibility of military action in the future.

# INDEX

Abkhazia, 162, 163, 165, 168, 173n
Action Council for Peace in the Balkans, 52
Afghanistan, 67, 182
Ahtisaari, Marrti, 23
Akehurst, Sir John, 102
Albania, 43, 65
Algeria, 185
Alton, David, 100
Ambartsumov, Evgenii, 158
Angola, 40, 72, 144, 182
Armenia, 4, 160, 161, 165n, 168, 171, 173n
Ashdown, Paddy, 100
Aspin, Les, 171
Atlantic Alliance, 106, 121, 130, 146, 147, 177, 189
Austria, 175, 183
Azerbaijan, 4, 72, 165, 168, 170, 173n

Badinter Commission, 16, 48
Bahr, Egon, 134
Baker, James, 22n, 48, 118
Balladur, Edouard, 123, 124n
Baltic States, 156n, 169, 173n, 180, 187
Barre, Raymond, 117
Barrot, J., 120n
Bashkorostan, 167, 169
Basic Law (Germany), 128, 129, 134
Baumel, Jacques, 121n
Beek, A. L. ter, 152
Belarus, 163, 178, 180, 187
Besse, Colonel, 123n
Biermann, Wolf, 128
Bosnia, 22, 24, 25, 26, 33, 41, 42, 43, 46, 60–7 *passim*, 72–3, 129, 179; EC and, 16, 29, 48, 180, 188; France and, 111–21; NATO and, 30; Netherlands and, 144, 147, 153; Russia and, 161, 167; UK and, 49, 59, 94, 96, 99–104; USA and, 32, 91
Boucheron, J-M., 121n
Boutros-Ghali, Boutros, 18, 20, 47, 51
Briquemont, Francis, 52

Broeck, Hans van der, 48, 148, 149n, 152
Bruckner, Pascal, 116, 119n
Brussels Treaty (1948), 146
Bulgaria, 43, 163
Bush, George, 38, 78, 84, 85, 86, 87, 89, 90

Cambadelis, 120n
Cambodia, 40, 51, 99, 129, 144, 150, 182
Canada, 52, 144, 145
Carrington, Peter, Baron, 16, 20, 48, 53
Castlereagh, Robert Stewart, Viscount, 35
Central America, 39, 92–3
Central Asia, 160, 180, 187
Centre for the Prevention of Conflict, 47
Chad, 139
Chalfont, Alan, Baron, 103
Chechnya, 169, 170n
Chevènement, Jean-Pierre, 117n
China, 54
Chirac, Jacques, 114n, 117, 120n
Christian Democratic Union (CDU), 132, 133
Christian Social Union (CSU), 132, 133
Christopher, Warren, 92
CIS *see* Commonwealth of Independent States (CIS)
Clinton, Bill, 11, 40, 45, 53, 55, 78, 85, 87, 91
Collective Security Agreement (1992), 161, 164, 168
Common Foreign and Security Policy (European Union), 15n, 46
Commonwealth of Independent States (CIS), 79, 80, 96, 155, 157, 158, 160, 173
Concert of Europe, 35
Conference on Security and Cooperation in Europe (CSCE), 7, 15, 16, 37, 43, 44–5, 47, 53, 125, 127, 132, 138, 173

191

Conventional Forces in Europe (CFE) Treaty, 160
Copel, Etienne, 119
Cot, Jean, 52
Council of Europe, 173
Council of Ministers, 15–16
Crimea, 169
Croatia, 3, 4, 6, 15–19 *passim*, 22, 25–9 *passim*, 41, 46, 48, 50, 62, 116, 179, 180; Germany and, 125, 126
CSCE *see* Conference on Security and Cooperation in Europe (CSCE)
Cyprus, 39, 94, 99, 103
Czech Republic, 5, 127, 161n, 175, 178, 179, 185

*Daily Telegraph*, 100
Delors, Jacques, 114n, 185
De Michelis, Gianni, 48
Deniau, Jean-François, 116, 117
Dniester Republic, 162, 163, 165
Dray, Julien, 120n
Dregger, Alfred, 139
Dubrovnik, 29, 46, 48
Duff, Sir Anthony, 100
Dumas, Roland, 116, 118, 121, 123
Duverger, Maurice, 116

East Timor, 58, 182
Eastern Europe, 82, 95–6, 98, 127, 184–5
Egypt, 185
El Salvador, 39
Engholm, B., 134
Enzensberger, Hans Magnus, 128
Estonia, 169, 173n
Eurocorps, 113n, 122, 137, 138, 148
European Community (EC), 72, 113, 125, 148, 176, 178; and Bosnia, 29, 41; Conference on Yugoslavia, 16, 20, 23; in Yugoslavia, 6–7, 15–17, 22, 48–9, 53
European Free Trade Association (EFTA), 43
European Security and Defence Identity (ESDI), 46, 55n, 123
European Union (EU), 5, 12–13, 44, 45, 127, 175, 176, 178, 179, 180, 183–9

Fabius, Laurent, 114n
Falklands War, 36, 58, 61, 94, 97
Farrar-Hockley, Sir Anthony, 102
*Figaro, Le*, 118
Fillon, François, 109n, 110n
Finkielkraut, Alain, 116
Finland, 175, 183
Fontaine, André, 115
Fox, Robert, 100
France, 11, 18, 24, 31, 32, 45, 51, 52, 95, 106–25, 144, 148, 149, 188
Free Democratic Party (FDP) (Germany), 128, 129, 132
Frewer, Barry, 52
Fuchs, Gérard, 119n

Galvin, John, 46
Gandhi, Mahatma, 57
Gansel, 134
Geneva Convention, 28
Genscher, Hans-Dietrich, 149
Georgia, 127, 160, 163, 165, 168, 173n, 180
Germany, 5, 11–12, 16, 43, 46, 66–7, 95, 125–41, 149, 172, 177, 180, 182
Giscard d'Estaing, Valéry, 117
Glucksmann, André, 116
Gorbachev, Mikhail, 90
Grachev, Pavel, 159, 160, 164, 167, 170
Greece, 43, 65, 179, 180, 183
Green Party (France), 117n
Green Party (Germany), 136
Greenwood, Christopher, 40
*Guardian*, 100
Gulf War, 8–9, 26–7, 42, 58, 67, 73, 81, 181; France and, 107–8; Germany and, 127–8, 129; Netherlands and, 143–4, 152; USA and, 88–9

Hailsham, Quintin Hogg, Viscount, 102
Hammarskjold, Dag, 39
Hercegovina, 14, 16, 17, 18, 19, 20, 22, 24
Higgins, Rosalyn, 49
Hungary, 5, 127, 175, 179, 185
Hurd, Douglas, 26, 30, 103, 149

## INDEX

*Independent, The*, 100
India, 39
Indonesia, 58, 60, 142, 143
Ingush, 170
International Conference on Former
  Yugoslavia (ICFY), 20, 21, 23
International Red Cross, 18
Iran, 155
Iraq, 2, 9, 38, 67, 77
Israel, 60
Italy, 144, 149, 178, 182, 188
Izetbegović, Alija, 21n, 55

Japan, 95, 172, 188
Jenkins, Simon, 100
Joxe, Pierre, 119
Juppé, Alain, 52, 110n, 123n

Kampuchea, 137
Karadžić, Radovan, 23
Karelia, 169
Kazakhstan, 156n, 161, 164
Keegan, John, 100, 102
Kenney, George, 100
Kent, Bruce, 100
Keynes, John Maynard, 185
Khasbulatov, Ruslan, 174
Kinkel, Klaus, 118, 129, 132
Klose, H-U., 128, 134, 135
Kohl, Helmut, 113n, 125n, 133
Korean War, 73, 105, 143
Kosovo, 19, 42, 48, 65, 120
Kouchner, Bernard, 115, 116n
Kozyrev, Andre, 157, 158, 161n, 166,
  167, 168
Kuchma, Leonid, 169n
Kundera, Milan, 116
Kurdistan, 97
Kuwait, 39, 61, 94, 97, 99
Kvitsinsky, Yuri, 44
Kyrgyzstan, 156n, 161, 164

Lacaze, Jeannou, 118
Lafontaine, Oskar, 135
La Gorce, Paul-Marie de, 116
Lalonde, Brice, 114n
Lamassoure, Alain, 114n, 116
Lanxade, Admiral, 119–20
Latin America, 92–3
Latvia, 169, 170
League of Nations, 35–6

Lebanon, 39, 67, 83, 103, 143
Lebed, Aleksandr, 163–4
Lévy, Bernard-Henri, 116
Lewin, Terence, Baron, 102
*Libération*, 118
*loi de programme militaire* (LPM),
  106, 108
Loza, Tihomir, 100
Luxembourg, 148

Maastricht Treaty, 5, 183
Macedonia, 4, 16, 18–19, 40, 43, 65,
  120
Major, John, 113n
Malaya, 101
Matthiesen, 128
Meacher, Michael, 100
Messmer, Pierre, 117n
Middle East, 39, 42, 96, 143
Military Staff Committee (UN), 36, 38
Millon, Charles, 114n, 117n, 120n
Milosevic, Slobodan, 16, 48, 114, 181
Mitterrand, François, 112, 113n, 115,
  116, 118, 119
Mladic, R., 51
Moldova, 127, 160, 163, 165, 170,
  173n
*Monde, Le*, 117n
Monroe Doctrine (Russia), 154–5,
  158, 170, 174, 180
Montenegro, 15, 20
Morillon, Philippe, 118, 121
Morin, Edgar, 116

Nabiev, Rakhmon, 164
Nagorno-Karabakh, 162, 165n, 168,
  173n
NATO, 7, 37, 43, 44, 47, 49, 55, 70,
  82, 125, 175; France and, 109, 123;
  Germany and, 128–9, 131, 136;
  Netherlands and, 143, 144–5, 146–
  8, 149; Russia and, 155, 158, 161,
  173; and the Yugoslavian wars, 15,
  30, 51, 52, 53–4
Netherlands, 12, 142–53
Niggemeyer, 135
North Atlantic Pact (1949), 149
North Ossetia, 163, 170
Northern Ireland, 11, 67, 94, 99, 103
Northern League, 185

193

Office for Democratic Institutions and Human Rights (ODIHR), 47
O'Kane, Maggie, 100
Operation Provide Comfort, 27, 144
Operation Sharp Guard, 37
Organisation of the Islamic Conference, 21
Owen, David, Baron, 20, 21

Pakistan, 39
Panama, 67, 93
Parsons, Sir Anthony, 103
Pasqua, Charles, 117n
PDS (Germany), 136–7
Pearce, Edward, 100
Petersburg Declaration (1992), 122
Pisani, Edgard, 116
Poirot-Delpech, Bertrand, 119n
Poland, 5, 127, 161n, 172, 175, 178, 179, 185
Poncet, Jean-François, 116
Poos, Jacques, 48
Portugal, 183
Powell, Colin, 83, 84, 86

Reagan, Ronald, 67
Rifkind, Malcolm, 36
Rocard, Michel, 121n
Romania, 163
Rühe, Volker, 131, 139
Rühl, Lothar, 118
Russia, 4, 12, 32n, 42, 45, 46, 54, 154–74, 175, 178, 179, 180, 185, 187–8
Rutskoi, Aleksandr, 174

Sakha, 169
Sandzak, 42
Sarajevo, 15, 17, 19, 24, 48, 52, 114, 118
Sarkozy, Nicolas, 114n, 120n
Scharping, R., 134, 135
Schmidt, Renate, 135
Schmitt, Maurice, 119
Schröder, G., 135
Schwarz-Schilling, C., 133
Scowcroft, Brent, 85
Serbia, 4, 16, 18, 21, 26, 29, 41, 46, 48, 61, 101, 181; France and, 112, 119, 121; Russia and, 166, 167; UK and, 101, 102; UN and, 20, 50; USA and, 24, 31–2, 102
Shalikashvili, John, 86
Shevardnadze, Eduard, 173n
Silajolžić, Haris, 21n
Single European Market, 182
Skokov, Yuri, 158
Slovakia, 5, 127, 161n
Slovenia, 6, 15, 16, 17, 22, 25, 29, 48, 116, 125, 126, 175, 179, 180
Socialist Review, 59
Somalia, 40, 65–6, 67, 70, 77, 84, 88, 89–90; Germany and, 130, 139–40
Sontag, Susan, 59
South Africa, 58, 60
South Ossetia, 162, 163, 165
Soviet Union, 37, 43, 44, 60, 64, 98, 177
Spain, 178, 183, 188
Social Democratic Party (Germany), 128, 129, 130, 131, 134–6
Stasi, Bernard, 114n
Stikker, Dirk, 148
Stoltenberg, Thorvald, 20n
Sweden, 175, 183
Syria, 185

Tajikistan, 159, 160, 161, 162, 164, 165, 171, 173n
Tatarstan, 167, 169
Thatcher, Margaret, 25, 100
Thornberry, Cedric, 18, 40
Times, The, 100
Transcaucasia, 127
Trittin, Jügen, 136
Tudjman, Franjo, 62
Turajlic, Hakija, 121
Turkey, 43, 60, 65, 128, 143–4, 155, 173, 179
Turkmenistan, 160

Ukraine, 4, 42, 163, 168, 169, 170, 173, 178, 180, 187, 188
United Kingdom, 68, 74–5, 94–9, 144, 149, 188; and Bosnia, 24, 25, 26, 49, 51, 52, 59, 99–104
United Nations, 2, 27, 36, 38–40, 70, 73–4, 89, 143; in Bosnia, 4, 29, 64, 66, 113; Charter of, 27–8, 36, 37, 38; France and, 110, 115, 118, 122;

Germany and, 128, 129, 131, 132, 135, 136, 139–40; Russia and, 159, 168, 170–1, 173; UK and, 98, 99, 103; USA and, 87–8; in Yugoslavia, 15, 20, 115n, 120
United Nations High Commissioner for Refugees (UNHCR), 18
United Nations Protected Areas (UNPAs), 17, 19
United Nations Protection Force (UNPROFOR), 17, 18, 19, 27, 33, 39, 50–2, 59, 65
United Nations Security Council, 8, 18, 19, 29, 36, 38, 39, 54, 123; Germany and, 131, 140; UK and, 95
United Nations Transitional Authority (UNTA), 50, 53, 144
United States of America, 37, 40, 42, 44, 45, 60, 68, 76–93, 102, 144, 177, 179, 180, 188–9; Russia and, 173, 174; former Yugoslavia and, 7, 19, 24, 29, 31–2, 46, 50, 51, 53, 55, 69, 85–6, 90–2, 149
Uzbekistan, 161, 164, 171

Vance, Cyrus, 17, 20, 21
Vance-Owen Plan, 21, 23, 24, 114, 166, 167
Veil, Simone, 117

Vietnam, 67, 68, 83, 86
Villers, Philippe de, 114n
Vincent, Sir Richard, 30
Voight, 134, 135
Vukovar, 46

Warsaw Treaty Organisation, 37, 43, 44, 47
*Washington Post*, 55
Weinberger, Caspar, 83, 84
Western European Union (WEU), 7, 15, 24, 37, 45, 48–9, 118, 129, 133, 143, 149, 175; France and, 122, 123; Russia and, 159
Western Sahara, 39, 99
Wiecorek-Zeul, Heidemarie, 135
Woollacott, Martin, 100
Wörner, Manfred, 30, 37

Yeltsin, Boris, 44, 45, 157, 158, 160, 161n, 166, 167, 169, 170, 171
Yugoslavia, 6–8, 15, 22, 29, 48, 51, 62–3, 68, 72, 75, 90–2, 102; Federal Republic of, 15, 19–20

Zhirinovsky, Vladimir, 155, 161, 171–2, 174
Zimmerman, Warren, 48

© The Political Quarterly Publishing Co. Ltd. 1994.